# Clearing a Vygotskyan Path
Phrase Play from Poetics to Prose

DANIEL BROUDY

# Clearing a Vygotskyan Path
Phrase Play from Poetics to Prose

© 2009 by Daniel Broudy
Waldport Press
Newport, Oregon, USA

The right of Daniel Broudy to be identified as the Author of this Work has been asserted in accordance with the US Copyright Act of 1976

All rights reserved. No part of this publication may be reproduced, stored in a retrieval system, or transmitted, in any form or by any means, electronic, mechanical, photocopying, recording or otherwise, excepted as permitted by the US Copyright Act of 1976, without the prior permission of the publisher.

First published 2006 Deakin University, Dewey Number: 808.042, Australian Library Collections Record ID, 41329874

First edition, published as *From Play to Poetics: Clearing a Vygotskyan Path to Prose*

*Library of Congress Cataloguing-in-Publication Data*

Broudy, Daniel S., 1964 –
   Clearing a Vygotskyan Path: Phrase Play from Poetics to Prose / Daniel Broudy
   *Revised Edition*
     p.cm.
   Includes bibliographical references and index.
   ISBN 978-0-9820534-0-9    (pbk.: alk. paper)

    1. Vygotsky        2. Psycholinguistics      3. Sociolinguistics
    4. Epistemology    5. Rhetoric

Printed and bound in the United States of America

The publisher's policy is to use permanent paper from mills that operate sustainable forestry policy, and which has been manufactured from pulp processed using acid free and elementary chlorine-free practices. Furthermore, the publisher ensures that text paper and cover board used have met acceptable environmental accreditation standards.

For further information on Waldport Press, visit our website:
www.waldportpress.com

## Acknowledgments

The author gratefully acknowledges the comments, critiques and patience of Professors Ron Goodrich, Catherine Beavis, Peter Elbow, Howard Giles, Gabriele Lusser Rico, Joe Moxley, Peter Simpson, Kevin Murphy, Barry Pollick, Bob Bailey, Richard Roberts, Henry Grubb, Sharon Flicker, Jeffrey Newbern, Margaret Borkowski, James Anderson, Randy Thrasher, and Burke Forrest.

The author also gratefully acknowledges the gut-honest criticism of style and usage meted out by writer and editor Frank E. Keyes Jr. as well as the thorough review offered by Professor Peter Wodarz. The author shall, nonetheless, take full responsibility for any long-winded passages which his readers may still perceive.

My gratitude, at last, goes to Jason Arbogast for both his critical comments on key chapters and expert camerawork.

## Dedication

To Yuna and Yena – wife and daughter

## CONTENTS

| | | |
|---|---|---|
| Tables | ............................................................................... | v |
| Abbreviations | ............................................................................... | vi |
| Foreword | ............................................................................... | vii |
| Introduction | ............................................................................... | 1 |
| Principal Questions | ............................................................................... | 2 |
| Explanatory Note on the Organization | ............................................................................... | 3 |
| Some Key Terms | ............................................................................... | 5 |
| Part 1. A Sketch of Linguistic Bias | ............................................................................... | 7 |

chapter / section

| | | | |
|---|---|---|---|
| 1. | Traditions and standards | ............................................................................... | 8 |
| | 1.1 Arguments from the Cheshire and Milroy Perspective | ............ | 11 |
| | 1.2 Public Concerns and Academic Policies | ............................... | 13 |
| 2. | Immigration and Cultural Capital | ............................................. | 23 |
| | 2.1 Responses to Perceived Linguistic Corruption | ...................... | 31 |
| 3. | The Current Traditional Paradigm | ............................................. | 37 |
| | 3.1 A Sketch of the Pedagogical Background | ............................. | 38 |
| | 3.2 The North American Paradigm | ............................................. | 56 |
| | 3.3 An Alternative | ............................................................... | 62 |
| 4. | Never End a Sentence with a Preposition | ................................... | 64 |
| | 4.1 Applying Linguistic Treatments | ........................................... | 72 |
| 5. | What is Meant by Knowledge of Language? | ............................... | 80 |
| PART 2. The Role of Play | | ............................................................ | 89 |

chapter / section

| | | | |
|---|---|---|---|
| 6. | Knowing and Doing | ............................................................ | 90 |
| | 6.1 Knowing That and How | ..................................................... | 93 |
| | 6.2 Meta-knowing | ............................................................... | 98 |
| | 6.3 Knowing How to Break Rules | ............................................. | 101 |

| | | |
|---|---|---|
| 7. | Writing: A Developmental Psychology Approach | 105 |
| 7.1 | Knowing & Doing in the Zone of Proximal Development | 110 |
| 7.2 | Playing in the Zone | 114 |
| 8. | Playing and Gestalts | 121 |
| 8.1 | The Gestalt of Meanings in Play | 124 |
| 8.2 | A Method of Playing & Discovering Form | 127 |

Part 3. The Practice of Play .................................................135

chapter / section

| | | |
|---|---|---|
| 9. | An Approach to Prose Through Play with Phrases in Poetry | 136 |
| 9.1 | Summary of Previous Observations | 138 |
| 9.2 | Hypothesis | 141 |
| 9.3 | Method Description and Aims | 141 |
| 9.4 | Case Study | 144 |
| 9.5 | Soliciting Participation | 144 |
| 9.6 | Participant Profiles in Experimental Group Workshops | 145 |
| 9.7 | Workshops | 148 |
| 9.8 | Research Methods Rationale | 149 |
| 9.9 | Methods | 150 |
| 9.10 | Epistemological Assumptions | 151 |
| 10. | Meeting 1 | 153 |
| 10.1 | Meeting 2 | 162 |
| 10.2 | Meeting 3 | 170 |
| 10.3 | Meetings 4 and 5 | 184 |
| 10.4 | Meeting 6 | 187 |
| 10.5 | Discussion of Case Study | 190 |

Conclusion .................................................196
Major Findings .................................................197
Limitations of Findings .................................................202
New Research Issues and Directions .................................................205

| | |
|---|---:|
| Appendices | 211 |
| Appendix A. Play Exercise | 212 |
| Appendix B. Kindergarten Cop | 213 |
| Appendix C. How About Dinner? | 214 |
| Appendix D. Miami Beach Bar Monty's | 215 |
| Appendix E. Scandal Meter | 216 |
| Appendix F. Untitled Prose | 217 |
| Appendix G. Untitled Prose | 218 |
| Appendix H. Untitled Prose | 219 |
| Appendix I. Untitled Prose | 220 |
| Works Consulted | 221 |
| Index | 237 |

**TABLES**

| | | |
|---|---|---|
| Table 1. The Process of Standardization | .......................... | 12 |
| Table 2. Schools of Composition Theory | .......................... | 41 |
| Table 3. Proficiency Levels for Writing Skills | .......................... | 54 |
| Table 4. Determining Pronoun Case Forms | .......................... | 59 |
| Table 5. Subject – Verb Agreement | .......................... | 60 |
| Table 6. Double Negatives are Illogical | .......................... | 67 |
| Table 7. Identifying Subordinate Clauses | .......................... | 70 |
| Table 8. Participant Profiles | .......................... | 147 |
| Table 9. Initial Experiment with Phrases | .......................... | 157 |
| Table 10. Subsequent Experiment with Phrases | .......................... | 158 |
| Table 11. Labeling Exercise | .......................... | 164 |
| Table 12. Many Mansions excerpt (Joan Didion) | .......................... | 166 |
| Table 13. Many Mansions Morphed into AAVE. | .......................... | 168 |

**ABBREVIATIONS**

| | |
|---|---|
| AAVE | African American Vernacular English |
| BBC | British Broadcasting Corporation |
| CTP | Current Traditional Paradigm |
| ESL | English as a Second Language |
| ETS | Educational Testing Service |
| IQ | Intelligence Quotient |
| L1 | First Language |
| L2 | Second Language |
| OED | Oxford English Dictionary |
| RP | Received Pronunciation |
| TESOL | Teaching English to Speakers of Other Languages |
| UK | United Kingdom |
| UMUC | University of Maryland University College |
| US | United States |
| ZPD | Zone of Proximal Development |

Clearing a Vygotskyan Path

# FOREWORD

This book represents a creative integration of Lev Vygotsky's socio-cultural theory of the mind (1978) and Michael Polanyi's theory of tacit knowing (1967 & 1975). It argues that some of the problems for college instructors in designing effective composition pedagogies can arise from misapprehending socio-cultural dimensions of and influences on language acquisition and use. The discussions are divided into three major Parts.

The first Part moves from the personal to the communal with a critical assessment of language norms, their historical development, and their underlying causes. By outlining causal relationships between conventional wisdom and prescriptive practices, this examination erects a basic theoretical frame through which to understand how popular and fallacious conceptions of and attitudes towards language use and users can affect classroom practices.

The second Part builds upon the first by reframing problems of classroom practice in the context of various socio-cultural distractions - critically focusing upon the epistemological, sociological and psychological underpinnings of language. This Part re-establishes a philosophical basis for an alternative way of teaching and assessing writing outside traditional prescriptive classroom methods, one which is the source for the development of practical tools that students, especially marginalized adult students at the college level, can use when apprehensions or similar distractions limit text production.

The third Part discusses a series of writing workshops that serve two principal aims. Firstly, by moving from theory to practice, it tests a playful, descriptive approach to writing that students can adopt when relying foremost on their creativity and tacit knowledge of the language. This method demonstrates how play with phrase structures can significantly enlarge abilities in generating ideas and thereby help resolve any difficulties of grammar at the sentence level.

Secondly, this Part demonstrates what the book as a whole upholds - a Vygotskyan approach to composition instruction that frees both college teacher and student from the dogmas of prescriptivism. —*Dr. Barry Pollick*

## *Introduction*

Many students of composition report that they are turned off by writing and by the traditions of academic English. I can empathize with them, perhaps for different reasons, but I still want to understand what precisely turns them off. This book represents an exploration of why and an effort of discovering how students' minds about writing can be changed for the better. While my early suspicions have often fallen upon potential flaws in pedagogical methods, I have also wondered if attitudes themselves about students' alternative discourse styles don't play larger roles in creating the sense of dread that these students tend to feel. This book teases out some potential answers to these sorts of mysteries and, as such, begins with some controversial contentions that question prescriptive traditions. Alongside these contentions unfold critical reviews of negative attitudes and their effects on developing writers.

Despite the early promise of alternative approaches to writing pedagogy in the United States since the Chomskyan revolution in linguistics (Hairston, 1982) and the emergence of composition as an important field of academic inquiry rich with theory, popular classroom approaches to composition still do not appear to meet the expectations of earlier theorists and the needs of composition students. This appears especially to have been the case in North American colleges where adult learners on the periphery, raised during the period in which pedagogic change could and should have benefited them most during the 1970s, must contend with their writing apprehensions and the cultural attitudes that shape the composition classroom dynamic. I consider the revolution to be ongoing and focus on both the internal and external writing distractions that students from periphery speech communities contend with but can resolve through creative playful ways in generating texts.

My principal interests throughout the text focus on Peter Elbow's concerns over the privileged place that academic discourse holds in the academy over alternative discourses—a view that "sensitizes [students] to the notion of differences in [rhetorical] form so that they may be more apt to look for [the accepted] cues and … pick them up faster …" (1991, p. 152). The generation of and experimentation with the kinds of textual forms of interest to me are both poetical and expository. That is, students begin with free experiments in poetry so as to move more easily into experiments with prose.

## Principal Questions

The primary aim of this work was to discover how adult learners in American community colleges can be better supported to confront and surmount their writing apprehensions and to disregard other related interferences in formal composition courses. Constructive answers to this concern will also require responses to the following additional kinds of questions: (a) From a sociolinguistic perspective, what is shaping their fears and apprehensions? (b) What is the literacy schooling context they have come from? (c) What have been the dominant paradigms of the literacy education they have received? and (d) What skills or awareness can be achieved through rhetorical play?

**Explanatory Note on the Organization**

The major sections of this book are organized somewhat unconventionally into three parts. Given the fairly complex cause-and-effect relationships connecting language to prevailing conceptions of correct usage and the pedagogies used to inculcate language users with a common sense of standardization, a tripartite approach to arranging the research, discussions and case study has proven necessary. While touching on key areas in psychology, linguistics and epistemology, this book traces the development of language norms emerging from associated schools of thought on pedagogy since the 1960s. These areas frame discussions of the kinds of attitudes that influence pedagogy in North American English composition courses, and their associated problems for minority or periphery students. Discussions throughout have implications, too, on ESL/EFL language learning inasmuch as nonnative speakers of English have had to deal with similar sorts of unequal access to the received standard variety in North America.

Critiques appearing in Parts 1 and 2 represent the theoretical groundwork and broad rationale for the proposed alternative teaching method critically examined in Part 3.

Discussions in Part 1, thus, provide a brief historical background and context to the concept of language norms set against what linguists Jenny Cheshire and James Milroy (1993) see as a perpetual process of standardization. In light of the development of standards and the sorts of attitudes necessary to encourage observance of rules and the preservation of a standard language ideology, Part 1 reveals how certain attitudes, however occasionally irrational, can give shape to North American language policies and approaches to teaching composition at the college level today. As a consequence,

Part 1 also includes discussions of various schools of composition, their related philosophical underpinnings, and how these approaches influence the knowledge and skills of students. Critical discussions of popular textbooks, influential authors, commentators, teachers and public figures provide a justification for offering an alternative means of approaching composition studies. Part 1, therefore, is an effort to trace to their recent beginnings various popular presumptions about English and use—the supposed corruption of the language, past and present; the major pedagogical movements in composition theory meant to serve students; and underlying attitudes that shape some of the methods used to treat periphery students.

Whilst discussions in Part 1 question conventional wisdom surrounding conceptions of linguistic corruption, competence and performance, Part 2 offers an alternative way of looking at language and teaching writing that suspends the often strong sense of compulsion teachers tend to have for prescribing rules and by focusing upon the potential linguistic creativity already inherent in students. Part 2 discusses the theoretical possibilities of play (Vygotsky, 1934/1978), the means by which apprehensive students[1] may generate sentence-level meaning, and a comprehensive rationale for seeing play as an ideal approach to scaffold increased know-how in composition studies. As prescriptive approaches to English composition tend to prevail in popular texts which presuppose linguistic deficits in students rather than differences, it is also necessary to interrogate the conventional wisdom surrounding the concept of linguistic ailments (Lippi-Green, 1997; Bolinger, 1980) and popular remedies used nowadays in classrooms to treat these problems. Part 2, therefore, addresses the following kinds of questions: What does it really mean to know a language and write in a

---

[1] As writing apprehension and writing anxiety are typically used interchangeably in the literature, no attempt to differentiate these terms is made in this study, although "apprehension" appears to have recently gained more popularity since Daly and Miller coined the term.

language? What kinds of actions stimulate growth in language skills, particularly in writing?

Part 3 features background material outlining the problem, hypothesis, detailed descriptions of the proposed method, and descriptions of a case study that discusses the effectiveness of play with phrase structures at the sentence level. Although the method for which I argue draws on positions taken up by scholars in rather disparate areas of knowledge, the marriage of Vygotsky's theory with a common rhetorical exercise and its application in the context of a composition classroom represents a new way of addressing an old problem.

As referenced earlier, Part 1 begins by addressing the concept of standardization set against the traditions and attitudes necessary to give prescriptive approaches to teaching English composition their form and import. It is necessary to commence, therefore, by examining how those attitudes are communicated and what connection they may have to a writer's sense of identity and power.

## Some Key Terms

According to the *Longman Dictionary of Language Teaching and Applied Linguistics*, the term "writing" is likened to a process of composing which can be categorized in three main stages: (a) rehearsing (or, namely, prewriting); (b) writing (or; namely planning, drafting, composing); and (c) revising (or; namely editing and postwriting) (Richards et al., 1999, p. 70). As the "composing process" (Murray, 1980; Koch & Brazil, 1978) suggests a wide range of complex and interrelated activities, the term "writing" will be used primarily throughout this study to suggest text production and the act of articulating meaning at the sentence level.

Beyond these uses of the simple term "writing," other features of the composing process will also be discussed and, as such, will be distinguished from "writing" as sentence-level text production. For example, in Part 3 of this book, discussions with case study participants feature other terms peculiar to the composing process, such as generating and brainstorming, which are often associated with the widely-used "Process Approach" to composition described by Peter Elbow (1973) and Donald Murray (1980).

Wherever noted otherwise, the term "writer" refers to the first-year student of college composition and rhetoric dealing with difficulties in grammar, meaning or mechanics or in generating and drafting text at the sentence level.

The term "periphery," adapted from Suresh Canagarajah's usage in *Resisting Linguistic Imperialism in English Teaching*, also appears throughout this study. Whereas Canagarajah describes the periphery as a set of less-developed post-colonial communities belonging once to the British empire, I adjust the term to represent the various sets of communities within North America whose people—whether immigrants or not—possess the less desirable social and/or linguistic power to contest the negative labels they are forced to bear.

Canagarajah also uses the term "center" to represent the "technologically advanced communities of the West which, at least in part, sustain their material dominance by keeping less developed communities in periphery status" (1999, p. 4). According to Howard Giles and Nikolas Coupland (1991), since stigmatized language varieties are sometimes used as markers for the members of marginalized sub-groups, the term "center" used throughout this study is as useful for representing those participants in the mainstream who possess the more culturally, economically, or politically desirable status. The term implies what is thought to connote superior status.

# PART 1. A SKETCH OF LINGUISTIC BIAS

## 1. Traditions and Standards

By no means is the contemporary tendency to complain in America about supposed corruptions of the English language and the decline of standards a recent phenomenon nor, indeed, are the undying public attempts to police these perceived defilements in speech and writing. To what depth, though, do notions of language corruption appear to sink? Having the roots of a "complaint tradition" (Cheshire & Milroy, 1993, p. 31; Claiborne, 1983, p. 223) buried in England's past, this phenomenon is said to have gained momentum in the academy following Henry Alford's *Plea for the Queen's English* (1866) (O'Conner, 1996, p. 182; Claiborne, 1983, p. 223; Pyles, 1971, p. 219). To contest attitudes about language corruption and standards today is, no doubt, to contest their traditions as well.

A brief outline of popular movements toward prescriptivism in communication should help frame contemporary notions of acceptability. Today's debate over how and when the prescriptive movement was conceived and why it still seems reasonable for some people to develop preferences for certain language varieties is best illustrated by a discussion of the word itself—*standard*. The following discussion briefly traces some notable features peculiar to these movements throughout the recent past when the sorts of attitudes about language norms have appeared in public and how these attitudes appear to have affected the opinions of those so concerned with language maintenance and standards today. This outline serves as groundwork for subsequent discussions of and references to personal, social or political power and the sorts of anxieties associated with a perceived loss of it and how these perceptions shape methods meant to encourage students of English composition to meet standards.

As Raymond Williams (1976, p. 296) indicates, the word *standard* has a rather complex etymological story. A study of the notions of standards in England's history could prove useful in better understanding the contemporary debate over language uses, since the word itself is linked today to a range of questionable attitudes and behaviors wherever English is the linguistic currency in the exchange of ideas.

According to the OED, the term, *standard*, entered use through the natural course of aphesis, the gradual dropping of an initial letter. Standard comes from the Latin *extendere*—stretch out. Of the thirty etymological strains defined, the very first, a reference to "a flag, sculptured figure, or other conspicuous object, raised on a pole to indicate the rallying point of an army" (1970, p. 814) is, perhaps, the most telling when one questions why linguistic standards have remained so staunchly defended. Given this Latin denotation, all contemporary notions of standards could be seen as figurative *extenderes*, and by further implication fair reasons why the sense of standards is connected to national identity and language use in times of war and peace (Simpson, 2000, p. 180). Consequent developments were, thus, able to allow a concerned public to speak of *rising* or *falling* standards, and to associate with them other analogies, such as the *call to maintain standards*—impressions of power connected to a monarch or, by extension in the United States, an elected guardian of the state. Related as well to these impressions are the public's notions of authority and who in society maintains power enough to define standards and subsequently mark what becomes seen as below or non-standard.

Terry Crowley describes two distinct strains in the etymological growth of *standard*. The first of these has the term as "a focus of unity," the second as an "authorised exemplar" (1989, p. 92). The latter distinction was also pluralized before long but continues to influence contemporary talk in so far as *Standard* English has been placed at the top of what now appears to be part of a natural power structure of many other dialectal types. To illustrate, Giles and Coupland suggest that a standard variety is the one that is most often associated with high socioeconomic status, power and media usage in a particular community (1991, p. 38).

So, what does the term *language* connote that the term *dialect* does not? Charles Fillmore observes that there is a misleading way of using words such as *language*, *standard* and *dialect* when "… one dialect comes to be the preferred means of communication in schools, commerce, [and] public ceremonies" (1997, ¶ 6). In Fillmore's view, "… what the linguist would … call the standard dialect is thought of as a 'language,' [while] the others as 'mere dialects,' [or subordinates] falling short of the perfection of the real language" (1997, ¶ 6).

Coincidentally, it seems self-apparent today that given the unremitting public debates, that a term such as *non-standard* has come to suggest *below standard* or *sub-standard*. As Jenny Cheshire and Jim Milroy have pointed out: "Some people confuse the concept of 'standard English' with the concept of 'standards of English', so that a non-standard feature, such as *I don't want none* appears … to be symptomatic of corruption and decay…" (1993, p. 15). In light of the historical growth of these notions of standard English and the contemporary debate over the acceptable uses of the language, it is not so surprising to find today the kind of continued confusion Cheshire and Milroy have outlined and the consequent turmoil that wields considerable influence in public discourse.

## 1.1 Arguments from the Cheshire and Milroy Perspective

Standardization, as Cheshire and Milroy (1993, p. 3) have noted, is best seen as an historically incomplete process. That is, one could reasonably argue that the standardization of English has not been and, barring the sudden and simultaneous demise of all English speakers, will never be complete. These contentions are more clearly illustrated with a summary of Cheshire and Milroy's major points elaborated in a chapter titled, "Syntactic variation in non-standard dialects." The standardization of language involves several stages, some of which never achieve their intended goal. Table 1 summarizes this view and Cheshire and Milroy's discussion of what must take place for the process to appear as though it were working.

Table 1

*The Process of Standardization*

| STAGE | GOALS |
|---|---|
| Suppression | The variability of spelling, grammar, vocabulary, punctuation, pronunciation and restriction of it occurs on all levels. |
| Selection | One variety is chosen from a pool of competing varieties. |
| Acceptance | The selected variety must be received by those who can influence other groups. (depending more upon social factors than on linguistic.) |
| Diffusion | The received variety must be dispersed socially and geographically through the writing system, the educational system, and discrimination against users of non-standard varieties. |
| Maintenance | Diffusion forces upon the received variety regular maintenance through education and literacy initiatives. |
| Elaboration of function | Diffusion forces the received variety into various administrative, scientific, philosophic, and literary functions. Users see a need for wider vocabularies and must borrow from other languages, as in the case of Latin and Greek. |
| Codification | The received variety must be codified so that interested persons can learn and use the "correct" forms that they believe will confer the likelihood for social or economic advancement. |
| Prescription | The codified forms in dictionaries and grammar texts subsequently become the lawful or legitimate forms whereas those forms not admitted in these texts become illegitimate. |

*Note.* Adapted from J. Cheshire and J. Milroy, 1993, pp. 4-6.

If the steps in this process are accurate, what follows is a discussion of how efforts to standardize the language have come to be construed as desires to achieve a remarkably unrealizable goal—immutable purity.

Projected upon contemporary American discourse conventions and popular notions of linguistic acceptability and correctness, what we see today are similar sorts of widespread attitudes competing for space among the inevitable migrations of peoples, their traditions and accents, and their continuing struggles for social and political identity. The following discussions, thus, examine the associations between past and present attitudes about language and use and approaches to enforcing the observance of standards.

## 1.2 Public Concerns and Academic Policies

Having established some of the principal connections between a desire to standardize English and the stages thought to be necessary in maintaining the process as if it were actually functioning, it would be useful to ask if the attitudes at work behind this desire have significant consequences for language users. That is to say, have attitudes about language use in the past come to shape popular attitudes and approaches to increasing competence and performance today? If so, then to what extent?

Howard Giles and Nikolas Coupland (1991) cite the work of Pear in the 1930s as a starting point for formal inquiries into the sorts of stereotypes and attitudes that surround language uses. They reference Pear's classic study that invited BBC audiences in the UK to offer personality profiles of certain voices they listened to over the radio to determine whether "voice parameters [i.e. RP versus Birmingham varieties] mirror someone's actual dispositional states" (1991, p. 33). Part of what Pear found was rather revealing. Judgment of personality appears to be a natural reaction rooted in preconceived stereotypes.

Ultimately, although there subsequently appeared to researchers little advantage to pursuing voice as an indication of actual personality, Giles and Coupland note that study after study in the decades that followed reveal a quite considerable consensus among those who judge and those who perceive stereotypical social traits associated with voice (language) (1991, p. 33). The so-called 'speaker evaluation paradigm,' according Giles and Coupland, traces its roots to Lambert et al's (1960) work, which adopted the *matched-guise technique* [2] (MGT), as a now-popular method for revealing the interrelationships among attitude, self-perception, speech and, by extension, writing.

According to Giles and Coupland, it was Lambert's work, though, that has, since 1960, spawned similar studies throughout the world revealing insights that show how "people can [and often do] express definite and consistent attitudes towards speakers who use particular styles of speaking" (1991, p. 33). Given the number of commentators engaged in devising and communicating various ways in which to encourage mass observance of language norms throughout the ages, the positions that citizens take on the issue of standards and usage today appear to have developed from fairly similar ideologies and perspectives to those that influenced talk long ago. Does the widespread propensity, though, to police speech publicly also have consequences for developing writers? Though apparent correlation does not equate to causation, it is, nonetheless, useful and important to note the patterns of expressed attitudes that surround notions of acceptability and correctness *en vogue* in written discourse as well.

---

[2] According to Giles and Coupland, "distrusting people's overt and public ascriptions as a true reflection of their privately held views," Lambert and colleagues "...formulated the MGT as a means of eliciting attitudes to users of different speech and language varieties." Giles and Coupland note that the "procedure is built on the assumption that speech style triggers certain social characterizations which will lead to a set of group-related trait inferences" (1991, pp. 33-4).

As an example, "Grumpy Martha's Guide to Grammar and Usage"[3] is merely one among a multitude of other worldwide websites offering visitors a long series of generally accepted prescriptions aimed at helping speakers and writers "sound smarter." As a "former spelling-champion" and present commentator on language norms, Martha Brockenbrough offers a helpful link to her site on grammar and usage with what appears a rather fitting title.

Many other similar titles turn up as well in cyberspace. Entering *standard english usage* in any capable search engine will yield the addresses of nearly 500,000 websites—some built by institutions, others by similarly concerned citizens. This number occupying cyberspace, though, seems to speak rather clearly to an overwhelming public preoccupation with linguistic correctness and uniformity. Though the true reasons for the public's fascination with standards and correctness today do not appear at first glance to be the same as those expressed long ago, they nevertheless appear to be, at least, indirectly connected to a perceived loss of power and control. The following discussion describes how these practices appear in public discourse today, why certain citizens may take part in them, and what may truly be at stake.

If, as Chomsky posits, languages are biologically acquired,[4] they are also provided with their distinctive features by a dominant social milieu. Roland Barthes suggests that language is "a social institution and a system of values" (1964/1999, p. 14). If this were so, the regional dialects that comprise languages are like verbal skin tones and verbal places of birth and are no more fundamentally altered than a speaker's hair color or curl (Schuster, 2003, p. 62).

In American schools, from elementary to university, what appear to be at stake in the broadest terms, at first glance, are the

---

[3] For more, see http://encarta.msn.com/encnet/features/Columns/?Article=grammarmain

[4] Responding to Barsamian's question about his theory of language, Chomsky remarks that "It starts from the fact, and it's not a very controversial fact, that the capacity for language is a species-specific property. That is, every normal human being has that capacity. As far as we know, it's biologically acquired" (2001, p. 204).

competences and skills that students develop to communicate a given level of it. *Standards*, then, remains the operative term of worth by which school districts, educators, and their students are measured. To best understand prevailing approaches to language teaching and popular conceptions of correctness that shape academic policies and public discourses, one must look across the Atlantic Ocean to England to the beginnings of a "progressive education policy" inspired decades ago (Blakeston, 2002, ¶ 2).

In his article, "Why do Britons Waive the Rules?" Rodney Blakeston reflects on some of the present-day problems in the British academy and traces their beginnings to the late 1960s when prescriptive grammars were largely dispensed with in favor of more liberal methods in English language teaching. He rails against well-educated academics who today ought explicitly to know canonized rules but who, because of those very policies, cannot even identify transitive or intransitive verbs (2002, ¶ 1). As a seasoned teacher/trainer at International House in London, Blakeston laments this "national shame [which he feels is] compounded by a … disbelief on the faces of German or Polish trainees when they discover that their British peers [don't even] know what the present perfect is" (2002, ¶ 3). Are Blakeston's impressions of any problems with the British academy necessarily prevalent, though, throughout Britain?

In a review of John Honey's book, *Language is Power: The Story of Standard English and its Enemies* (1997), Peter Trudgill addresses the sort of panic that those of Blakeston's camp have been known to create. In his "fully researched" text filled with "errors, half-truths … and willful misrepresentation" of the facts, Honey's principal intent is to uncover some elaborate and deceptive academic scheme. He argues that there is for the public a "conspiracy afoot on the part of linguists to keep nonstandard English-speaking people in their deprived state by persuading them that there is no need to learn Standard English" (1998, p. 457). As a "skillful self-publicist," according to Trudgill, Honey is "not at all a linguist" but indeed rather "a clever scholar" who with "the weight of uninformed journalistic opinion on his side" is actually better equipped to "[c]ourt attention through his polemics" than contribute anything useful to linguistic scholarship (1998, p. 457). Although not inevitably prevailing, the viewpoints that academics like Blakeston and Honey champion have a visible effect on the public discourse and the attitudes that ultimately shape academic approaches to English language teaching.

Some speakers of English across the Atlantic in America feel just as strongly, too, about the perceived failings of the academy. For example, in his article, "Random Thoughts on the Decline of English," columnist Fred Reed developed a discussion of the problems he has seen with his fellow citizens and with academics in particular, and he dispenses a series of prescriptions with a level of disdain matched, it seems, only by that which can be generated in talk of politics or religion. He sees deplorable uses of the language in writing, "your" for "you're" and in saying "me and him was talking" (2004, ¶ 1). He deplores "Ebonics" and poses with pointed contempt what he seems to feel is a clever and unanswerable rhetorical question: "… how in Ebonics does one say, 'The entropy of a closed system tends to remain the same or to increase'?" (2004, ¶ 12).

As an elderly Caucasian male posing at his website as a kind of free-thinking liberator of the inarticulate masses, he laments the disappearance of the great writers, the G.K. Chestertons, C.S. Lewis', Ambrose Bierces, Mark Twains, Hunter Thompsons, and Joseph Hellers of this world, and closes his critique with a series of eloquent but dogmatic remedies for recapturing the glories of English past, such as suggesting that universities divest themselves of academics who are prescriptively hostile to elitist values (2004, ¶ 10).

Reed's approach seems to give voice to the sorts of sentiments that aren't usually shouted so loudly in public discourse but which, I suspect, are nonetheless present in the attitudes of those who feel obliged to protect English from foreign invaders, from domestic "periphery users" (Canagarajah, 1999) and from the consequent decay they are thought to produce. "Good English," Reed contends, "depends upon a cultivated elite to preserve it. A pride in language is needed to prevent degradation from seeping upward from the lower classes, and only careful schooling instills the fine distinctions that make the difference between the literate and those who recognize words vaguely, like half-forgotten relatives" (2004, ¶ 7). Such hasty conclusions, though, seem nearly as impulsive as they are mysterious. While degradation to Reed appears to defy the forces of social gravity and to taint the higher classes, he also perceives that it is unnecessary to identify in this article which words, precisely, the lower classes themselves are unable to recognize.

Although Reed is not noted for his scholarship in language studies per se, it is worth noting the extent to which commentators of his sort reflect and influence popular attitudes about language uses in the public sphere and how these sorts of feelings, which border on xenophobia, pervade public discourse. It should be further noted that concerned citizens across the political spectrum can develop irrational preferences for the concept of purity in language. When these citizens have opportunities to call mass attention to their fears about what they perceive to be some imminent linguistic collapse on the horizon, those who sense this sort of threat most strongly will not hesitate to sound the level of alarm that Reed, Blakeston, and others like them feel they must. The sense of dread they feel turns out to be real for them as they see society slipping down the slope into linguistic oblivion.

What Rosina Lippi-Green saw as a kind of *schizophrenic* (1997, p. 109) view of language usage seems to develop in those who feel they face daily chaos and disorder and a disappearance of standards, hearing in popular media and mainstream discourse the kinds of peripheral varieties advanced by the so-called "uncultivated" and "unwashed" (Reed, 2004, ¶ 10). But, can this sort of behavior in Reed and others necessarily be seen as neurotic i.e., irrational?

Colonel Brian Cavallo and Frosty Woolridge echo similar worries with a similar sort of xenophobic tone tingeing their commentary, "American Politicians Serving Foreign Constituencies." They point to polling data as clear indications that Americans:

> ... want to preserve their language and culture. The message is loud and clear: ... our Lords and Ladies in Washington ... have other plans, ... like corporate welfare, multiculturalism, ... courting votes from growing numbers of illegal aliens and anything else that will compromise and undermine America's English language, culture and heritage. (2003, ¶ 1)

Given the passionate tenor in these observations too, it should likely be evident to the casual observer that the rise of illegal immigration as well as popular culture's varied and growing economic endowments are a few of the primary precipitating causes of the mounting campaigns for tougher standards waged over the airwaves and in the press today. Other responses to the problem, from noted academics, seem to hit the mark. As Camille Paglia observes, "...popular culture, with its stunning commercial success, has gained strength until it is now no longer the brash alternative to organized religion or an effete literary establishment: it *is* the culture ..." (2004, p. 1 [author's emphasis]).

It should be noted, nevertheless, that observations regarding language norms communicated to the masses on both sides of the Atlantic Ocean are not generated by a lunatic fringe, but by presumably rational people in social or professional positions that they feel—it seems—provide fitting opportunities that warrant their actions. Given their positions, can commentators such as Reed, Cavallo and Woolridge be motivated by a nobler sense of civic or national obligation and, if so, does this make their views of language more valid?

Barker and Giles suggest that popular campaigns, such as the English-only initiatives mounted in various states "... appear to embody a pattern of concern among Anglo-Americans about their position relative to other ethnic groups—particularly Latinos" (2004, p. 78). The true motives, though, behind such popular crusades may be considerably more complex than simply pointing to the public's alarm at ever-increasing immigration rates, a kind of perceived socio-cultural invasion or conquering force of "illegals" that appears, presumably, to shift the balance of economic power away from the center.

Other factors may, of course, contribute as well. Rather than having purely political antecedents, the upheaval, Paglia observes, may find its fuel in the excesses of the culture itself. As a classroom teacher for over thirty years, Paglia submitted at a conference, titled "Living Literacies: What Does it Mean to Read and Write Now?" that she has "become increasingly concerned about evidence of, if not cultural decline, ... cultural dissipation since the 1960s—a decade that seemed to hold such heady promise of artistic and intellectual innovation" (2004, p. 2).

Ironically, too, for all of the lip service still paid to the "progressive movement," fewer popular campaigns appear so progressively conservative and traditional. In national American politics, for example, conservatives are traditionally criticized by the left for their inability to perceive some of the most fundamental and obvious social and economic inequalities (Lakoff, 1996, p. 25) that exist in their constituencies, to recognize that all citizens do not come into the world equipped with equal opportunities for self-determination and success. Liberalism, on the other hand, connotes the opposite, the so-called "bleeding hearts," champions of the downtrodden, who are typically thought to be perceptive enough to sense that the playing field is actually sloped in favor of the socially and economically advantaged. These distinctions can even apply to how one views a language variety and a set of language users.

A recent example can be located in linguist John McWhorter's eloquently argued book, *Doing our Own Thing: The Degradation of Language and Music and Why We Should, Like, Care* (2003). In it, he observes that "modern linguistics focuses on speech rather than writing, ... the structures of language as spoken spontaneously" (2003, p. xiv). He identifies the decline of oratory as stemming from "the counterculture's permeation of the national consciousness ... [which] has created a new linguistic landscape (2003, p. xiii). In

McWhorter's estimation, "… our new sense of what American English is has upended our relationship to articulateness, our approach to writing … interest in poetry … [and] response to music …" (p. xxiii).

Like Paglia, McWhorter cites the 1960s as a time of dramatic change in American cultural mores, a period of momentous social upheaval that forever changed the appearance and sound of American English, and not for the better (2003, pp. 47-9). Of that period, he cites some pillars of proof in the public discourse. Because of the many "modern" lexical features it contains, Jane Fonda's declaration of protest heard over Radio Hanoi is trivialized as "normal" for its preferred casual tone and absence of any kind of "careful pace in length and balance" (McWhorter, 2003, p. 54). It would seem worth asking, though, whether casual tones such as Fonda's are not still sometimes struck in the "normal" social register with meiosis—a kind of verbal irony that draws even more attention, than hyperbole might, to a message protesting the injustices of, say, an unjustifiable war. Some simple parsing of Fonda's statement/speech reveals a few other rhetorical gems besides: parallelism, alliteration, ellipsis, asyndeton, and polysyndeton.

Nevertheless, McWhorter argues that this period represented a turning point in American discourse styles as speakers, like Fonda, began positioning themselves, much more than their message, "front and center" in the public consciousness. As the front of formality erected in past discourse styles tended to subordinate the speaker and create the necessary tone of objectivity, this new counter-cultural way of being heard where the speaker gains more attention has become, for McWhorter, one of the precipitating causes of the decline in the American variety of English. In his "Reflections on American Discourse," Elbow does not appear particularly surprised by this phenomenon as he observes that "… many academics seem more nervous about changes in discourse—than about changes in ideas or content or doctrine" (1991, p. 152).

While the public discussion over language norms may appear at first glance to rest upon, say, ever-increasing threats from popular culture's widely perceived unrefined *nouveau riche*, paradigm shifts in discourse styles, or an ever-growing influx of newly naturalized settlers who can "barely use English," the truth may exist somewhere between—in the space amid the illegal immigration issue and the issue over linguistic inconsistencies thought to exist among native speakers of English who are often said to use language in inappropriate or incorrect ways. As to the process of standardization described by Cheshire and Milroy, the goal of such a movement seeking unrealizable linguistic uniformity, purity and immutability can, it seems, be safely reduced to myth.

Apart from the widespread passions surrounding linguistic variability that saturate mass media, the scholarly literature features much more precisely defined characterizations of the debate which reveal the attitudes of a surprising mix of public figures on both sides of the political divide. Section 2 below will address some problems of language and use in North American discourse framed by Pierre Bourdieu and Jean-Claude Passeron's conceptions of cultural capital.

## 2. Immigration and Cultural Capital

> If English was good enough for Jesus Christ,
> it ought to be good enough for the children of Texas
> —*Governor Ma Ferguson*
> *All Pianos Have Keys, 1994*

> Whoever controls the language, the image, controls the race.
> —*Alan Ginsberg*
> *The New Yorker, 1968*

When James Crawford was asked during the early stages of his research in the mid-1980s, as he began investigating the possible roots of English-only (*also known as* language restriction) activism and whether these movements were connected directly to ultra-conservative groups, such as the Ku Klux Klan or the American Nazi Party, he admitted his alarm when he uncovered the identity of the founder, a former national leader in liberal groups such as the Sierra Club, Planned Parenthood and Zero Population Growth (2000b, ¶ 2). With the assistance of Senator S.I. Hayakawa, John Tanton was able to found the language policies think tank, U.S. ENGLISH Inc. (Dicker, 1996, pp. 157-8). Crawford observes that self-appointed guardians of English have always been with us, but never before in the shape of a high-powered Washington lobby, replete with political action committee pledged to defend our common language (1992 [1988], p. 171).

Since the organization's inception, U.S. ENGLISH Inc. has enjoyed endorsements from various other leading public figures besides the late Senator. According to Crawford, such proponents of Tanton and Hayakawa's English-only movement included former Senator Eugene McCarthy, former President Richard Nixon, and literary figures Saul Bellow, Norman Cousins and Gore Vidal. More recently, actors such as Whoopi Goldberg, Charleton Heston, and Arnold Schwarzenegger and other prominent figures in the public eye have signed onto the movement (2000b, ¶ 4). "Recognizing that fluency in English is necessary for full integration into the American mainstream" (Toonkel, 2003, ¶ 4), the members of U.S. ENGLISH Inc. neglect seeing or acknowledging the needs of the periphery. As the subtitle of their website might suggest, "Toward a United America," its creators presuppose that *only* linguistic uniformity in such a culturally, economically and politically diverse nation as the United States can create unity.

In her article, "Doing-English-Lessons in the Reproduction or Transformation of Social Worlds?" Angel Lin counters the conventional misconceptions uncovered by Crawford in the public domain by providing more precise descriptions of the stark divisions that exist in the public's notions of linguistic correctness and the academy's. Citing the work of Pierre Bourdieu and Jean-Claude Passeron (1977, p. 73), Lin describes their notion of

> … *cultural capital*, [which] refers to language use, skills, and orientations, dispositions, attitudes, and schemes of perception (also collectively called *habitus*) that children are endowed with by virtue of socialization in their families and communities. Bourdieu argues that, through their familial socialization, children of the socioeconomic elite receive both more of and the right kind of cultural capital for school success (i.e.,

their habitus becomes their cultural capital). (Lin, 1999, p. 394)

Despite the relative limitations of the *cultural-capital* metaphor that frames the debate, with its antecedents to and imagery rooted in an exclusively Marxist conception of capitalism, the term *habitus* seems useful enough for synthesizing the complex social and linguistic phenomena that characterize children's worlds. According to Lin, one theme that Bourdieu returns to is the idea that children do not begin from equal starting points in their races toward success (1999, p. 394). That is, those children from underprivileged groups with a *habitus* incompatible with that already inherent in schools and, also, incompatible with those coming from the socioeconomic elite do not have access to comparable starting blocks from where to begin the pursuit. In the case of an historically marginalized community, its members hear about the supposed corruption of their social, economic or political condition as well as the ignorance of their speech long before they reach the academy (Schaff, 1964, p. 152; Cameron, 1995, p. 9; Baugh, 1999, p. 67).

Speech and, by extension, writing are believed to mark the speaker as belonging to a particular class or a particular region or possessing a particular set of manners, morals or aptitudes. That is to say, as they signify disparities in *standard* versus *non-standard* usage, the slight details and differences of pronunciation or misspelling can carry the resonance of class and competence and with their echoes of prestige can assume critical social, political or economic significance. In revisiting Labov's earlier argument (1969), Giles and Coupland suggest that, "even a single vowel or consonant sound, contrasting with others or with our expectations, can have evaluative repercussions for its utterer (1991, p. 32).

They also cite Huspek (1986) who had suggested, for example, that images evoked in response to someone saying 'he went jogg *in* last night …' rather than 'he went jogg *ing* last night …' differ to the extent that, even if the utterance is the same in all other respects, the speaker in the first case will be afforded less respect than the speaker of the second." Common stereotypes and attitudes about linguistic correctness are, thus, inextricably bound by language varieties.

Another way of framing this discussion, too, emerges from Tajfel and Turner's work in the 1970s. Whereas Bourdieu and Passeron's theory of discrimination and language relates more to the perceived differences in social class, Tajfel and Turner's theory relates more to the concept of personal and group identity and how these categories of self-perception are affected by inter-group communication. Their concept of social interaction embodied in two opposing extremes, or "poles," helps researchers categorize rather simply and, thus, apprehend the complex attitudes at work in personalized and depersonalized styles of discourse. Rejecting wholesale acceptance of the theory, Giles and Hewstone's later adjustments (1982) consider Tajfel's bipolar model as "… essentially two separate and independent continua, each with extremes that can be labeled 'high' and 'low' … [such as when] the participants in trade union-management talks are trying to come to terms not only with the group stances of the other party, but also the personal styles of their representatives" (1991, p. 17). Of course, depending principally upon the context and who holds the position of power, either should likely fit as well as the cultural-capital model in classrooms where periphery students contend with others' negative attitudes and their own apprehensions.

Returning again to the cultural-capital metaphor, the formation of stereotypes arises from attitudes uniquely peculiar to class and privilege, as those in positions to do so feel inclined to make choices about language and the manner of its use a means of excluding the vulgar and thereby affirming their distinction (Bourdieu & Passeron, 1977, p. 118).

> Rhetorical devices, expressive effects, nuances of pronunciation, melody of intonation, registers of diction or forms of phraseology by no means solely express the conscious choices of a speaker

> preoccupied with the originality of his expression …: all these stylistic features always betray, in the very utterance, a relation to language which is common to a whole category of speakers because it is the product of the social conditions of the acquisition and use of language. (Bourdieu & Passeron, 1977, p. 117)

Social stratification, according to Lin, thus, exists before the appearance of students in classrooms (1999, p. 394). While it has traditionally been the business of liberals to call attention to what should already be rather obvious socioeconomic disparities that students bring to schools, educationists have used the notion of habitus to characterize the disadvantaged position of ethnic and linguistic minorities and to question the belief that state-run education in modern societies is built on meritocracy and equal opportunity (Lin, 1999, pp. 394-5). Such efforts, though, do not appear to square well with a public claiming to be concerned about literacy, with its widespread belief in a single standard language, and especially with politicians or members of school boards who, when intent on maintaining their relative power, can appeal widely to the citizenry with campaigns to maintain or raise standards.

Another term appearing in Lin's article is Bourdieu's idea of "symbolic violence," which describes how failure in schools can easily be ascribed to individual cognitive deficit or lack of effort and not to unequal initial share of the "institutionalized habitus" already prized and legitimized (Lin, 1999, pp. 395-6). Is it necessarily obvious, though, to policymakers that the system inherently is symbolically violent towards students while attempting to "suppress" (Cheshire & Milroy, 1993) linguistic features peculiar to "periphery" (Canagarajah, 1999, p. 4; Lippi-Green, 1997, p. 107) varieties of English? That is to say, is the school system indifferent to the needs of those students exhibiting "linguistic capital" (Bourdieu & Passeron, 1977, p. 73) contrary to that already valued in schools? Bourdieu believes so and contends that the dominated classes, nevertheless, permit the struggle

> ... to be imposed on them when they accept the stakes offered by the dominant classes. It is a ... reproductive struggle, since those who enter this chase, in which they are beaten before they start ... implicitly recognize the legitimacy of the goals pursued by those whom they pursue by the mere fact of taking part. (quoted in Lin, 1999, pp. 395-6)

For Bourdieu and Passeron, such an arrangement should not be entirely surprising since, in broadly Marxist terms, education systems, which are extensions of the political/ideological superstructure in capitalist societies, and the economic infrastructure are interdependent (1973, p. 55). While Bourdieu and Passeron's characterization of the relationship between economics and politics may or may not be valid and even still relevant to contemporary American education systems, this sort of interdependence has not prevented sharply different attitudes about and views of linguistic capital to enter the debate over how best to treat students in need of more valuable or other kinds of capital.

Two viewpoints on dialect have emerged since the deficit versus difference debate of the late 1960s and early 1970s. What was, perhaps, hastily thought by Basil Bernstein's contemporaries at the time to be Bernstein's (1971) model of linguistic deficit—wrought by cultural deprivation—prompted William Labov's response (1969), propounding, instead, cultural difference as the schism that separates classes and determines cultural capital. Labov's famous preemptive reaction in "The logic of nonstandard English," (to be addressed in Part 1, Section 5) precipitated a fundamental change in academic thinking towards periphery speakers, their communities and dialects. Although Labov furthered understanding of an important alternative point of view—that of the periphery speaker—composition pedagogies that reflect the deficit perspective continue to occupy a central presence within the North American paradigm.

In light of these differences in thinking about dialect, Donna Christian points out that attitudes toward linguistic capital, nowadays, can affect the quality of education received by some students in significant ways (1987, ¶ 4). For example, in citing dialect differences and their potential to interfere with their children's ability to acquire new information and educational skills, such as reading, a group of black parents in Ann Arbor, Michigan sued the local school system in 1979 for denying equal educational opportunity because of their own language background (Chambers & Bonds, 1983, p. 47; Farr Whiteman, 1980, ¶ 3). In this precedent setting case, the parents successfully argued that the schools were failing to teach their children to read because the educators had not taken into account the language differences represented by their children's vernacular dialect.

In Christian's view, the social consequences of belonging to a periphery dialect group may be quite subtle but just as important. The attitudes of teachers, school personnel, and other students can have a significant negative effect on the educational process. In keeping with Lambert's observations from the 1960s, Christian contends that those who hear a vernacular dialect make erroneous assumptions about the speaker's intelligence, motivation, and even morality (1987, ¶ 6)—a behavior that case study participants (to be later discussed) assumed about themselves as well. At last, according to Frederick Williams, research has shown that there can be a self-fulfilling prophecy in teachers' beliefs about their students' abilities (1976, p. 48).

If teachers confuse and conflate dialect differences with cognitive deficits and, thus, underestimate students' potential abilities, certain students will likely do less well in school perhaps as direct results of negative expectations. In some cases, students are "tracked" with the so-called slower groups, or even placed in special classes for the mentally handicapped because of their vernacular speech patterns (Christian, 1987, ¶ 6). Christopher Hurn notes that the first and best known attempt to apply this concept of tracking and its effects to the classroom was made by Robert Rosenthal and Lenore Jacobson (1968). Hurn points out that if labels applied to students by educators

> ... are consequential for future behavior and future evaluations, the same should be true of the official labels schools apply when students are ... track[ed] or stream[ed] on the basis of ability. Thus, when a teacher is confronted with a class described by other teachers as 'slow learners' we should expect that this official label will also shape that teacher's expectations and future behavior (Hurn, 1993, p. 171).

What Rosenthal and Jacobson did for their experimental group was to create in teachers entirely different expectations by deliberately misidentifying their prospective students as having unusual intellectual promise. Rosenthal and Jacobson had hypothesized that this misidentification would produce radically different attitudes in teachers, that they would treat these students differently and in turn the students would learn more. Although correlations said to exist between high IQ and language remain tenuous, the original experiment, according to Hurn, was quite successful in producing higher scores.

Of course, tracking or streaming students still remains a fairly common practice (Ansalone, 2003, p. 3; Ansalone, 2004, p. 258). The sorts of erroneous or hasty assumptions about certain speakers and underestimations of their ability, though, voiced in public discourses nevertheless emerge from the very attitudes that appear to shape the strategies used to treat perceived linguistic deficits among students— reactionary ways of staving off what many concerned citizens see as an imminent collapse of the language.

Often, it seems, therefore that the most pragmatic, objective and quantifiable means of preventing the perceived impending destruction of the language are coveted and put forward as the best.

Hence, the popularity of prescriptive grammars which can aim visible treatments at what sounds on the surface like rather obvious linguistic deficits in the mouths of "periphery" users (Canagarajah, 1999, p. 4).

The periphery is where prevailing teaching methods appear to meet most of their resistance, where the institutionalized forms of "suppression" (Cheshire & Milroy, 1993) work on varieties beyond the civilizing influences of the academy. Tolerance, recognition, approval are more likely to be realized only when those of the periphery adapt, "select" (Cheshire & Milroy, 1993) and master the more widely accepted standard forms. The responsibility of encouraging speakers to adapt, select and master those forms falls upon academics who themselves are expected to recognize the needs for standards by acknowledging the public's often inexorable pressure.

## 2.1 Responses to Perceived Linguistic Corruption

In his book, *Language, the Loaded Weapon*, Dwight Bolinger discusses some of the extremes to which some people might go in coercing others to meet standards. He reminds readers that a "comparison of two dialects is always misleading when one is taken as a standard" (1980, p. 47). While speakers of AAVE, for example, tend to omit the cupola *is*, i.e. "You out the game," he points out that the same sort of omissions occur in Standard English, i.e "George here? I can't believe it!" Bolinger wonders, therefore, whether speakers of AAVE omit, or if speakers of Standard add the copula. For him, the lure of calling attention to dialect differences and thus making value judgments may be tied to the act itself of isolating features in a dialect that appear deficient, i.e. non-standard.

He points to the occasional public campaigns for standards and some of the ways in which some American academics have had to respond to and approach the literacy issue, suggesting that misdiagnoses of language deficiencies become self-fulfilling (1980, p. 49). Since language users generally see themselves as inseparable from their language and implicitly understand that their speech patterns and accents are constructed by their social experiences, prescriptive approaches to discussing matters of competence and performance in classrooms appear to do more than simply underscore supposed linguistic inadequacies, but further highlight as well the pre-existing socioeconomic deficits present in the periphery.

That learners of all ages are completely unaware of the extent to which the idiosyncrasies of their speech are scrutinized in the academy when it publicly tests their variety in classroom discussions seems uncertain. Nevertheless, Carolyn Adger points out that a "pitfall in labeling students' language as inconsequential or wrong concerns the [very] social identity function that language serves" (1997a, ¶ 3).

For all of the irrational public fears associated with the perceived decline of language and civility, academics of more prescriptive persuasions appear to feel as though they must, nonetheless, respond to those fears with observable efforts and time-tested pedagogical methods. Amid public discussions of these supposed declines where suspicion seems often to intersect with televised nightly news scenes of illegal border-crossings from Mexico, American academics concerned with literacy issues and an ever-growing population of "illegals" must address the needs of periphery learners while contending with what seems an ever-widening scope of debate.

It can be argued that the dimensions of the standards debate in America, nowadays, are generally influenced by the conservative elite, by those who feel they must, by virtue of social station or professional position, overtly respond to the continued public calls for tougher or higher standards with editorials that aim to capture and communicate widespread public misgivings with national political policies related, in large part, to immigration.

Cultural critics also frame the debate of standards in terms of the academy's perceived inability to deal adequately with the problems of English language education, immigration and acculturation. Critics such as John Leo, a routine contributor to *US News and World Report*, can leave some readers contemplating the very survival of American English. In a lucidly penned article, referenced at times by my own colleagues, "The Answer is 45 Cents" (1999), Leo illustrates his keen contempt for, yet apparent ignorance of, the process school of composition. Perhaps seeing only one side or one minute feature of process theory, Leo assumes that the process approach to writing equates to a dispensing with logic. As he excoriates those professors who abide by its premises, he is, thus, in a good position to affect the tone or direction of the public debate:

> In some ways, this anything-goes movement is an attempt to patronize a new wave of unprepared college students, largely members of minority groups, by saying that standards aren't really all that important after all. Mac Donald writes: 'Confronted with a barrage of students who had no experience in formal grammar or written language, it was highly convenient for professors to learn that students' natural ways of speaking and writing should be preserved, not corrected.'
>
> But the good-hearted professors who disparage 'the myth of basic skills' are doing students no favors. At some point they have to leave the university and find a job, usually one offered by a company that cares less about oppression and feelings than about those basic skills. (1999, p. 14)

It would, of course, be easy to concede that basic skills are fundamental to the socioeconomic growth of the individual, but just as easy to question the means by which basic skills are developed in students. Staunchly prescriptive assessments of speech and writing, such as those advocated by Leo, can often communicate implicitly what cultural imperialists manage to convey explicitly: "non-mainstream varieties of US English should be restricted to the home and neighborhood, to play and informal situations, to the telling of folktales and stories of little interest to the *wider* world" (Lippi-Green, 1997, p. 109 [author's emphasis]). Vast portions of the public debate appear occupied by concerns over the best means of maintaining the accepted variety at the center, with the view that children at the periphery should be drilled with the more widely-accepted methods and standard prescriptions of enlightenment.

Historically, though, not all academics have boarded the same language-policies bandwagon. In 1963, for example, John Holt called attention to some of the problems in militantly prescriptive approaches to the study of communication when he observed in his book, *How Children Fail*: "...that for most children, school was a place of danger, and their main business in school was staying out of danger as much as possible" (2000 [1963] p. 230). Scholarship, at the time, appeared able, in part, to encourage change in politics as then-governor Ronald Reagan signed California legislation in 1967 authorizing bilingual education, ending a nearly 100-year-old state mandate that "all schools shall be taught in the English language" (Crawford & Lyons, 1998, ¶ 1). The 1960 Census also contributed to obvious change when it revealed that English-only schooling harmed Hispanic, Asian, and Native-American students. At a time when militancy on civil rights issues dominated the national political landscape, the Census must have revealed rather startling statistics to public policymakers. Fifty percent of California's Mexican-American residents, aged 18-24, had dropped out of school before completing the 8th grade (1998, ¶ 1).

The question remaining today is whether schools or approaches to the communication arts have changed enough and for the better since the early 1960s. What appears to have changed, most significantly, since the 1960 Census was reflected in the very latest Census Bureau report in 2003: "nearly one American in five speaks a language other than English at home, with Spanish leading and Chinese growing fast" (Schmid, 2004, ¶ 7). It was not until the late 1990s that Proposition 227, a state referendum, marked a noticeable return to a nationalistic view of and approach to language norms. The so-called "English for the Children" initiative launched by Californian businessman Ron Unz had put the English-only model back in the hands of a public wanting and plotting out new formulas as a response to rampant illegal immigration (1998, ¶ 2). According to James Crawford, twenty-three states since the 1980s have adopted Official English measures (2000/2001, ¶ 1). In Crawford's view, the present campaigns to "… 'officialize' English in the United States rests on the absurd claim that the most successful and dominant world language in history is under siege in its strongest bastion" (2000a, pp. 5-6).

The political responses to public outcries since 1998 have clearly been in favor of moving away from bi-lingual education—a trend that in Lippi-Green's view should not be altogether surprising. In commenting on this trend, she observes that the relationships between shifting power-bases and the public consciousness of language uses often focuses on legislation of one type or another (1997, p. 218). Crawford supports this view in his paper, "Anatomy of the English-Only Movement," when he points out that language politics are ultimately determined by material interests—struggles for social and economic supremacy—which normally lurk beneath the surface of the public debate (2000b, ¶ 23). Another scholarly response to these recent campaigns appears in John Baugh's book, *Out of the Mouths of Slaves*. Baugh contends that against the background of the competitive global economy, the linguistic diversity embodied throughout the American population is an underutilized resource. The educational implications of squandered linguistic assets have been politicized within debate on the value of bilingual education and growing legal and illegal immigration to the United States (Baugh, 1999, p. 156).

How do these phenomena, though, relate to teaching adult periphery students academic modes of composition? As normative pressures mount upon speakers in academic contexts—forcing upon them a perceived belief to self-correct or "hyper-correct" (Giles & Coupland, 1991, p.6)—similar pressures also mount upon student writers trying to communicate but finding themselves confounded by a range of other difficulties. As the practice of "verbal hygiene" (Cameron, 1995) embodies judgmental attitudes that converge on speech situations that shape a speaker's self-perception, similar sorts of attitudes are also involved in "shaping a student's self-perception" and, hence, ability to communicate in writing (Cheng, Horwitz & Shallert, 1999, p. 436).

The groundwork having been laid for the possible imposition of popular attitudes and judgments on speech and the movements toward tighter restrictions on language policies, the following discussions extend the interest in these relationships to the teaching of writing. Apart from some of the irrational attitudes surrounding language and use, scholars have since the mid-1960s developed a number of useful approaches to composition studies grounded in rather diverging schools of academic inquiry. Discussions of the three major schools of composition follow.

## 3. The Current Traditional Paradigm

> Our common language is ... English.
> And our common task is to ensure that our
> non-English-speaking children learn this common language.
> —*Secretary of Education, William J. Bennett,*
> *compiler of "The Book of Virtues" (1993)*

In some ways, the forces of popular campaigns for stricter language policies possess both positive and negative charges. If they call greater attention to already existing social or economic inequalities, they can also reshape and distort the dimensions and tone of public debates about which institutional strategies should work best in pulling periphery students from their marginal status.

As discussions of prevailing strategies and descriptions of their effects on pedagogical approaches are in order, this section addresses the following concerns: (a) What is the theoretical background of popular composition pedagogies? (b) What appears to be the dominant North American paradigm and how and where does it fit? (c) How does my approach to be demonstrated in Part 3 differ from this dominant paradigm?

## 3.1 A sketch of the pedagogical background

In the early part of the previous century, Vygotsky observed that "... to this point, psychology has conceived of writing as a complicated motor skill ... and paid ... little attention to the question of written language as ... a particular system of signs that designate the sounds and words of spoken language, which, in turn, are signs for real entities and relations" (1934/1978, p. 106). Many areas of the composition landscape have, fortunately, since developed. As Patricia Bizzell suggests, most research that shapes our current knowledge of composing, that is turning thought into a system of signs, has been published since 1970 (1992, p. 178). According to Bizzell, a majority of so-called composition specialists in the 1960s saw themselves primarily as writing teachers, not researchers. Yet, their work has since, nevertheless, influenced current research, not only in what it tells us about composing but also in the professional agenda it establishes for composition studies (Bizzell, 1992, p. 178).

A useful starting point for a discussion, therefore, of research in composition theory is Maxine Hairston who argued in the 1980s that a new paradigm had been emerging in composition and rhetoric (1982, p. 77). The title of this chapter, hence, borrows its name from Hairston's influential yet controversial essay, "The Winds of Change: Thomas Kuhn and the Revolution in the Teaching of Writing," which attempted at the time to paint a realistic portrait of prevailing teaching practices in composition. Re-introduced in Hairston's essay, the term "Current Traditional Paradigm" (CTP hereafter) was originally used by Virginia Burke in 1965 yet still appears to maintain currency, a point I shall briefly expand on here.

In determining the focus of this section, I was aware of the variety of theories supporting each of the major schools of composition in the United States. As each school features its unique theoretical underpinnings, each also appears to intersect at points when theory is turned into practice. Thus, the term *sketch*, more than *portrait*, appearing in the subtitle above, would better represent the qualities of these interrelated and intersecting approaches. That is to say, whilst no teacher of composition is likely to abide strictly by the practices typical of a single category, as, say, a traditional prescriptivist or liberal descriptivist, no single label could best exemplify them or their approaches, a point echoed by Richard Fulkerson (2005, p. 658-9).

The associated features of what Canagarajah sees as three major North American schools of composition are set out in the succeeding table, a variation of his outline. It must be noted beforehand, however, that competing characterizations and categories of the North American paradigm have emerged since Canagarajah's 1999 explication and are just as useful for gaining another perspective on the wealth of current approaches and theories. In his survey of composition studies at the turn of the 21st Century, Fulkerson observes, for example, that (a) critical/cultural studies, (b) expressivism, and (c) procedural rhetoric now form the basis of the North American paradigm. Consequently, one alternative perspective would hold that recent scholarship and practice drawn on the work of Peter Elbow, Donald Murray and others have pushed expressivist approaches to the forefront of practice. As with the procedural rhetoric and the critical/cultural schools referenced above, expressivist approaches are said to naturally incorporate a "process" perspective (Fulkerson, 2005, p. 658)—a method that does not appear in Canagarajah's original rendering.

Another alternative set of descriptive terms applied to the North American paradigm had been put forward by James Berlin. In his influential paper, "Rhetoric and Ideology in the Writing Class," Berlin argued that contemporary approaches to composition exist within an ideological frame rather than an ideology existing in rhetoric (1988, p. 477). As composition and "rhetoric [are] regarded as always already ideological," Berlin observed that the three schools of composition having emerged as most apparent were (a) the rhetorics of cognitive psychology, of (b) expressionism, and of (c) the social-epistemic (1988, pp. 477-8). Further complicating efforts to organize a comprehensive and cohesive description of the North American Paradigm is a recent personal communication from Elbow who sees "process" as the more precise term and remains rather critical of the term "expressivism" as it suggests to him a way of "labeling people [prescriptivists] that others disapproved of" (December 14, 2006).

Given the various alternative ways of surveying the composition and rhetoric landscape in the North American paradigm, the field seems to remain unsettled territory where pedagogies compete for prominence. The following table is an initial attempt to categorize this variety of diverging philosophical approaches to teaching writing and to show how these intersect at points within the North American paradigm. Whereas Canagarajah's original table (1999, p. 152) features the primary pedagogical focus as the heading of each approach, my adaptation features three generally recognized labels among eight major North American schools of rhetoric. It should also be noted that Table 2 provides not so much a detailed representation of all of these schools with strict categories as it does a general outline of what appears the most prominent features.

Table 2

|  | Structural | Generative | Genre |
|---|---|---|---|
| **Primary focus** | form (textual) | writer | content / reader |
| **Language connection** | current traditional paradigm | cognitive process theory | discourse analysis |
| **Pedagogical strategies** | writing modeling | generating editing revising processes | rhetorical analysis |
| **Linguistic base** | American structuralist | transformational generative | communicative competence |
| **Intellectual base** | behavioral Skinnerian inductive empirical normative | rational Chomskyan deductive | social Vygotskyan relativistic situational naturalistic expressivist |
| **Ideology** | instrumental | interactional | assimilationist |

Adapted from Canagarajah, 1999, p. 152

While Canagarajah saw fit not to cite Chomsky's influence on the generative school as helping form the intellectual base for many approaches to composition today, I felt that including this source would be not only important, but necessary for framing references to Chomsky's work in later sections.

Another reference absent in Canagarajah's original rendering is an expressivist approach to composition, which is thought to emerge from a Vygotskyan perspective on speech development and its implications for the development of writing skills. Elbow, for example, observes that a flawed assumption is that speech and writing are distinctly characterizable media, a point Vygotsky had reported on from investigations that show "…speech development follows the same laws as the development of all the other mental operations involving the use of signs…" (1986, p. 86). As writing is the deliberate use of signs, Elbow argues, rather, that "…each medium can draw on and foster *various* [author's emphasis] mentalities" (1985, pp. 283).

Other helpful terms which appear as amendments to the generative category are *generating* and *processes*—key words that turn up at times in critical discussions of pedagogies, but which are assumed to support all contemporary approaches to composition (Fulkerson, 2005, p. 658). The discussions that follow, many of which borrow from Canagarajah's explications, outline a variety of current practices and summarize their various strengths and weaknesses.

One well-known remedy for treating linguistic ailments in classrooms comes in the form of drills (Bizzell, 1992, p. 178; Cameron, 1995 p. 104), when students are required to commit to memory any number of the parts of speech and to repeatedly pronounce their definitions in class. Activities of this kind are often seen as an 'essential exercise' as one passionate high school teacher recently advocated in a private discussion while expressing her 'serious concern' over falling standards. Whilst widely known as drills, this strategy, grounded in the American Structural School, has its focus on correct form, for it "conceives of writing as the mastery of correct grammatical and rhetorical structures for text construction" (Canagarajah, 1999, p. 148). The means by which correctness is achieved, though, can be further interrogated. Apart from putting students through a regimen of drills, some approaches also tend to rely on sentence-combining exercises, parsing or various other similar methods in which students can imitate model essays in order to achieve academic success.

According to Canagarajah, approaches such as these derive their roots from the CTP that was dominant in the mid-1960s in first-language pedagogy and which attended to the textual structures in the finished product (1999, p. 148). Given the academic value placed upon the correct form of the finished product, it is also worth noting, here, another term sometimes used to describe Structuralist Approaches. Carl Smith cites the research of Warchow and Gustavson (1999, p. 5) who suggest that "modernist approaches" such as these force students to accept the standard five-paragraph structure for text production prescribed by the teacher. This model, though, often fails to encourage students to develop and fully explore their own ideas. In seeing no academic value in, say, creative writing, these modernist approaches completely ignore the personal, creative force behind text production (Smith, 2000 ¶ 14)—requiring instead the production of a body of quantifiable, systematically constructed knowledge (Warchow & Gustavson, 1999, p. 11).

Since the CTP was, nevertheless, part of a revival of classical Greco-Roman rhetoric, it was, thus, assumed to be grounded in great Western literary traditions (Canagarajah, 1999, p. 148)—hence, the compliment *traditional* for *paradigm*. As Bizzell observes, instructors came to hope that the study of classics such as *Walden* and *Sons and Lovers* would open up in students the floodgates of correct, intelligent and stylish prose (1992, p. 106)—a likely precursor to later developments in the genre school. The CTP is also said to be undergirded by American linguistic structuralism and behaviorist psychology in its assumption that abstract textual structures could be drilled into students through controlled exercises in order to "cultivate habitualized writing skills" (Canagarajah, 1999, p. 148).

Is the CTP necessarily still current, though? As I aim to illustrate in the following section, the North American paradigm represents unique academic territory where the Genre, Generative and Structural schools both clash with and complement one another. Of course, while some of the major byproducts of Structuralism, for example, have resulted in exercises such as sentence-combining, diagramming and drilling students with meta-linguistic terms, that can be controlled, these tasks are also located farther away from the more immediate, subjective and practical tasks involved in generating and drafting. Expressed another way, if a noun is, according to the often-repeated classroom maxim, 'a person, place or thing,' it is worth wondering, too, how this abstract bit of knowledge translates precisely into real writing situations and further shapes for the better figurative or literal uses of the language.

Adger supports this observation in her article, "Language Policy and Public Knowledge," arguing that grammar drills separated from language use haven't made much of a dent in students' language use in the past. She argues that simply refocusing this approach so that it helps students add another dialect rather than stamp out the one they have is not promising (1997a, ¶ 2). This current observation was also given attention in the late 1960s as James Moffett argued that students are being asked, in effect, to prefer the dialect of a speech community to which they do not belong and to disavow the ways of communicating that they learned from parents or others upon whom their sense of personal and social identity depended (1983, p. 156-7).

Deborah Cameron speculates more recently why strategies such as drilling or diagramming appear to hang on in classrooms. Perhaps they remain current because of certain subjective convictions that words themselves are solemn or pseudo-sacred tools of our swollen intellect, that they somehow speak of our power over those things we routinely identify and name. Cameron likens this sort of behavior to "magical thinking"—when there is a symbolic connection deeply embedded in human culture between exerting control over language and exerting control over things and events in the world (1995, p. 219). In offering a set of six "elementary" prescriptions for "expressing thought," Orwell's "Politics and the English Language" (1946) best exemplifies the general tendency towards exerting control over language.

To illustrate further, a virologist goes to certain extremes to commit to memory a number of the terms peculiar to her vocation, the instruments she uses, the pathogens she isolates, the tissues they invade. In communicating the results of her analysis, she depends on these terms but may feel empowered in locating an elusive, previously unidentified virus, recognizing its unique features, and ultimately naming it. Conversely, student writers forced along the American Structural path must go to some lengths to memorize a wealth of specialized terms. In communicating their analysis of a particularly problematic passage of prose whose meaning may be as elusive to them as the virus is to the researcher, these students will also need to draw upon their knowledge of meta-linguistic jargon. Precisely identifying and naming the problem has its rewards, but the difference for the student of writing ends there.

The difference is that the virus—a minuscule but nevertheless concrete thing—is not a thought—the electrical impulse of a developing idea transformed into symbols that will represent the thought (Vygotsky, 1934/1978, p. 106; 1934/1986 p. 218). The difference is quite significant because it is the concrete world in which the writer and germ researcher exist. More than merely identifying grammatical problems or naming parts of speech, the student writer is often more concerned with finding an expedient way towards the expression of thought precisely and clearly.

The second category in Table 2 summarizes Generative approaches which stem from cognitive process theory in first-language research and which attend more to the thought processes and cognitive strategies typically employed by writers while shifting attention away from the finished product. Seeing *essay* as more of a verb than a noun, as a complex cognitive activity that is recursive, generative, exploratory, and goal-oriented, practitioners of this approach find their philosophical roots buried in the "Chomskyan revolution of transformational generative grammar and the related rise of humanistic psychology" (Hairston, 1982, p. 77).

Canagarajah observes that since Generative approaches connect acceptable academic writing to the knowledge base which informs the texts of the respective disciplines, it tends to ignore the local knowledge (i.e. day-to-day classroom insights and first-hand observations) of writing of teachers and students. Nor is this approach informed by the knowledge traditions of other minority communities from which periphery students usually come (1999, p. 149). These methods also fail to account for the literacy conventions, hermeneutic models, and communicative modes traditionally practiced by periphery communities. For Canagarajah, methods arising from the Generative tradition pose challenges for periphery students

> ... from constructs developed in the center. Moreover, the acquisition of these structures is considered a matter of habit-oriented automatic skills. In line with behaviorist pedagogy, students are expected to master these textual structures through constant practice and imitation. However, by excluding 'thinking' from writing, the school treats writers as lacking agency, subjectivity, individuality. The students are prepared for formulaic writing, bordering on mechanical, thoughtless modes of text construction, similar to those demanded by bureaucratic institutions in a technological society. (1999, p. 149)

As Linda Brodkey describes them, Generative approaches, which tend to focus more on the idealized writer, also obscure the implied institutional power that teachers hold over students. That is to say, although they are "pedagogies of process and personal experience," they "fail to the extent that they deny that composition teachers *are* the designated institutional representatives of the power and authority of language" (Brodkey, 1996, p. 145 [author's emphasis]). As techniques typical of the Generative School permit researchers greater opportunities to understand the unique challenges that periphery students face, the much larger focus on the particular acts of text production are likely to prevent a deeper understanding of the socio-cultural, affective, and situational pressures that impinge upon writing itself (Canagarajah, 1999, p. 150).

Advocates of this school are said to maintain that most students can learn and make use of a set of universal cognitive strategies that help them generate effective writing and that those who exhibit these abilities are considered skilled while those who don't are seen as unskilled. This school, though, can largely overlook the significant generating and drafting differences that students cannot help but bring to the task of producing texts. In seeing those students whose strategies are different as unskilled, the Generative School implicitly or explicitly labels such students as cognitively deficient. Thus, simple cultural differences brought to the task of text production can be misdiagnosed as a kind of deficiency (Canagarajah, 1999, p. 151). John Leo's hasty misdiagnoses, for example, discussed earlier in Section 2.1, serve as a fairly good illustration of the sort of misinformed and, thus, misdirected criticisms sometimes leveled at Process practitioners.

The third category outlined in Table 2 summarizes Genre approaches. Canagarajah argues that the Genre School has its own set of problems and limitations in that the approaches, which are content and/or reader focused, impute egalitarian and democratic attitudes to discourse communities (1999, p. 152). Although practitioners of these approaches accept that discourse conventions are different in different communities, they consider that all of these conventions are equally accessible to all writers and, therefore, hold equal value. To students of the periphery, the more highly valued conventions associated with cultural capital become, in effect, alien dialects while the *equal value* to which Canagarajah points is, more likely, a mere myth in classrooms where prescriptions for correctness remain a last resort. While these approaches recognize that differences do exist,

> … they do not relate [those differences] to power. As a result, they [overlook] the threat faced by minority

> students, in being dominated, alienated or ostracized by the academic community. On the motive of inculcating communicative competence to talk to the chosen academic community, these approaches can indoctrinate … students with the values behind these communities. (1999, p. 152)

In the broadest terms, then, assimilation becomes their key to academic success and, thus, future economic success. In adopting as his or her own the accepted Genre, though, to what extent does a student's ability to adapt and assimilate weigh upon his or her capacity to develop effective writing skills? In more specific terms, Brodkey addresses this difficulty by observing that

> …composition instruction appears to have succeeded best at establishing in most people a lifelong aversion to writing. They have learned to associate a desire to write with a set of punishing exercises called writing in school: printing, penmanship, spelling, punctuation, themes, book reports, and library research papers in college preparatory and advanced placement courses" (1996, p. 135).

Brodkey wonders, too, whether successful students are not the sort that are able to learn early on that writing assignments represent opportunities for them to demonstrate their ineptitudes and for their teachers to correct them and not invitations to write about ideas (1996, p. 136).

Increasingly more sophisticated reading drills, for example, rooted in thinking that only repeated exposure and practice make perfect are the usual implications for, say, first-year college students seeking increases in their linguistic capital. These so-called punishing exercises about which Brodkey writes can become, ultimately, fundamental to strategies of composition praised for their adherence to the concept of standardization discussed by Cheshire and Milroy (1993).

Moreover, as Canagarajah argues, if these so-called punishing approaches "impute egalitarian and democratic attitudes to discourse communities," Karen Hornick discusses how this might be so. In "Teaching Writing to Linguistically Diverse Students," she observes that since standard written English is taught by representatives of the academic community itself, the cultural orientations of educators ultimately determine school literacy. That is, as objectivity and explicitness are valued in academic discourse, especially in writing, the characteristic, competitive patterns intrinsic to the received academic register conflict, in Hornick's view, with "the communal cooperative verbal styles typical of nonstandard English speaking communities" (1986, p, 1).

She argues that most "...research on high school writing instruction points to a single great need: better trained teachers" (1986, p. 1). Though emerging from studies of composition theory and practice in the 1980s, Hornick's observations, even so, remain current. Edgar Schuster supports this view more recently in "Reforming the English Language Arts" (1999). In his article, Schuster argues that these sorts of traditional approaches to teaching writing extend throughout the grades, even into college and represent a staggering waste of time and money (1999, p. 512).

Brock Haussamen and colleagues clarify why by arguing that the problem with traditional schoolhouse approaches to grammar has not been

> ... grammar itself as much as it has been the way grammar is usually taught. Instead of helping students to focus on real literature or on the actual paper they are writing, traditional grammar pedagogy requires students to divert their attention to the isolated and often contrived sentences in a textbook.

> It encourages students—and teachers—to believe that the authority for Standard English is that separate book of rules rather than literature and the language of those with power and prestige in the living culture. It focuses on errors instead of on the understanding of language. (Haussamen et al., 2003, p. 4)

Given the range of periphery students in adult continuing education programs grappling with ways in which to develop not only acceptable writing but, often simultaneously, an acceptable verbal academic register, what are the likely implications for students engaged in the composing process?

The sorts of problems in standard usage drills that Brodkey, Hornick, Schuster and Haussamen call attention to and which are often fundamental to stereotypical composition courses seem to present a twofold difficulty for periphery students. In conflating the troubles they perceive in their writing with the problems they perceive in their own oral communication and not wanting to recreate these problems on paper, they may sense a relative futility of composing in writing what they already do naturally in speech.

Could any limitations to Generative or Genre approaches arise simply from the differences inherent in discourse communities and the variety of styles that their participants bring to academe? The communication problem in the classroom remains, in Xin Liu-Gale's view, "intrinsic to teaching" (1997, p. 54) which is, according to Bourdieu and Passeron, the "symbolic imposition" (1977, p. 7) of a cultural arbitrary by an arbitrary power. If it is the mission of schools to conserve and reproduce knowledge (the cultural arbitrary) which is made legitimate by the dominant class, then to fulfill its obligation to the dominant class, the institution must create the context for "pedagogic communication" (1977, p. 7). In this context, teachers maintain the legitimized institutional power

> ... over students, and the latter [are forced to accept] whatever is taught to [them] without resistance. As a consequence of these [unbalanced] power relations ..., pedagogic communication between teachers and students is characterized by coercion, by students' submissiveness and obedience, by the affirmation of teachers' values, by the infallibility of teachers [themselves], and by the absence of a genuine interest in what is being communicated. (Liu-Gale, 1997, p. 56)

Hornick discusses some of the consequences of pedagogic communication, arguing that unsuccessful attempts in American high schools to address fully the needs of all students often pose a dual difficulty for those who come from linguistically diverse backgrounds. She points out that those who "... speak nonstandard English are often ... penalized simply for using the language ... they do at home" (Hornick, 1986, p. 1)—observations also made by case study participants and to be discussed in Part 3. As these ways of responding to writing are embedded in thinking in dichotomies of good and bad or correct and incorrect, Haussamen asks practitioners to first reflect on the very meanings of "correctness" and "incorrectness." That is, when we feel moved to tell students that they are wrong in their uses of language, we should also consider the context and circumstance of such a criticism. Haussamen observes that the "simplistic and absolute judgment that a piece of language is right or wrong can be, at its root, an attempt to judge people" (2003, p. 11).

Nevertheless, the categories that Canagarajah creates and his explications are useful insofar as each class helps simplify understanding of the great range of approaches and the cross-borrowing of each at work within the predominant North American context. The purpose of this discussion, thus far, has not been to encourage rejection of insights developed in these schools of composition, but to call even greater attention to the "...form, content, reader and writer in the social context" (Canagarajah, 1999, p. 153) of text production.

To echo once more Canagarajah's key position, an expedient method should also surpass the usual ways of "...perceiving the discursive challenges of periphery students into dichotomies such as first-language vs. second-language, native discourse vs. Anglo-American discourse, vernacular community vs. academic community, or native culture vs. Western culture" (1999, p. 152). Perhaps it is worth taking Canagarajah's critique a step farther and asking, too, whether the common pedagogical materials, templates or structures themselves, such as those to be discussed in Section 3.2, impose upon speakers and writers boundaries and rules which cannot be crossed or broken. That is to say, do popular approaches that emerge from the CTP divide language in ways that are unnatural or counter-intuitive to the language learner, whether, say, the sociological acquisition of a grammar (standard or otherwise) or even the socially constructed patterns of argument in discourse communities? If questions like these are relevant and important to students of composition, another way of seeing and simplifying further the complexities of the process is recognizing foremost the range of natural linguistic abilities and interests that students already possess and enter classrooms with, a discussion of which is to be taken up in Section 3.3.

The major schools of North American composition theory described herein ultimately feature a few fundamental similarities that cannot be easily denied but can, perhaps, be more easily overlooked. From each will develop certain levels of prescription which will invariably force practitioners into obligations they feel that they can likely not avoid. Combined with the expectations of the institution and those imposed by the self or society, typical American teachers of English composition must do much to prepare students while contending with a vast range of student abilities and self-destructive attitudes.

As the judiciary fulfills its duty to the public through the maintenance of judicial laws, the university does so through the maintenance of linguistic laws. Nowhere does Cheshire and Milroys' concept of 'maintenance' (1993) appear more apparent than in composition classrooms where approaches informed largely by the American Structuralist school seek observable, quantifiable, and measurable outcomes of writing behavior and final product. What appears to be their growing popularity may hinge upon two reasons. Firstly, the recent dramatic negative changes in the public's attitudes towards corporate citizenship have forced more strident calls for responsibility and accountability into the public discourse. The infamous corporate accounting scandals at Worldcom and Enron, to name a few, seem to have precipitated serious reflection on values in all sectors of public life, namely too including public universities. Secondly, in seeing themselves increasingly more as pseudo-corporations than public institutions of higher learning, North American colleges intent on maintaining survival and sustained accreditation for public funding now move more visibly with trends toward outcomes assessment and other quantifiable forms of knowledge (Combs, 2001, p. 85; Isserlis, 1998, ¶ 12).

Adapted from the Educational Testing Services (ETS) website and now part of University of Maryland University College's efforts in assessment, the following table illustrates the objectively verifiable and testable niceties of English composition.

Table 3

Proficiency Levels for Writing Skills

| | |
|---|---|
| At level 1, a student can: | …recognize agreement among basic grammatical elements (e.g., nouns, verbs, pronouns, etc.). <br> …recognize appropriate transitions. <br> …correct (as a verb) word choices. <br> …order sentences in a paragraph. <br> …order elements in an outline. |
| At level 2, a student can: | …incorporate new material into a passage. <br> …recognize agreement among grammatical elements (e.g., nouns, verbs, pronouns, etc.) when these elements are complicated by intervening words or phrases. <br> …combine simple clauses into single, more complex combinations. <br> …recast existing sentences into new syntactic combinations. |
| At level 3, a student can: | …discriminate between appropriate and inappropriate use of parallelism. <br> …discriminate between appropriate and inappropriate use of idiomatic language. <br> …recognize redundancy. <br> …discriminate between correct and incorrect constructions <br> …recognize the most effective revision of a sentence. |

Adapted from Educational Testing Services at
http://www.ets.org/hea/acpro/proficiency.html#writing

Beyond the useful divisions of theories and practices outlined thus far, the predominant North American paradigm of tertiary composition courses remains current and traditional as the instruments of measure themselves beget rules that once broken clearly mark the writer as a member of a particular class (Giles & Coupland, 1991, p. 32).

These rules and the efforts made in maintaining the selected variety with its conventions of usage produce diametrically opposed classes of language users: those who break the laws and those who follow them. Students who reject or who remain unable to observe the rules by dint of their socioeconomic station may likely continue facing the kinds of contempt typically reserved for the abject quarters of society. As Cheshire & Milroy (1993) argue, the laws that govern usage, thus, require teachers or other guardians of linguistic uniformity to "suppress" varieties that compete with the selected one so that subjects may always agree with their verbs, pronouns with their antecedents, commas and all other mechanical marks with their codified prescriptions. It may be worth asking, ultimately, if popular methods meant to maintain the process of standardization are actually elitist or merely pragmatic approaches to developing higher levels of literacy.

As a major critic of the "institutional politics of composition" in the United States, Susan Miller (1998) feels that they are predominantly elitist and argues that compulsory composition courses perpetuate class differences by holding the non-elect in courses that expose them to insignificant forms of writing, while students from qualified backgrounds, exempted from first-year writing courses, are promoted quickly to rhetoric courses in which they learn to speak and write for powerful forums.

In keeping with Cheshire and Milroy's notion of "suppression" and "selection," Kathryn Fitzgerald, notes too that composition theorists today have unearthed what they call "… the elitist, undemocratic aspects of the field's past that [continue to] disturb many contemporary [researchers] who see their aim as extending the opportunities available through education to all social classes by introducing students to discourses of power" (2001, p. 225).

Furthermore, as Fitzgerald notes, "… students held in first-year composition [are] convinced that their linguistic roughness disqualified them from serious public participation" (2001, p. 225). And what of the college textbooks nowadays meant to codify and embody the received variety? Fitzgerald observes that in their attempt to convert complex oral and literary rhetorical theory into writing instruction for first-year college students, these textbooks reduced the theory to sets of formulaic generalizations that were inadequate to their task both conceptually and practically. Certainly, in light of some of the more popular texts (to be critiqued in Section 3.2) nowadays with The University of Maryland University College, Fitzgerald's observations still hold.

Finally, another difficulty of constructing an accurate portrait of prevailing methods in teaching composition lies in the disparate policies that govern local school boards throughout America. Whereas state legislatures set general policy, local school districts and their boards of education must interpret state guidelines in light of the perceived needs of local students and the district's own financial means of carrying out policy (Shafer, R. 1999, p. 381). Furthermore, academic freedom itself permits teachers to choose one approach over another, so teaching writing remains "the result of an infinite number of choices" (Bishop, 1999, p. 12). Like various interpretations of laws that compete for validity in the public arena, the various approaches to English composition compete for validity in academic practices. Whether embodied predominantly in traditional schoolhouse grammar methods replete with codified prescriptions of correctness or in cutting-edge progressive approaches, a more comprehensive depiction of North American writing pedagogy will need further explanation.

## 3.2 The North American Paradigm:

Given the general outline of a few major divisions and characteristics of composition studies in North America, what kinds of practices appear to be the foci for composition teachers? For all of its progressive and wide variety of theories, the North American paradigm, namely one which subsumes all three approaches discussed in 3.1 as well as those cited by Berlin and Fulkerson, is still, broadly speaking, a prescriptive movement retaining some remnant features of nineteenth century traditional grammars (Van Essen, 1997, p.1). To illustrate, Wartchow and Gustavson contend that modernist approaches fail to encourage students to think creatively by expecting them to follow closely to the widely held ideal of the five-paragraph pattern which embodies "quantifiable, systematically constructed knowledge" (1999, p. 11).

Beyond missed opportunities in classrooms for creative interaction and thought sharing among students, the notion of an ideal discourse style set within the boundaries of an ideal five-paragraph pattern seem to arise from an implicit acceptance of the sorts of arguments that give English-only movements their life in the public fray. For Bruce Horner, the problems in composition practice emerge from "… a pervasive, tacit policy of 'English-only' in composition and of a constellation of assumptions about languages, and language users, that continues to cripple both public debate … and compositionists' approaches to matters of 'error'" (2001, p. 742).

In spite of major efforts to regain from state legislators the control over curricula they had usurped from local school boards during much of the 1980s (Shafer, 1999, p. 383), the attempt at a consensus in composition pedagogy among practitioners and the promise of a new unified direction after Dartmouth II[5] (1987) has not yet entirely found its way into practice. As Horner goes on to argue, "the dominant approaches to language and 'error' have failed to understand language as material social practice, and so have persistently produced strategies at odds with the realities teachers,

---

[5] Darmouth II is the moniker for a June 1987 invitational seminar attended by sixty members from eight English language associations whose aim was to "discuss English curricular and chart the course of English studies for the 1990s and beyond" (Shafer, 1999, p. 383).

students, writers, and the public confront daily in their interactions with one another" (2001, p. 742).

Examples of the North American modernist bent towards correcting errors and dispensing prescription abound not only in the expressed attitudes of concerned citizens in public discourse, but also in some popular academic texts. Of course, texts do not define how compositionists approach their practice, but it must be noted that textbooks do represent academic efforts to reflect current scholarship. If conservative attitudes toward language and use, such as those discussed earlier, have any influence on scholarship and textbook production, then this connection could not be more apparent than in Susan Fawcett's *Evergreen: A guide to writing with readings* (2004). Taking as its predominant feature a structuralist approach to language, each new edition has remained a staple in the first-year writing program at the University of Maryland University College for at least the past twelve years. Chapters such as "Exploring the Writing Process," "Prewriting to Generate Ideas," and "The Process of Writing Paragraphs" feature useful discussions of the complex cognitive processes at work in the minds of those engaged in the process of writing, while the major emphasis of the book lies in much more structuralist approaches.

The various textual discussions prescribing correct ways to identify and label lexical items in terms of the traditionally endorsed eight word-classes (i.e. noun, pronoun, adjective, article, verb, adverb, preposition, conjunction), as well as to use punctuation, dominate the rest of the text. The following table, adapted from a discussion of pronoun case forms in compound constructions, and a subsequent practice exercise illustrate the general pattern of prescriptions adult learners with UMUC confront.

Table 4
Practice 6
Determine the case required by each sentence, and circle the correct pronoun.

1. (He, Him) and Harriet plan to enroll in the police academy.
2. A snowdrift stood between (I, me) and the subway entrance.
3. Tony used the software and then returned it to Barbara and (I, me, myself).
4. The reporter's questions caught June and (we, us) off guard.
5. By noon, Julio and (he, him) had already cleaned the garage.
6. These charts helped (she, her) and (I, me) with our statistics homework.
7. Professor Woo gave Diane and (she, her) extra time to finish the exam.
8. Between you and (I, me) I have always preferred country music.

Reproduced from *Evergreen: A guide to writing with readings*, by Fawcett, 2004, p. 421

Cheshire and Milroy's reference to *codification* and *prescription*, here, communicates to adult learners the academy's firm emphasis on the concept of correct form. Any response beyond the boundaries of the parentheses is intolerable. As a variation of the cloze exam, Practice 6 suggests, as well, that deviation from the norm is improper and potentially embarrassing to the student who misrecognizes and, thus, announces in classroom discussions the unacceptable case form. In keeping with the prescriptive gist of the *Evergreen* text, a popular companion workbook, *English 2600: A programmed course in grammar and usage*, features even more stringent and archaic approaches to language teaching. The following table, adapted from the *English 2600* test booklet, illustrates the typical kinds of exercises students must contend with if they are to learn anything useful about English composition in at least one North American institution of higher learning.

Table 5
_____

Unit 1-A  The Verb and its Subject
_____

**True or False**
After each statement write *T* or *F* in the space at the right. (2 points each)
1. A sentence might consist of only two words                          1. __
2. The subject of a sentence usually comes after, not before, the predicate.  2. __
3. The most important word in the predicate is the verb.               3. __
4. A noun but not a pronoun can be used as the subject of a sentence.  4. __
5. A pronoun can be used to avoid repeating a noun.                    5. __

**Indicate the simple subject and the verb in each by writing, under the proper heading, the letter of each word you select. (2 points each)**

|  | Subject | Verb |
|---|---|---|

6. A small fire quickly spreads to a large area.        6. _____    _____
   a   b   c   d    e    f  g   h    i

7. Everybody in the room talked at once.                7. _____    _____
   a       b c  d   e    f  g

8. The voice with a smile wins.                         8. _____    _____
   a   b   c d  e   f

9. The local train stops at every small town.           9. _____    _____
   a   b   c   d     e    f    g    h

10. Tornadoes often occur there in the spring.         10. _____    _____
    a          b    c    d    e   f   g
_____

Reproduced from *English 2600: A programmed course in grammar and usage*, (Blumenthal, 1989, p. 5)

    Of particular interest here is the original publication date and the many subsequent reprints of this text since 1960, which appears to signal that Structuralism, for example, has not entirely lost its appeal. The *True* or *False* quiz, one of the hallmarks of structural approaches, is typical of the heavy reliance on meta-lingual knowledge still tested as prerequisite to good writing. One wonders, too, what sort of knowledge periphery student writers, hoping to find success, must draw upon here to solve such a series of non-sequiturs. Besides the unrelated difficulties of generating and drafting, the sample sentence at number 9 may present other problems too, wherein *stops* is seen as a noun rather than a verb. The de-contextualized uses of the language here present additional difficulties for some students who might ask why an auxiliary verb and main verb to complete the noun phrase do not appear in this sample.

As for the importance of developing a more extensive meta-language lexicon, students must also work through the "simple subject and verb" test that follows. While this test is a variation of parsing exercises that were popular in the 1970s, it demonstrates the limitations of meta-linguistic knowledge. Adult learners who are coping with problems in composition, such as their own well-entrenched apprehensions, are forced to revisit old academic territory and cope with a wealth of arcane terms they had likely encountered in primary or secondary school during the 1970s or 1980s.

In the face of Bizzell's reference to widespread professional self-reflection and positive change in the field of composition (1992, p. 178)—that is that "writing teachers became convinced ... that [their] initial assumptions about the need for grammar drills were simply wrong"—the exercises illustrated in Tables 4 and 5, nevertheless, closely resemble those still in vogue today. As the use of something may, thus, suggest its perceived widespread necessity, textbook exercises such as these seem to contradict Gretchen Owocki and Yetta Goodman's observation that "contemporary researchers ... no longer view [writing] as something to be taught through grammar, spelling, and penmanship drills" (1997, p. 178). That is to say, the gaps between contemporary research in composition, pedagogy, and textbook content may be too narrow, at times, to even discern.

In light of the variety of perspectives that characterize the North American Paradigm, the ways of assessing the utility of pedagogies, texts and student abilities, Horner and Trimbur insist that "... compositionists must learn to resist thinking of identifying students and teaching in terms of fixed categories of language, language ability, and social identity, however natural and inevitable such categories can seem to be in our daily work and in the arguments we make to the public in defense of our work" (2002, p. 622).

## 3.3 An Alternative

In what school does my approach to composition find its roots? As suggested earlier in this section, labeling teachers as adherents to only one school or another does little to further understanding the depth of the real problem. While one teacher may typically take up Generative approaches, he or she may also see the need at times to introduce methods emerging from the Genre or Structuralist paradigm. What appears to dominate, though, and stifle the creative potential in students are those normative structural approaches peculiar to the current traditional paradigm, wherein behaviorist traditions remain alive and well.

The three dominant schools of composition outlined in Table 2 (page 41) account for most, but not all of the ways that knowledge of a language figures into the development of writing as a skill. As Canagarajah situated Vygotsky in the genre paradigm (1999, p. 152) for his contributions to the socio-psychological dimensions of language development, Michael Polanyi's contributions (1958, pp.132-33) for understanding the epistemological dimensions of language and their implications on knowing and using the language also figure prominently in the debate over which approaches work well and when. It is both Vygotsky's work in general as well as Polanyi's notion of tacit knowing, the idea of making use of what is known implicitly, what is often unarticulated but known by the body, that makes the approach for which I am arguing novel.

This method grounds its practitioner in the Genre paradigm, which draws on the situational, naturalistic phenomena present as writers work together towards a common rhetorical solution. It also asks how play, an activity paramount to child development (Vygotsky, 1934/1978, p. 96), extends to adult learning in light of the tacit knowledge of language (Polanyi, 1958 p. 70; 1967, p. 91) brought to the task of generating and drafting. So, this primary approach crosses Canagarajah's categories and focuses on the writing process (generative) as well as on the content (sentence level) where meanings intersect with genres and rhetorical devices.

This point at which students superimpose rhetorical devices upon intended meanings in certain genres and wrestle with how best to deal with the problems of clarity and precision is still part and parcel of the debate in contemporary composition theory. Should prescription reign over all other approaches where adult periphery students, speaking a wide variety of nonstandard dialects and dealing with a variety of apprehensions, come to have their language skills polished for use in the wider world? The following sections attempt to grapple with this problem and the problem of relying too heavily on popular normative approaches to language and use.

## 4. Never End a Sentence with a Preposition

> This is the sort of bloody nonsense up with which I will not put.
> —*Winston Churchill*
> *(in E. Gowers' Plain Words 1948)*

If a pen were mightier than a sword, then language is a double-edged weapon. Languages can both liberate and bind. The "...sliver-tongued orator... [6]" Barack Obama, both ridiculed and praised for his oration, must see his uses of language as self-apparent weaponry that can cut his opponents, but himself as well. For those speakers of English wishing to emerge from the periphery, the double-edged qualities of language beyond rhetorical styles ring especially true for those who are often bound and confounded by certain "prescriptive rules [that] make no sense on any level" (Pinker, 1994, p. 373). "They are," in the words of Steven Pinker, "bits of

---

[6] One of Mr. Tom Buffenbarger's various epithets for Sen. Barack Obama during the 2008 campaign for the Democratic nomination for president (2008).

folklore that originated for screwball reasons [arguably] several hundred years ago and have perpetuated themselves ever since" (1994, p. 373). Still considered, for example, the language of the learned and powerful in eighteenth century England, the perception was that Latin [a language whose grammar is governed by entirely different rules] was the model of "precision and logic to which English should aspire" (1994, p. 373). What Pinker refers to as "folklore," Patricia O'Conner identifies many examples thereof in a chapter titled "The Living Dead"—an appropriate name for the sorts of "mythrules" (Schuster, 2003, p. xii) still circulating in classrooms and public and academic discussions of language uses.

Like Theodore M. Bernstein, H.W. Fowler, and George O. Curme before her, O'Conner attempts to put to rest a number of these linguistic legends still propagated in schools. Hers is a more contemporary response, it seems, to William Strunk and E.B. White's *The Elements of Style* that features more prescriptive and less descriptive approaches to discussing language uses. Ending sentences with prepositions, beginning them with conjunctions, splitting infinitives, using double negatives, using *whose* to refer to inanimate objects, using *it is I* instead of *it is me*, and many others appear with complementary descriptions and discussions outlining why these prescriptions are based on erroneous claims and should, therefore, be ignored rather than attended to.

As forms of spoken and written discourse, American varieties of English are fairly well policed modes of expression. Wayne C. Booth speculated decades ago "…why so many of our fellow citizens think of us as unfriendly policemen: it is because too many of us have seen ourselves as unfriendly policemen" (1963, p. 247). It appears that little has changed since in the minds of those students routinely cited for linguistic infractions. Neither, too, should the term *policed*, here, with its antecedents to law and order, come as a surprise to readers, as the following discussion should reveal the extent to which some citizens feel moved to protect the language with popular appeals to the authoritative "mythrules."

In 1957, White observed that "[years] ago, students [had been] warned never to end a sentence with a preposition, [but] time, of course, has softened that decree" (1979, p. 77). Have those engaged in language teaching today, though, since softened their stance and left the prescriptive traditions that White had spoken of buried in the past? While even popular prescriptive grammar reference texts, such as *The Little, Brown Handbook*, feature sensible discussions of usage and suggestions for clarity and precision, many so-called "mythrules" have maintained some currency.

While these sorts of myths have been exposed as such and discussed extensively for at least a hundred years, they appear to remain active in the minds of those who still wish to negotiate their supposed import. "I was told that you can't begin a sentence with conjunctions like *because*," is one often-heard refrain. A five- to ten-minute counterargument calling attention to this sort of nonsense must invariably ensue if I am to persuade at least half of my students that such a prescription sinks to the level of legend. Yet, some of these myths, such as the double negative, can also easily be located in prescriptive academic texts such as *The Little, Brown Handbook*.

Its editors, for example, offer only a terse one-sentence description of how double negatives can be useful when intended for understatement, as in *She was not unhappy*, but Fowler and others appear to focus—perhaps unconsciously—even more attention on the so-called faulty uses of double negatives. Their implied intention here was that students should, perhaps, completely avoid double negatives in order to reduce any further risk of potential error or imprecision. Also, since the header that identifies this section of the text was titled "Watch for double negatives," it seems even more likely that such a suggestive prohibition could serve teachers well as they engage in the business of dispensing useful and easily remembered prescriptions.

Jenny Cheshire explores this alleged prohibition in greater detail and finds it to be based more on legend than on any abiding linguistic truths. In her aptly named article, "Double Negatives are Illogical," she cites a number of examples when, throughout the developmental course of English, such constructions were both scorned *and* accepted. Drawing on more contemporary uses of the double negative, Cheshire collected samples taken from casual responses to a simple question she posed to strangers on a "typically grey London day." Their replies appear in the following table.

Table 6

Double Negatives
Do you think it looks like rain?

Oh no, I don't think so.
Definitely not, it was like this yesterday and it didn't rain.
No no, it's going to be fine later.
Not to me it doesn't.
Well, they didn't forecast rain on the radio this morning.
No, but I wish it would, then I could go to work by car without feeling guilty.
Maybe, maybe not.

Adapted from Cheshire in Bauer & Trudgill, 1998, p. 116.

Cheshire observes that, unlike computers, when humans communicate with each other, we do not deal exclusively in simple two-way distinctions: there are many other important aspects of meaning that we convey at the same time as the factual information (1998, p. 116). So, phrases such as *not untrue* or *not unkind*—while reviled by Orwell in "Politics and the English Language"—reveal our occasional needs as communicators to move past the strictly black-and-white categories of binary communication.[7] The communicator who reflects on how we actually use language everyday will invariably notice that there are "very few distinctions that are clearly one thing

---

[7] This is a reference to forms of spoken and written communication that emerge from binary thinking.

or the other" (p. 116). To be fair to Orwell's point, though, the examples offered by Cheshire are drawn from casual conversation, a fairly different form of communication than formal writing. Nevertheless, usage of the questionable double-negative construction varies in writing with one of the cleverest examples offered by Douglas Adams who describes in *The Hitchhikers Guide to the Galaxy* a machine that dispenses "... a substance almost, but not quite, entirely unlike tea" (1979). Other double-negatives appear as well in more formal writing as variations of litotes[8], the use of understatement that helps deny the contrary.

While we must sometimes express meaning somewhere between solid affirmation and solid negation, these conventional expressions that we routinely use without much thought do help communicate our position somewhere amid the two extremes. Perhaps this is one reason why the present American president's policy on being "either ... with [him], or ... with the terrorists" (Bush, 2001, ¶ 29) has met with so much resistance. While such an over-simplification of policy clarifies his political position, it effectively reduces humans, capable of analyzing complex matters, to automatons able only to bifurcate complicated issues.

Even though opposite meanings, such as negatives and affirmatives, are best seen as helping to form a continuum rather than mutually exclusive alternatives, Cheshire observes that this has not stopped people's reactions to them. It is, thus, worth asking also why commentators do not apply the same flawed *mathematical reasoning* (Cheshire, 1998, p. 114) to double positives. If the first meaning of *very* is *complete and absolute*, and *best* is the superlative of better, as in, *This is the very best defense of double negatives I've read*, then why don't these sorts of expressions receive similar sorts of public rebuke? If there were anything illogical about double negatives, it is the "... knee-jerk responses offered up in public discourse: some hate them, some love

---

[8] i.e. She is not so unkind. There isn't a day that goes by that don't think about her kindness.

them; some … both love and hate them; some people laugh at them whilst others, like BBC correspondents are appalled" (1998, p. 119).

Perhaps, without having to belabor students of composition with the niceties of usage and with details about when conventional expressions like double negatives *could* be useful, prescriptivists appear to employ these sorts of dogmatic treatments as succinct and easily recalled maxims that students ought to observe if they are to realize success. Expressed another way, it would be easier, of course, to deem double negatives illogical or illegal than it would be to describe all of their uses and their potential utility to hedge definitiveness (1998, p. 120).

Perhaps the various prescriptive approaches to teaching composition usually prevail because they are, by their very nature, dogmatic. That is, prescriptions for linguistic ailments assume their effective power precisely because of their pith, transparency, purported claims to authority, and their uncanny ability to condense the vast complexities of actual speech into a set of "codified" (Cheshire & Milroy, 1993) and effortlessly identifiable equations for eloquent and acceptable writing.

Schuster offers some further perspective. He observes that anyone who has attended "American schools will recognize the classic methodology of the school grammar classroom: Definition, Example and Drill" (1999, p. 520). As he sees the difficulty, contemporary methods presumably rely too heavily upon a flawed requirement—a student's acquiring an explicit knowledge of meta-language. Schuster's opponents appear to believe, though, that greater knowledge of meta-language, committing to memory the many terms used in discussions of language itself, has direct, immediate, positive effects on understanding language. And understanding language in this explicit way is, according to the CTP and those campaigning for tougher standards, a first step toward using language with power and grace. When literacy is weighed by these scales, by the presupposition that true and complete knowledge derives from and can be measured by one's repertoire of meta-language, then the tendency to focus on and overemphasize its utility in classrooms invariably increases, and may soon outweigh the minute benefits enjoyed in identifying and naming the various parts of speech.

As discussed earlier, for example, the popular grammar reference text, *The Little, Brown Handbook* features an extensive mix of rhetorical descriptions as well as prescriptions for standard usage and exercises for students to assess their own knowledge of the material and the depth of their meta-language lexicon. The discussions of style and usage throughout are cogent, yet most of the exercises meant to reinforce lessons presuppose extensive knowledge of terms typical of the rather specialized jargon. The example in the following table illustrates this point:

Table 7

EXERCISE 14
Identifying subordinate clauses

Identify the subordinate clauses in the following sentences. Then indicate whether each is used as an adjective, an adverb, or a noun. If the clause is a noun, indicate what function it performs in the sentence.

1. Scientists who want to catch the slightest signals from space use extremely sensitive receivers.
2. Even though they have had to fight for funding, these scientists have persisted in their research.
3. The research is called SETI, which stands for Search for Extraterrestrial Intelligence.
4. The theory is that intelligent beings in space are tying to get in touch with us.
5. The challenge is to guess what frequency these beings would use to send signals.

Reproduced from The Little, Brown Handbook, edited by Fowler et al., 2001, p. 27.

My own students, who had already demonstrated above average skills in written expression, endured an intensive two-hour lecture in the standard uses of complements, yet were still unable afterwards to finish *Exercise 14*, or, more significantly, to even explain precisely what the actual goals of the exercise were. Such has been the case with scores of students I've seen since the mid-1990s. Their general inability to apprehend the full meaning of meta-linguistic terms seemed to suggest that grammar lectures alone did little to deepen the kinds of knowledge necessary to demonstrate in practical ways a tacit knowledge of the rules they had already clearly internalized. Of course, other factors, such as miscommunication or their inattentiveness, could have influenced their responses to the exercise, yet this class was not unlike previous ones wherein students would experience significant difficulties reflecting the kinds of explicit knowledge asked of them.

When I was asked in the midst of a discussion of "clauses that act like modifiers" about whether "modifiers" differed from "complements," it did not take long to understand the expressions of confusion written on the faces of students still grappling with the meanings of the term, "modifiers." Perhaps another notable reason why students become increasingly confused and frustrated is that they hear not only a wealth of unfamiliar and abstract terms used interchangeably in composition classrooms, but they also hear what they perceive to be many contradictory rules. For example, their awareness of the meaning of the term, *transitional expression* (Fawcett & Sandberg, 2000, p. 52), was confounded by other like terms, i.e. *connector*, *connective* (Buscemi et al., 2000, p. 53) *bridge*, *transition*, *transition device* (Richards et al., 1999, p. 388) *transitionals* etc.

The conspicuous absence of a standardized meta-language lexicon multiplied by either an unwillingness or inability of many teachers to use the same terms will, more likely, equal confusion on the part of those students required to take hold of the jargon and use it to better their writing. While Deborah Cameron speculated about this kind of "magical thinking" (1995, p. 219) and its relationship to culture and control over language, none of this supposedly valuable knowledge gleaned from grammar lectures has utility if it cannot be truly applied.

## 4.1 Applying Linguistic Treatments

Of particular relevance to the present 21st century debate in America is George Orwell, the renowned 20th century British essayist who, in his still often-cited and coveted indictment of deplorable language practices, remains a major figure. From rhetoric textbooks to essay anthologies, Orwell's work and advice abound. Borrowing a quotation from the author himself, Peterson et al. submit in a recent Norton anthology that

> ... [most] of us share a belief that: language is a natural growth and not an instrument which we shape for own purposes: Orwell, on the other hand, refuses to take a passive stance; rather, he actively seeks to purge the English language of errors, obfuscation, cant, and corruption. He does more than diagnose its illnesses; he offers prescriptions that are practical—though not painless. (2000, p. 148)

Of interest here are the editors' uses of *diagnose, illnesses, prescriptions,* and *painless*—terms in keeping with CTP traditions which conjure images of the university "writing laboratory" or "writing clinic" where students suffering various linguistic ailments might drop in for quick and painless relief. Who, precisely, are those in need of painless treatments for their linguistic illnesses? Though White[9], for example, offers no specific name for them, he suggests that "[only] the writer

---

[9] The attribution of E.B. White as exclusive commentator on style here comes from the author's admitted "prejudices, ...notions of error, [and] ... articles of faith" (1979, p. xii).

whose ear is reliable is in a position to use bad grammar deliberately; only he [the writer] knows for sure when a colloquialism is better than formal phrasing; only he is able to sustain his work at the level of good taste" (1979, p. 77).

The problems with this sort of reasoning are at least twofold: Firstly, "good" being a subjective label assumes all members of all audiences understand what "good" writing really is. Does White's conception of "good" include, for example, alternative discourse communities or only those privy to the author's special understanding of "good" prose style?

Secondly, such a view of language expressed by White, Orwell, and others in their camp today fails to recognize their presumptions that "good" means the center and that the center was and remains the place where all must be politically, socially and economically—a feat wholly unrealizable despite the very best teaching efforts inspired and advanced by those at the political left *or* right. Recycled notions of "good" discourse styles seem to turn up when those who already possess the *cultural capital* (Bourdieu & Passeron, 1977) are in positions to comment on speech and, thus, mark the boundaries of good or acceptable usage.

In *Successful Writing: A Rhetoric for Advanced Composition*, Maxine Hairston, an American rhetorician, analyzes and lauds Orwell's prescriptions. She imbues her discussion with many Orwellian-flavored linguistic remedies, imploring her audience to be vigilant in its search for only "good nouns and verbs" and to dispense with what Orwell calls "decorative adjectives" such as *spectacular*, *splendid*, or *tremendous* (1981, p. 114). Ironically, a number of the words that Orwell singles out in 1949 are of Latin origin, a language from which English has traditionally borrowed heavily. Orwell's urging his audience to dispense with foreign words and phrases also lacks a valid foundation. Since few other language speakers have borrowed, and still do, as much and as often from others as do speakers of English, such a suggestion obscures a fairly apparent reality.

In American academic discourse, Orwell still embodies all that is "good" and just in the standards movement with its accompanying prescriptive treatments of correct usage. As an attempt to describe these sorts of behaviors and commentaries voiced at the center, Deborah Cameron uses the term *verbal hygiene* to capture the level of oral cleansing that some observers feel must be achieved if the language is to survive decay. She points out that these sorts of attempts at purification appear

> ... whenever people reflect on language in a critical (in the sense of 'evaluative') way. The potential for it is latent in every communicative act, and the impulse behind it pervades our habits of thought and behaviour. [She has] never met anyone who did not subscribe, in one way or another, to the belief that language can be 'right' or 'wrong', 'good' or 'bad' more or less 'elegant' or 'effective' or 'appropriate.' (1995, p. 8)

In the face of her critique stands "Politics and the English Language." In the North American context, Orwell's consistently anthologized essay remains a "justifiably famous" (Peterson et al., 2000, p. 148) and impressive achievement in political discourse analysis. It also remains a model discourse for framing the standards issue, yet for reasons Cameron perceptively questions. As an important treatise for the more or less prescriptive teacher, Orwell's essay outlines the supposed reasons for suppressing "corrupted" spoken and written forms which, in Cheshire and Milroy's scheme of standardization, further fuels the perceived need to "maintain the selected variety" (Cheshire & Milroy, 1993, p. 5).

As is often the case with attempts to suppress some corrupted form, the consequences seem twofold. Firstly, by virtue of its repeated codification, Orwell's essay, for example, also helps legitimize the perpetually reified illusion that a single accepted variety remains a static and, thus, easily acquired form whose mastery can be reduced to a set of easily apprehended prescriptions. Secondly, the accepted form becomes itself a metric by which students in the process of acquiring the skills, but who regularly fall short, can be measured and implicitly reminded of their depraved condition. Whereas speech is an often spontaneous and ephemeral form of communication, allowing for immediate real-time resolution of ambiguity or vagueness, writing remains visible, permanent and, thus, open to another way of reflecting on its form and content. The tendency to judge each form as inseparable is sometimes tied to "… education systems themselves [which] … concentrate on inculcating a … high degree of literacy, with little attention paid to the nature of spoken language as an everyday social activity" (Cheshire & Milroy, 1993, p. 5). Thus, for periphery students seeking more valuable linguistic capital and freedom from the margins, the very academic freedoms they seek in class sometimes include the potential communication risks they want to avoid.

Interestingly, students alone are not immune from being assailed by custodians of American English. Even experts of public discourse make fitting targets for ridicule. A recent example of "verbal hygiene" practiced at the highest academic levels in the United States appears in *The Chronicle of Higher Education* (2002). As Dean of the College of Liberal Arts and Sciences at the University of Illinois, Stanley Fish highlights the irony of a preeminent academic who "commits three grammatical crimes [in] a short … sentence" yet who, as Fish points out, "maintains his position as 'Harvard's caped crusader for scholarly rigor'" (2002, p. 37). One might imagine labeling Lawrence Summers with the "caped crusader" moniker, with its negative antecedents, would represent enough justified public disapproval to humble or humiliate him in his tower at Cambridge. While Fish's caustic tone seems to dominate the article and obscure his intended message, his approach to the practice of verbal hygiene is certainly not unique. Having exhausted the space to communicate what seems his personal contempt, Fish also neglects calling greater attention to the bigger issue—the perceived decline of standards.

In explicating a single line from a speech given by Summers, Fish aims to convince the public that steps must be taken to stave off the imminent collapse of American English whilst ignoring the fundamental differences that exist between oral and written communication. Rosina Lippi-Green points to a potential cause of rampant institutionalized verbal hygiene in a chapter titled "Appropriacy Arguments." In light of attitudes such as those expressed by Fish, she notes that these sorts of arguments illustrate an inability or, perhaps, unwillingness to keep separate the written and spoken language (1997, p. 107). For her, the issue of rightful authority in determining standards for language use obscures some principal distinctions in communication: "speech and writing lend themselves differently to standardization" (1997, p. 20).

M.A.K. Halliday further points out why, suggesting that "... writing and speaking are not just alternative ways of doing the same things ... [but] ways of doing different things" (1989, p. xv). That is, speech and writing will appear as "different ways of meaning" (Halliday, 1987, pp. 79-80). As these ways of communicating differently tend to impose upon communicators linguistic bars of correctness, the "judgments about ... correctness in speech are therefore often made on the basis of what is correct in writing" (Milroy, 1998, p. 64). Perhaps, in the North American context, it is ultimately a "system-wide adherence to standard language ideology" (Lippi-Green, 1997, p. 106) that provides enough of the impetus for conservative claims about our supposedly dying language to figure so prominently and to appear so frequently in the public discourse.

Notwithstanding the common practice of conflating the "speech act" (Searle, 1969, p. 22) with writing, North American

English composition studies remain, as John Holt once observed, foremost about not making mistakes—about negotiating the tenuous, treacherous path toward enlightened or, at least, more informed writing and speaking. Barbara Kamler verifies Holt's observations in her book, *Relocating the Personal*, by pointing out that what she learned most powerfully from her schooling in America was fear and a strong sense of inadequacy (2001, p. xiii). It may, thus, be worth asking about who feels best endowed with the cultural capital to identify and mark the kinds of model language uses that should be most coveted in the wider world.

Connected also to contemporary notions of standard written and spoken English are the terms *acceptability* and *correctness*. The current debate surrounding literacy and language uses in American schools appears, nevertheless, to be clouded by confusion over the meanings of these terms. In the public discourse, one term often appears to be used interchangeably for the other. When advocates of English-only campaigns speak of the attributes of correctness, they typically appear to hope for all of the positive connotations of acceptability to enter the periphery of the discussion as well. So, popular notions of correctness today appear to hinge upon mainstream ideas of acceptability. In his book, *The Language Instinct*, Steven Pinker uses the following examples to illustrate how native speakers of English trouble themselves over arguably small discontinuities in dialects and how those various dialects affect how we tend to judge their acceptability:

> But though the language engine is invisible to the human user, the trim packages and color schemes are attended to obsessively. Trifling differences between the dialect of the mainstream and the dialect of other groups, like *isn't any* versus *ain't no*, *those books* versus *them books*, and *dragged him away* versus *drug him away*, are dignified as badges of 'proper grammar'. (1994, p. 28)

Whoever deems speech or writing acceptable will likely point to standardized texts coveted by the center as evidence of correctness since, as conventional wisdom follows, only the center can create linguistic norms. One may further conclude that examples of the rules describing the correct sentence can be easily found "codified" (Cheshire & Milroy, 1993) in widely accepted or selected grammar texts. Since the turns of speech Pinker cites, though, are certainly less likely to be found in accepted grammar texts, one may reason that these are incorrect in all contexts and, therefore, unacceptable. The questions that concerned citizens appear to generally have about acceptable uses of language, though, deal not so much with correctness, but with varieties typical of the periphery. In her discussion of attitudes towards regional varieties of English, their acceptability and favor, Cheshire and Milroy further clarify this point:

> Because standard English morphological and syntactic forms are typically used in written English and in the spoken English of the more powerful and influential people in society, their use has come to be seen as an indication of being educated and 'cultured'. It is hardly surprising, therefore, that these are the forms that are now considered as 'correct' and 'proper' English. This attitude is reinforced by the fact that these are the forms ... taught to non-native learners, and that histories and grammars of the language usually describe not 'standard English' but simply 'English', as if no other varieties ... had a right to the name. (1993, p. 14)

In the minds of those so concerned at the center about declining standards, about, perhaps, the social, political and economic encroachments of those from the periphery on mainstream life, the meanings of terms such as *acceptability*, *correctness*, *competence*, and *performance* (Chomsky, 1965, p. 200-1) seem to collapse under the weight of what appears to be the center's greatest expectation of those on the periphery—their ability or inability to adequately assimilate.

As I have tried to show, the fight for standards has many fronts: within academia where language uses can be negotiated; within cyberspace where *language mavens* [10] seek to purge English of corruption; within political institutions, such as the U.S. Congress, where intolerant movements seek to outlaw languages other than English in the public domain (Cameron, 1995, p. 23); within the columns of mass media language commentators and political pundits whose strident calls for purity do not appear to rest easily. Is it the perceived potential loss of control and order that worries those who continue to so vehemently defend standard language ideology practices? Perhaps, since so many of our verbal idiosyncrasies have political and economic consequences, we hear of concerns raised often in the public discourse: "How will the children learn how to speak or write or get good jobs if they don't know the language?"

---

[10] Pinker's term in *The Language Instinct* (1994, p. 373) for those who see themselves as experts of language use and, thus, feel compelled to offer prescriptions of usage to members of the general public.

# 5. What is Meant by *Knowledge of Language?*

> If our students can't even speak, how can we expect them to write?
>
> —*UMUC professor at the "Teaching Effectiveness Conference" Tokyo, 2002*

    The hyperbole appearing in the above epigraph, which frames the following discussion, is central to the debate over language and its acceptable uses in the North American academy nowadays. This quotation, I suspect, is a fairly good caricature of the various attitudes that typically prevail in public discourses but which leach into composition courses where students come to have their language skills cleaned up for use in the wider world, well beyond institutional walls. To speak in any informed way about language use, though, political pundits and other sorts of language mavens in the public discourse must have been first willing to accept what it means to know a language.

Much of the research in language awareness, according to Arthur Van Essen (1997, p. 4), began to grow in the 1960s from a universal disenchantment with how languages were taught in schools and academic institutions. Demands for change, led by functional linguist M.A.K. Halliday and contemporaries, led to new programs that could develop in students greater awareness of what language is and how it is used and to extend their competence in handling the language (Doughty et al., 1971, pp 8-9). This new program was to provide a common ground for discussing language issues in a common vocabulary, thus bridging the gap between English, ethnic minority mother tongues, foreign languages and English as a second language (Van Essen, 1997, pp. 4-5). Principal goals were to create opportunities when linguistic variety could be discussed openly so that stereotypes, prejudices and parochialisms could be stamped out and learners could grow in confidence and in understanding how more formal or conventional patterns could be used to their advantage. Admirable goals, but what is the North American legacy of this chiefly British movement from the 1960s?

Carolyn Adger paints a fairly grim portrait in "Language Policy and Public Knowledge," when she observes that much of the national discussion about "policies on standard English instruction suggests a lack of awareness about how language works. The view that there is one correct, standard English and that variations from that standard are deviant—a view still manifesting itself in the public discussion—is an example" (1997a, ¶ 1). As with the various popular usage and diction myths discussed earlier, circulated within each new generation, the prevailing misconceptions that surround human language continue to survive in public and academic discourses and should prove to lie near the center of the debate over how best to treat perceived language deficiencies among children, and adults, in classrooms.

So, what is language, and how does one come to be judged deficient in it? As I shall try to show by the slightly varied answers given to this question, the answers themselves speak of an overarching necessity, nonetheless, to see language in an unusual light, one that is entirely free from various ad populum fallacies that some uses of a language are debased because of their perceived disconnection to the more widely accepted forms in mainstream discourse.

William Labov's 1969 research still serves as a useful departure with data that can deflate arguments claiming as valid the various hypotheses of linguistic depravity which stir the public interest. After bringing an end to his now-famous study of the speech patterns that children from a Harlem ghetto exhibit, Labov concludes that linguistic depravity among impoverished children is a dangerous myth. Then, the widely accepted view was that these children were verbally deficient because of the impoverished social environments that inspired their language uses:

> The viewpoint which has been widely accepted, and used as the basis for large-scale intervention programs, is that the children show a cultural deficit as a result of an impoverished environment in their early years. Unfortunately, these notions are based upon the work of educational psychologists who know very little about language and even less about [black] children. The concept of verbal deprivation has no basis in social reality: in fact, [black] children in the urban ghettos receive a great deal of verbal stimulation, hear more well-formed sentences than middle-class children, and participate fully in a highly verbal culture; they have the same basic vocabulary, possess the same capacity for conceptual learning, and use the same logic as anyone else who learns to speak and understand English. (1969, p. 179)

Despite his generalization that black children "hear more well-formed sentences," a contention that seems not only unverifiable but also inconsequential, and his limited sampling of participants, one child and one adult, Labov recognizes a vitally important aspect of the overall issue. What he argues quite convincingly is that "grammatical" uses of a language hinge upon the "consistent rules in the dialect of the speakers" (1969, p. 179). If social experiences, therefore, inform knowledge, if uses of language themselves contain interpretations and projections of such knowledge, it then follows that a theory that ties social poverty to linguistic poverty is suspect.

Derek Bickerton elaborates by pointing to a similar false assumption sometimes made about the complexities of a language and its supposed relationships to societal sophistication. He suggests that if there were any connection

> ... between cultural complexity and linguistic complexity, we would find ... the most complex societies had the most complex languages while simpler societies had simpler languages. We find [no] such thing, [and] nobody has managed to produce a metric for linguistic simplicity. If you measure by the number and variety of inflections, English and Chinese, the languages of two highly complex cultures, are extremely simple; if you look at their syntax, it's another story. Simplicity over here always seems to be paid for complexity over there. (1995, p. 35)

The reasoning typically used to tie a socioeconomic poverty to a linguistic one turns an enormous and convoluted circle when those with, say, the power to affix labels identify a marginalized subgroup as linguistically inadequate because the members thereof and their discourse conventions appear (on the surface) to diverge so widely from the norm. Widespread uses of labels such as these appear to arise from various logical fallacies—hasty generalizations that have, in their turn, evolved from a false correlation between linguistic phenomena and socioeconomic phenomena. What's more, these sorts of labels are more likely to stick to the stigmatized subgroups because the members thereof obviously lack the socioeconomic power to contest effectively how others view them.

Notwithstanding this rather complex circular pattern of reasoning, language appears to remain a broadly misunderstood human trait. Today, in more recent discussions of the very same concerns is Dennis Baron's comments about why arguments still rage and why the case for, say, standardization has not yet been adjourned: "What linguists say about language variation contradicts what people feel they know about standardization and the rightness and wrongness of language use. Educators, legislators, and the public at large are not yet ready to buy into the notion that stigmatized varieties of a language may be rule-governed, let alone useful anywhere but on the street" (2000, p. 11). Despite a wealth of research in twentieth century linguistics alone, significant changes in academic approaches to teaching writing do not appear very apparent in classrooms (Adger 1997a, ¶ 1).

Given Labov's and Baron's discussions and conclusions surrounding the ongoing and sometimes obsessive debates over language and use, it is worth clarifying what language and use actually mean and how they diverge. Bickerton contends that the term language

> …has been put to a variety of uses, or misuses. We hear about the language of flowers or body language; people speak of animal language or the language of bees. Because so many people confuse language with communication, pretty well anything that communicates may be called a language" (1995, p. 11).

Susanne Langer also cites problems in this way of thinking, referencing the kinds of category mistakes that take hold in the mind when, for example, philosophers who have recognized the symbolical character of so-called 'sense data,' especially in their highly developed uses in science and art speak quite naturally of a 'language' of the senses, a 'language of musical tones, or colors, and so forth (1979, p. 94). She suggests that these and other similar metaphors lead to rather deceptive ways of speaking about language.

In recognizing some of the fundamental flaws suffused with the conventional wisdom, Bickerton uses the following illustrations as a means of clarifying some neglected distinctions:

> First, there is the persistent confusion between a thing and the use of a thing. This should not be a problem at all. People who blithely say 'Language is (a form of) communication' do not confuse cars with driving, scissors with cutting, or forks with eating. If language were a visible tool that you physically used, the confusion could hardly arise. But language is more abstract than cars or scissors, and when thing and use are both abstract the absurdity of conflating them becomes less apparent.
>
> The second part of the misunderstanding arises because animal communication systems, and all the other things illegitimately described as languages, differ from language in that they can do nothing but communicate. Language has additional capabilities … e.g. one can-not think in body language, or use an animal communication system to store information. (1995, p. 11)

Why is it useful to outline and reemphasize these distinctions? If Bickerton's cars, scissors and forks analogies were valid, one may also ask quite reasonably whether the apparent widespread commission to criticize language uses so sternly is just as valid.

Where and when language and power are concerned, users of language and seekers of power cannot often help but slip, it seems, into this popular dichotomy of finding linguistic differences between themselves and others (Fairclough, 1989, p. 12; Giles & Coupland, 1991, p. 32), a perspective within which poor usage appears inseparable from poor user. Bickerton continues by arguing that "If one envisages language as no more than a skill used to express and communicate the products of human thought, it becomes ipso facto impossible to regard language as the Rubicon that divides us from other species" (1995, p. 9).

What seems clear enough, though, is that social stereotyping (Lakoff, 1987, pp. 85-6) humans for their supposed inferior uses of language is an often inescapable tendency. Perhaps this sort of behavior is entirely natural, that our conceptions of the rightness and wrongness of language spring from rather natural ways of making sense of the world and others in it as our own subjectivities color our critical approaches to all phenomena. What Derek Bickerton seems to suggest most importantly is that when we are too busy evaluating what lies beyond our bodies, we are not prepared to consider the limitations of our bodies.

That is to say, critics of a walking style do not use their legs to communicate critiques of someone else's walk. Nor would these sorts of critics ordinarily use their opposable thumbs to communicate critiques of someone else's poor grip on a coffee mug. The use of language, like the use of the spine or an appendage, suggests the use of a tacit skill, a discussion of which will be taken up in the following chapter. What Bickerton contends is that critics of language use, though, fail to hear their own voices, fail to realize the irony in the inherent luxury of using words to criticize the various uses of words themselves.

If the uses of language, like the uses of limbs for walking upright, simply are, if they are simply features of humanness, how does one legitimately posit concerns about the degeneration of a language itself? One may express concern for ways of combating enduring degenerative conditions, such as scoliosis or osteoporosis, but one does so for much different reasons. If, therefore, the clarity and precision of a communicated message hinges more upon the context and intention of a speaker or writer rather than on a strict observance to the codified rules of a language, how does one justifiably measure correctness?

Apart from the distinctions that Bickerton and Baron call attention to, what remains part of the public discourse, nonetheless, are various undercurrents of relative ignorance that engender what often seems to be overtly a kind of extreme linguistic intolerance. Although use depends to a large degree on context and speaker/writer intention, it also figures prominently in the social or intellectual value judgments we make of others (Giles & Coupland, 1991, p. 32). The often-repeated concern echoed by students in schools, now seen, it seems, as a universal folk maxim, testifies to the fairly widespread belief that knowledge of language does not necessarily translate into a knowledge of how to actually use a language—"If we write how we speak and our speech is incorrect, our writing must be also."

One difficulty of separating language user from language variety and exploring radically different ways of approaching the teaching of composition is compounded by what T.R. Johnson sees as the relative absence of our own discourses about our students' "'resistance' to our pedagogies" (2001, p. 624). In composition studies, he submits that "we have some clues, some inklings about how students take pleasure in learning how to write" (2001, p. 624). At last,

> … if we can pin down what authorial pleasure is, we can then suppose that this assemblage of possibilities is what many students can't seem to access; we can

think about why and what we might do to make the pleasures of writing more available to them (2001, p. 624).

These authorial pleasures that *can* certainly be experienced in composition lie in the writer's own active involvement in the process—in discovering the tacit linguistic knowledge the writer possesses, in exploring the boundaries of individual creativity, interacting creatively with the tools of composition, and witnessing firsthand the emergence and coherence of the writer's thoughts. By what manner of creative expression, though, can coherent thought converge in the writer's workspace, be it a computer screen, note pad or chalk board? That is to say, if the CTP were merely collections of expressivist pedagogies, what then initiates self-expression?

One answer for composition classrooms where student writers struggle with generating and working out coherence at the sentence level may lie in a rather ordinary but typically unnoticed characteristic of human behavior—play. The following discussion is a theoretical outgrowth of observations and criticisms of language norms and attitudes put forward thus far. It re-examines approaches to composition in light of some of the overlooked aspects of play, the sort of knowledge that must be available and accessed in play, and the potential value these aspects of behavior possess for those engaged in the process of generating and expressing meaning at the sentence level.

# PART 2. THE ROLE OF PLAY

## *6. Knowing and Doing*

The following discussion represents the theoretical groundwork that supports a new pedagogical approach to generating and expressing meanings at the sentence level. In the broadest sense, the initial discussion of knowing and doing will serve as a foundation for later discussions of knowing language and doing (using) language. This section, therefore, asks about certain kinds of knowledge, whether they are useful or superfluous, whether they produce higher forms of awareness or belabor learners with unnecessary or trivial truths. In light of the discussions developed throughout Part 1, the goal is to allow a new method to emerge unencumbered by popular assumptions about language users, their apparent knowledge or lack of knowledge of language, and the more irrational biases favoring certain forms of language use.

What follows is meant to serve as a potential answer to questions involving longstanding assumptions carried into classrooms about written and spoken forms of language, as well as to demonstrate the extent to which these assumptions can distort the well-intentioned goals of teaching methods in composition. A secondary aim, therefore, underpins the entire proposition put forward herein. Before critical assessments of writing can be voiced in the classroom, this new approach is intended to encourage its practitioners to permit the learner's tacit knowledge of language to inform the skills he or she brings to the task of writing so that self-awareness of emerging skills can better strengthen the learner's inherent sense of the self as a generator and communicator of meaning.

To begin, a sandcastle, for example, might serve well as a general illustration here. What kinds of knowledge must the castle maker have of sand in order to produce stable sandcastles? How does the novice maker of a castle come to a full knowledge of the value of, say, a foundation and its density and then the castle's overall dependence upon these two aspects of castle making? Must the maturing maker of castles come to an explicit knowledge of the nature of sand itself, its essential molecular components, its peculiar adhesive properties when combined with water? Would such explicit knowledge necessarily lead directly to much sounder sandcastles?

Given the confusion often voiced in discussions of English language varieties and their variety of uses, can we truly understand what it means to know a language by assessing the various ways in which that knowledge is expressed through the language? Expressed another way, can we accurately assess an individual's knowledge of language by evaluating an individual's linguistic output? As with many kinds of artful expression, the use of language, like, say, the use of sand on a beach, can evoke a range of responses—some rooted in truth, others in misconception.

As with building a sandcastle, developing meaning in an essay is as much an art of doing as an art of knowing. Both efforts require certain measures and numbers of intellectual and physical tools. While physical ones, such as a shovel and pail on a beach or pen and pad in a classroom, can be set aside or dispensed with altogether, intellectual tools cannot, since they are developed and rooted in a social context within which and from which the doer or practitioner cannot readily remove himself or herself (Sveiby, 1997, ¶ 34). If, say, writing requires more deliberate and extensive uses of intellectual tools than sandcastle construction, the developing writer ought to feel more confident in that social context when consciously following certain rules in order to make full use of the physical and intellectual tools at his or her disposal.

It might, therefore, be useful to frame the following discussion with references to Bertil Rolf's hierarchy of knowing based on how humans tend to follow rules. According to Carl Sveiby, Rolf sees knowing as embodied in three levels (1995). As the lowest of these levels, *skill* is the ability to act according to rules which depend on feedback from a non-social environment, such as building a sandcastle. The agent is, thus, able to assess whether the action has been successful or not (Sveiby, 1997, ¶ 38).

Next, *know-how*, to be explored in greater detail, is the ability to act in social contexts, which implies problem solving and the ability to reflect on the result of an act. The boxer, surgeon, and poet, for example, are all able to apply their special skills as they carry out their work and are considered by observers to be good or bad creatively, not because of their ability to reflect on what they are doing as they carry out their work but because of the result of their work (Ryle, 1949, p. 28-9).

Lastly, *expertise* is know-how combined with the more skillful ability to reflect on and influence the rules within a certain social system, domain, context or tradition. Expertise, then, or "competence" (Polanyi, 1975, p. 4), is not a "… property but a relation between individual actors and a social system of rules. A person is an expert within a tradition: in a competent mental act, the agent does not do as he pleases, but compels himself forcibly to act as he believes he must" (Sveiby, 1997, ¶ 40). While the novice maker of sandcastles may possess some sense of know-how on the beach, his or her success in castle making does not depend upon the same level of competence that the novice maker of meanings in an English composition course needs. In a castle-making contest, of course, judged by sandcastle "connoisseurs" (Polanyi, 1975) some degree of expertise will come into play, but not the level brought to the task of text production.

To abandon briefly the sandcastle metaphor and be more specific, the following sections explore what knowledge of language means as well as the means by which humans appear to arrive at this sort of knowledge. Central to understanding what is meant by the *knowing a language* premise, though, would be a brief outline of the present contentions.

## 6.1 Knowing That and How

The current debate is best framed by a reference to Gilbert Ryle and his argument for seeing human knowledge as embodied in two predominant human responses: people say "I *know that* ..." when accessing declarative knowledge, but "I *know how* ..." (1949, p. 28) when referring to procedural knowledge: e.g. I *know that* Vincent van Gogh was a painter, and I *know how* to recognize van Gogh's work respectively. For his part, van Gogh, one might say, proceeded to demonstrate a *knowing how* to use paint, brush and canvas to represent knowledge of his subject matter visually while he declared, at least implicitly, a *knowing that* impressionism was a suitable means through which to express his knowledge of, say, a sunflower.

As Jason Stanley and Timothy Williamson point out, however, distinctions such as these contain a few intrinsic problems. In developing counterarguments that cross into philosophy of mind and philosophy of language, Stanley and Williamson present a similarly forceful case for seeing *knowing how* as merely a species of *knowing that* (2001, p. 412). Given the apparent contentions presented by Ryle's dichotomy, discussion of the following illustration is prefaced with a number of qualifiers.

If, say, van Gogh's work represents or communicates the artist's impression of his subject matter (a *knowing how* to use paint and brush to express), then language—like the tools of an artist—may permit impressions or representations of knowledge to be expressed (a *knowing how* to use *a lexicon and a grammar*) (Langer, 1979, p. 94) to communicate impressions of the world, or to even acquire further knowledge of it (Hirst, 1973, p. 96). Attributing to each mere brush stroke on a canvas more meaning than each singularly deserves, this analogy stretches the connection between these two ideas, but the concept is, nevertheless, useful for seeing more clearly what Susanne Langer described as and meant by discursive and presentational forms. That is to say, "the elements [or presentational forms] that the camera represents [or a van Gogh rendering of sunflowers] are not like the elements that written language represents [the discursive forms]" (1979, p. 95).

For P.H. Hirst, the problem lies in seeing knowledge as strictly embodied only in the *knowing how – knowing that* dichotomy. In his search for a coherent and just definition of liberal education (1965, p. 32), Hirst, later abandoning seven distinct forms, had argued that human knowledge is comprised of seven irreducible kinds that diverge and vary widely in appearances that cannot be so easily separated, simplified and categorized (1973, p. 84). "Differentiated into a number of logically 'distinct' forms," (1965, p. 46) none of which are ultimately reducible and expressible in such simplistic halves, human knowledge for Hirst is a much more complex weave of theoretical, practical, propositions, beliefs, and moral codes that defy clear bifurcation.

For Hirst, even the fine arts, for example, should not be precluded, for they too, while symbolic forms of expression, have meaning and, thus, qualities compatible with those in propositions (2002, p. 51)—or in the "discursive forms" described earlier (Langer, 1979, p. 95). But, are the problems of production and expression of meaning in the arts analogous to those acts carried out in a composition classroom? Both areas of inquiry, no doubt, require their practitioners to draw upon their *skills* and *know-how* (Sveiby, 1997, ¶ 38). Perhaps, though, their widespread acceptance as good practitioners of their art depends principally upon the relationship they maintain between themselves, their audience, and that "certain social system of rules" within which they practice expression and produce meaning (Sveiby, 1997, ¶ 40).

In recent years, Jim McKenzie revisited Hirst's principal argument to clarify and adjust it in light of new knowledge in logic and semantics, asking whether it is just a matter of discourse types (1998, p. 27). Whereas Hirst had contended that even the arts were "symbolic expressions having meaning" and thereby presumably possessing "properties logically equivalent to those of propositions" (1973, p. 97), McKenzie claims that we can discriminate among forms of knowledge "by the fact that there are argument patterns which are valid in some kinds of discussion and not in others" (1998, p. 39).

While Hirst and McKenzie had originally considered the expression of knowledge and meaning on many more complex fronts, Ryle's dichotomy, it seems, is just as useful a model by which to further an understanding of the kinds of knowledge that all students appear to generally access when dealing with problems in a given discipline. In many disciplines, if perhaps not all, teachers typically aim to raise awareness of explicit kinds of knowledge. Students of physics, for example, "know more than they can tell" (Polanyi, 1966, p. 8). That is, they may know tacitly that some mysterious force called gravity anchors them to the surface of the earth, yet be unable to *tell about the particulars* (Polanyi, 1966, p. 9) of *how* (Ryle, 1949, p. 29) explicitly or precisely gravity acts upon their bodies. While they are attending *from* a tacit awareness of their own ontological position on the surface of earth, they are—in a physics classroom—attending *to* a particular set of physical laws that describe motions and forces (Polanyi, 1966, p. 10; Lakoff & Johnson, 2004, p. 562). The teacher's goal beyond this is to expand the student's understanding of this force, to move beyond mere knowledge of what the student may name towards knowledge of what the student can explain.

When, for example, students say they *know that* gravity is a force that works on all material objects on earth, they are drawing on a declarative kind of knowledge, which may be a kind of parroted version of something they may have heard someone else say, well before they entered a lecture hall. Beyond the customary pull of gravity experienced each day, this sort of testimonial knowledge, it may be said, lacks a tangible context that might further help the learner develop a greater depth of understanding, such as that felt in an antigravity chamber. When students say they *know how* gravity acts upon objects, they are accessing a deeper sort of procedural knowledge wherein explanations or illustrations, for example, may be given to flesh out more fully, say, a listener's rather limited tacit knowledge of gravity. Knowing *how* to apply $F=Gm_1m_2/r^2$ means that the student has moved from attending to a tacit understanding, a knowing *that* he or she will not float away to the heavens because of this invisible force, to something more explicit and useful—effectively rooted in the experience.

Of Polanyi's dissections of tacit knowing into four strains, his discussion of the "semantic" aspect should help better explain this illustration (1966, pp. 10-14). Just as the physics student's tacit awareness of gravitational forces may or may not help further shape her explicit knowledge of formulas describing physical laws, so, too, the composition student's tacit awareness of language may or may not help further inform her explicit knowledge of certain linguistic laws. For example, in uses of regular and irregular verbs, the L1 speaker should likely know tacitly *that* and *how* she must morph to shift the tense of a verb, but be unable to tell explicitly *how* in some verbs *d* or *ed* is needed while in others these affixes aren't.[11] In seeing her language represented on paper, the student attends from her "proximal" (Polanyi, 1966, p. 10) tacit awareness of morphological changes to the particulars or semantic aspects located at a distance from her on a page, but even through continued practice in writing may come no closer to explaining *how* it is that these oddities, or

---

[11] Pinker references this tendency in *Words and Rules* when he suggests that regular past-tense verbs are predictable in sound and generated freely because they are products of a rule that lives in the minds of children and adults (1999, p. 16).

morphological irregularities, appear in the language. Is knowing the *how* in this instance necessary to her development of writing skills?

Knowing *that* and *how* may not be enough. Applying their tacit knowledge of the rules of morphology to a noun, such as *kudos*, has not prevented some speakers or writers from choosing the plural form, *are*, as an attempt to agree with what is sometimes perceived to be a plural form of praise. Likewise, transposing the same sort of knowledge used in contracting *will* and *not*, as in *won't*, will sometimes produce either *Ain't I clever boy* for *am* and *not*, or its often preferred problematic alternative, *Aren't I a clever boy*. Such is the case with speakers and writers attending *from* their tacit proximal awareness of morphology *to* the semantic particulars.

Does "teaching" or does exposure to the right kinds of usage increase the kind of knowledge that language teachers are interested in communicating? Polanyi uses the "probe" analogy in his talk of the "semantic" aspect of tacit knowing to illustrate how a blind man might through practice with a cane transpose meaningless feelings into meaningful ones: "We become aware of the feelings in our hand in terms of their meaning located at the tip of the probe to which we are attending" (1966, p. 13). Even speech for the speaker, much like writing for the writer, will sometimes require "an interpretive effort" (p. 12).

The speaker may become more aware of the meaning in the message she utters in terms of its meaning manifested in the expression on the face of her interlocutor to whom she is attending. She may know *that* her intended message was received but be unable to tell precisely *how* she was able to perceive this fact. For the speaker, was there something she saw in the face of her interlocutor that encouraged her to re-adjust the locution on some meaningful level? For the writer, was there something in the sentence that looked or sounded strange? The speaker and writer know *that* adjustments to the message must be made but may be unable to communicate precisely *how* they knew or even how precisely they might proceed. Does "teaching" a student rules, therefore, apprise her of certain linguistic facts that govern the uses of a language, or do the student's own innate acts of perceiving and interpreting the media (the facial expressions of others or the contextualized words on paper) play larger roles in deepening, extending, or increasing explicit awareness? Answers to questions such as these are certainly worth pursuing but lie just beyond the scope this book.

## 6.2 Meta-Knowing

Ryle's conception of knowledge also has considerable value in psychology, in an area known generally as meta-cognition. In the case of a child declining, for example, conjugating and constructing compound and complex sentences, Vygotsky observed that writers "know neither how [they do] this, nor that [they are] doing this, ... in effect, [they know], but [do] not know that [they know]" (1983, p. 6). Meta-cognitive awareness is, thus, "our knowledge, awareness, and control of our cognitive processes, [which] is important because our knowledge about our cognitive processes can guide us in arranging circumstances and selecting strategies to improve future cognitive performance" (Matlin, 1994, p. 256). Margaret Matlin's illustration may have considerable value for the teacher of languages—especially for the teacher of composition.

For example, like the student of physics who brings certain tacit forms of knowledge to the classroom, students also carry with them a tacit knowledge of their first language. When a teacher wonders if students actually know their native language, a teacher can confidently respond with an affirmative. No special definition of "know," notwithstanding its "intuitive" status, is necessary in this sense, that is if the teacher does not confuse a student's use of a "nonstandard" variety for not knowing the language. But, if teachers are interested in whether students have an explicit knowledge of their language, a teacher can reasonably voice some doubts. As Noam Chomsky observes in *Language and Mind*, the person

> ...who knows a language has mastered a system of rules that assigns sound and meaning in a definite way for an infinite [or, perhaps more accurately, vast] class of sentences ... [but] the person ... has no consciousness of having mastered these rules or of putting them to use, nor is there any reason to suppose that this knowledge of the rules can be brought to consciousness. (1972, pp. 103-4).

The principal goal of "teaching" English, or any other language for that matter, nevertheless remains. It is to enlarge students' explicit knowledge of their language in explicit ways, their awareness of a standardized grammar so that the unique needs of a certain audience may, more likely, be addressed more attentively in the written message. Precisely how, though, does the teacher help increase the kinds of explicit knowledge needed to help students become more aware as they develop the skills in communicating the message they intend?

Typical answers to this kind of question set up one of the principal opposing arguments that will be developed throughout this discussion. As I will attempt to show in later sections, teachers have generally relied on traditional exercises that encourage students to memorize various terms peculiar to the meta-linguistic lexicon or to diagram sentences into their constituent parts. Indeed, these tasks are practical and procedural and are, given the influence of the Generative paradigm, still thought to represent some of the most effective means by which to help students create much deeper, more lasting forms of knowledge.

Of course, this is not altogether surprising, given the nurtured and natural increases in knowledge humans enjoy when attending to the particulars of a subject of inquiry (Polanyi, 1958, p. 117; 1975, pp. 32-3). It would seem reasonable to conclude that students who are not only able to talk, but to talk about their language in explicit ways, have moved beyond accessing merely declarative knowledge (e.g., knowing *that* cat is a noun) and have arrived at accessing a much deeper procedural knowledge (e.g., knowing *how* I can apply this knowledge to expressing a range of meanings, e.g., cat can serve as a noun, verb, adjective etc.). This is the sort of hope that teachers have traditionally looked toward in exercises that develop abilities in diagramming and knowledge of meta-linguistic discourse[12]. If, for example, a student has proven able to parse or diagram, identify and discuss the constituent parts of a sentence, the assumption usually follows that he or she is quite able to express himself or herself effectively, or even eloquently, on paper.

In some classrooms, this view remains a well-guarded belief but arises, it seems, from a post hoc fallacy—analogous to the film critic who can adeptly diagram the flaws in the plot of a motion picture yet who remains unable to apply his or her critical and explicit knowledge of cinema to the drafting of a compelling screenplay. Do a critic's artful or sophisticated analytical skills suddenly increase his or her ability to conceive cinematic productions and articulate their particulars on paper? What seems ignored or accidentally overlooked is the developmental path one must negotiate which precedes the mastery of an art, the experiential movement from novice to critic. Full of difficulties and opportunities for error, this is the route all students must take which is fundamental to the development of skill, know-how, and the higher forms of awareness peculiar to expertise.

To best understand the kinds of sentence-level problems that students of writing typically face, one must ask whether increases in the ability to adeptly parse or to engage in meta-lingual discourse truly furthers the skills of developing writers, or do these sorts of increases come from the many mistakes that students of composition naturally make, a kind of *learning from one's mistakes*. That is to say, which of these two routes, the procedural or the declarative (the *knowing how* or the *knowing that*) leads to the knowledge that teachers so concern

---

[12] Martha Kolln observes that when we study grammar we are bringing to a conscious level of awareness the rules of the language that we already "know" subconsciously (1994, p. 4).

themselves with communicating in traditional classroom exercises in grammar? As I shall try to show, both forms are valuable, but the means and order by which we have traditionally tried to stimulate their growth seem disputable.

An expedient alternative ought to build further upon the potential strides that students can make in more explicit forms of knowledge, a method that certainly presupposes the value of meta-cognitive forms yet offers first more practical opportunities for students themselves to "arrange circumstances and select strategies to improve future cognitive performance" (Matlin, 1998, p. 256). Returning, at last, to the much earlier sandcastle metaphor, it seems worth asking how students come to apprehend the potential value of the words they choose that serve as foundations upon which they build their intended meanings. If humans generally develop demonstrable skills in language use (Pinker, 1994, p. 19) at such early ages, is it necessary that students of writing must acquire first an explicit knowledge of the nature of words themselves, their particular meta-lingual meanings, the labels they assume when "strung together in discrete ways" in assorted contexts (Langer, 1979, p. 80)? And, would this sort of knowledge initially and necessarily lead directly to greater skill in writing? A discussion of potential answers is taken up in subsequent sections.

## 6.3 Knowing How to Break Rules

Disobedience and rule breaking seem a natural consequence of free will. If they are to learn, grow and develop, humans cannot help but test the limitations of their physical and mental facilities. More than meeting certain needs, experiment and invention appear to be a major consequence of the will and fascination with the creative powers of the mind. Composition classrooms, though, whether in high school or college are places where creativity, experiment and invention are too often subdued in favor of rule learning. This has long remained a major feature of English composition courses in the North American academy.

As discussed in Part 1, Section 3.1, prevailing approaches to teaching composition usually imply that developing writers must turn their tacit awareness into explicit knowledge in order to know a standardized grammar, the "linguistic etiquette, and rules of usage imposed by society" (Kolln, 1994, p. 10). Only the student whose "ear is good" and "knows the tricks of rhetoric" is able to discern when to legitimately break the rules of linguistic etiquette, like, say, splitting an infinitive phrase (Strunk & White, 1979, p. 78). Constance Weaver rejects the Strunkian injunction and argues in a chapter titled "Toward a Perspective in Error" that "writing growth and error go hand in hand" (1996, p. 69).

In the case of developing writers, what may be ignored or overlooked too often are the valuable "practical and procedural" mistakes that help lay the foundations for the future mastery of a skill. An initial step towards teaching composition might first encourage students to take liberties, to experiment and break rules in order to know them. Such a path seems to represent more closely the natural developmental course of growth in skills.

For example, in his discussion of infants experimenting with the tools of speech—the mouth, tongue, lips and larynx—Pinker uses the "complicated audio equipment" metaphor to illustrate how infants might make such remarkable strides in linguistic facility in so short a period. While "listening to their own babbling and mimicking the sounds they hear," Pinker suggests that "babies write their own instruction manuals as they fiddle with the tools of speech" (1994, p. 266). In much earlier studies of the developmental course of speech play in children, Mary Sanches and Barbara Kirsenblatt-Gimblett observed that "... as babbling is essential to the acquisition of language, the acquisition of language may be essential to controlled and disciplined speech play which may in turn be essential to the acquisition of poetic discourse" (1976, p. 105).

How do these illustrations relate to the development of skills in written discourse? Writing is itself a discursive activity, an action replete with experimentation and a variety of strategies students must test for themselves to discover the optimal path, the fluid movement of thought from the mind to the fingertips (Langer, 1979, p. 81).

As speech may appear to the casual observer to be a merely "biological adaptation" (Tomasello, 2003, p. 290) developing naturally alongside other intrinsic human skills, like intellectual or motor development, the learned ability to write may seem to be, on the surface, little more than a natural extension of the developing literate person—like the ability to run might seem to the developing toddler (Lightbown & Spada, 1993, pp. 7-8). To Vygotsky, the connections between thought and word that produce speech are more complicated than seeing speech as merely an adaptation. In *Thought and Language*, Vygotsky points out that language

> ... is not a thing but a process .... Thought is not merely expressed in words; it comes into existence through them. Every thought tends to connect something with something else .... An analysis of the interaction of thought and word must begin with an investigation of the different phases and planes a thought traverses before it is embodied in words. ... such a study distinguish[es] between two planes of speech. Both the inner, meaningful, semantic aspect of speech and the external, phonetic aspect, though forming a true unity, have their own laws of movement. (1934/1986, p. 218)

The difficulty of this movement for the writer is compounded, though, by what Vygotsky sees as a "double abstraction: an abstraction from the sound of speech and ... from [an] interlocutor" (1934/1978, p. 181). To the child, writing is an entirely new and peculiar undertaking. It is, for Vygotsky, written speech—a conversation with a blank sheet of paper or computer screen (1934/1978, p. 181). Like the child who writes her own instruction manual, discovering just how to articulate ideas manually, a certain amount of invention and experimentation must precede and/or accompany the development of the skill.

Despite receiving seemingly countless lectures on how best to move ideas from the mind to, say, a pad of paper or computer screen, students, whether children or adults, will ultimately write their own "instruction manuals" for coping with the various problems that the task and subject of writing sets before them. Their experiences in coping force them to fiddle with the intellectual switches, so to speak, to find the most expedient means of perceiving and interpreting and turning their thoughts into words that represent more precisely what they mean as writers. Related to these characteristics of language acquisition and development is Lev Vygotsky's notion of play as an innate feature of cognitive development, a way of coping with the physical world and increasing skills to face the problems in it.

# 7. Writing: A Developmental Psychology Approach

Lying also near the center of the debate over effective teaching practices in composition classrooms and connected at least remotely, albeit indirectly, to perceived language deficiencies is a pervasive underestimation of the range of difficulties that sentence-level drafting presents to developing writers. Throughout Vygotsky's work in developmental psychology, his observations of children at play helped him apprehend the extent to which the development of skills and intellectual growth hinge upon active participation in a social context.

His insights helped further the development of positions from which one could argue that writing represents the culmination of a complex series of cognitive and physical acts carried out in accord with the developmental level of the learner. Of course, these were to also shape the subsequent advance of pedagogies that consider and employ these connections. These positions consider three inherent aspects of intellectual growth: the actual level of development, the potential, and the area between where teacher and student may meet (Lantolf & Appel, 1998, p. 10). How, though, do these developmental levels relate to the development of writing skills? In *Mind in Society*,

Vygotsky points out that to move from first-order symbols, drawings and doodles, to second-order symbols,

> ... written signs for the spoken symbols of words, [the] child must make a basic discovery—namely that one can draw not only things but also speech. It was only this discovery that led humanity to the brilliant method of writing by words and letters; the same thing leads children to letter writing. From the pedagogical point of view, this transition should be arranged by shifting the child's activity from drawing things to drawing speech (1934/1978, p. 115).

The method for which I am presently arguing presupposes that difficulties in drafting arise when the student writer feels no thought worth sharing is present in the mind. The writer feels that no idea he or she has is significant or valuable enough to move from the mind to the page and, thus, feels no necessary compulsion to generate words essential to fleshing out the requirements of, say, a writing assignment. Along with Vygotsky's insight, though, is an assumption that the generation of a thought and its articulation on paper require that the writer has first conceived of an idea he or she feels is worth communicating (Bizzell, 1992 p. 94).

For most developing writers, writing is the most painstaking form of language use, which depends, at least initially, not so much on sound but on the conscious and deliberate use of signs. Before arriving at the question over which particular signs to choose, a writer must generate a thought, acquire a corresponding set of words or images that adequately represent it, and transform either set into the sequenced symbols peculiar to a written language. Vygotsky saw this rather sophisticated movement from thought (inner speech) to the "consciously elaborated system of conventionally accepted signs" (1934/1978, p. 183) as "deliberate semantics" (1934/1978, p. 182)—a deliberate structuring of the web of meaning. He goes on to conclude that

> ... (a) the essential difference between written and oral speech reflects the difference between two types of activity, one of which is spontaneous, involuntary, and nonconscious, while the other is abstract, voluntary, and conscious; (b) the psychological functions on which written speech is based have not even begun to develop in the proper sense when instruction in writing starts. It must build on barely emerging, immature processes. (1934/1978, p. 183)

To underestimate the fundamental importance or to ignore the distinction that Vygotsky makes here is to overlook a significant reason why the act of writing at the sentence level could represent such a difficulty to the frustrated student who complains, for example, that the hands do not easily obey the mind's intention to convey the intended thought. Seeing, therefore, the difference between these two actions which Vygotsky spells out is crucial to understanding why the presumably simple act of writing for some may appear to others to be such a monumental feat. It is here precisely that these distinctive types of activity, nevertheless, influence and shape the course towards furthering the development of skills. Vygotsky's notion of the "spontaneous, involuntary and non-conscious" aspect of speech finds further value in both composition pedagogy and in Polanyi's talk of tacit knowing discussed earlier.

To illustrate, as the immense expansion of knowledge opened up by the acquisition of speech foreshadows all articulate knowing, it is the human desire to explore and achieve intellectual control that also prefigures the shaping of personal knowledge (Polanyi, 1975, p. 132). If, as Polanyi observes, personal knowing is shaped by our desire to explore and achieve intellectual control, this observation ought then prove useful to the design of pedagogies that aim to kindle in learners abiding, spontaneous, and non-conscious desires to explore and solve, with a fellow learner, some stimulating academic puzzle. The sort of puzzle to which I here refer is to be discussed in Section 8.2.

Nevertheless, Polanyi further points out that the structure of personal knowledge becomes all the more apparent when we "recognize personal participation as the universal principle of knowing" (1975, p. 42). That is to say, all knowing is grounded in action. If therefore, as Polanyi argues, dwelling in our own bodies brings us, at least, to a subsidiary knowledge of our surroundings, and if speech, whether verbal or sign, further informs and shapes that knowledge, then dialogue as a means of aiding the search for and refinement of meanings ought to occupy a much more significant role in writing instruction. For student writers developing further means by which to generate and communicate intending meanings, it is the way in which they "dwell in these particular subjects in achieving [their] knowledge of them (Polanyi, 1975, p. 42)" that underscores not just the value of active participation but also the evidence of their difficulties while contending with the particulars of a given subject.

If as Polanyi contends that "all knowing is personal," then Vygotsky pointed out how personal knowing figures into the process of overcoming difficulties presented to developing writers when he suggested that written language is more abstract than speech, has no interlocutor and is addressed to no one in particular (1934/1983, p. 4). The problems that solitary writers have in generating ideas prefigure the sentence-level difficulties they must invariably face. These difficulties can be treated with simple solutions. As Gordon Wells observes, human "...understanding is constructed in the process of people working together to solve problems that arise in the course of shared activity" (2000, p. 66). Hence, a simple dialogue between developing writers who can dwell in their subject, draw on personal knowledge, and address to one another whatever writing burdens or difficulties of expression they face will compel both writers to engage in a considerably important act—the active and collaborative pursuit of precise meanings.

An example of dwelling in a subject and drawing on personal knowledge to transform existing knowledge comes from Vera John-Steiner and Teresa Meehan. In "Creativity and Collaboration in

Knowledge Construction," John-Steiner cites an exchange she had recently had with a colleague:

> While discussing dialectical concepts with one of [her] collaborators, [the researcher's] questions and her responses to [them] created an environment for joint understanding. At the same time, the interaction contributed to clarification and reorganization of [her] own thinking. (2000, p. 35)

John-Steiner later reflected on the significance of that experience, suggesting that knowledge, therefore, is both reconstructed and co-constructed in the course of dialogic interaction. For John-Steiner and Meehan, this way of seeing the structuring and re-structuring of knowledge is rooted in both the socio-cultural and the individual cognitive experience.

In "Considering Culture in the Selection of Teaching Approaches for Adults," Linda Ziegahn takes the socio-cultural position in the classroom and elaborates on the value of this kind of social interaction. For her, "…the social construction of knowledge might be fostered through collaborative group learning, which emphasizes the process of listening to and respecting others, understanding alternative views, challenging others, and negotiating meanings" (2001, ¶ 17). As discussed earlier, Wells also seems to echo Polanyi's explication of personal knowledge as he observes further that knowledge "is created and re-created between people as they bring their personal experience and information derived from other sources to bear on solving some particular problem (Wells, 2000, p. 67).

Developing writers would best be served in their studies of and experiments with composition and rhetoric, it seems, when they are encouraged to engage in dialogues that aim them toward the answer to, say, a mutual research question—an intellectual space where the relative ignorance of one learner may be promptly transformed by the relative knowledge of another. This "space" is part of an important theory developed by Vygotsky: the zone of proximal development (ZPD). It would therefore be best to turn to this Vygotskyan metaphor to determine how it can serve as a tool for understanding the development of writing skills in the midst of play.

## 7.1 Knowing and Doing in the Zone of Proximal Development

Expressed simply, the ZPD is the area within which humans develop new knowledge and skills, the space between present ability and potential. According to Vygotsky, problem solving and other skills assume three categories (1934/1978, pp. 86-7): (a) those performed independently; (b) those that cannot be performed even with help; and (c) those that fall between the two extremes, tasks that can be performed with help from others. This last category is the ZPD—the area or time within which development occurs.

Vygotsky points out that the ZPD "furnishes psychologists and educators with a tool through which the internal course of development can be understood, … [permitting them] to take account of not only the cycles and maturation processes that have already been completed but also those … that are in a state of formation, that are just beginning to mature and develop" (1934/1978, p. 78). More significantly, he further observes that "…what is in the [ZPD] today will be the actual developmental level tomorrow—that is, what a child can do with assistance today she will be able to do by herself tomorrow" (1934/1978, p. 78).

Why is Vygotsky's notion of the ZPD significant to the development of writing skills? In a classroom, for example, dialogues effectively stimulate intellectual interactions among learners as they approach solving a writing problem. The process of writing is both communal and solitary, and the communal aspect of this action permits one learner to contribute to the shaping of knowledge and the generating of ideas for the other. Put another way, among other acts that contribute to knowledge gathering and extending skills, speech itself, when used in a meaningful way in a mutual search for meanings, refines old ideas, generates new ones, and, thus, shapes the writing that later approximates those ideas on paper.

The image on the proceeding page illustrates the role that dialogues take in the ZPD as the mutual search for interesting phrases can serve as building blocks for more expanded and meaningful expression.

UMUC students negotiating the relevance and usefulness of a particular phrase.

Dialogues can displace relative ignorance (or generalities) with certain possibilities (or particulars) and can serve as a useful means of erecting the theoretical scaffolding, or operationalizing Vygotsky's concept of the zone of proximal development (Wells, 1999, p. 127).

The scaffolding metaphor (Wood, Bruner & Ross, 1976, p. 90; Wells, 1999, p. 127) is really an illustration of how experiences performed with help from others can help construct the building of skills. Relevant to the future development of writing skills are the particular features of scaffolding: (a) joint problem solving; (b) intersubjectivity (working together, same goal, negotiate differences to arrived at shared perspective); (c) warmth and responsiveness; (d) teacher's job – keep child in ZPD, adjusting challenge and intervention; (e) promote self-regulation – teachers relinquish control as students work independently; (f) distancing to promote problem solving (Berk, 1995, pp. 30-3) and, more relevantly for writing, also provide "sentence frames" for completion by the learner (Cazden, 1983).

In his article, "Collective Scaffolding in Second Language Learning," Richard Donato points out that this idea, "which derives from cognitive psychology and [first language] research, states that in social interaction a knowledgeable participant can create, by means of speech, supportive conditions in which the novice can participate ..., and extend, current skills and knowledge to higher levels of competence" (1998, p. 40). Much like the supports that construction workers use, scaffolding is intended to be temporary. It remains principally as an aid for the completion of a task and is eventually disassembled. Dialogues, in the same way, may be used as scaffolding in the midst of a learner's ZPD for the completion of a writing task. Simple dialogues engage the minds that conceive ideas, ears that receive them, mouths that negotiate their precise meanings or potential rhetorical effects, and the hands that act upon them with pens or pencils. Polanyi's illustration of the conscious attention to detail and the efforts made in understanding a subject of inquiry has value for writers engaged in dialogues and collaborating in a pursuit of meanings and clarity of expression. He points out that

> ... our knowing lies in recognizing or understanding a thing, [and] the effort involved in acquiring such knowledge may be ... guided by our attention. A biologist, a doctor, an art dealer, ... acquire their expert knowledge in part from textbooks, but these texts are of no use to them without the accompanying training of the eye [and] ear .... Only by attentively straining their senses can they acquire the right sense, or feel, for identifying a certain

> biological specimen, the symptoms of a certain sickness, [or] a genuine painting by a certain master.... By such training the expert develops an exceptional fastidiousness, which enables him to act as an appraiser of the value or meaning of certain objects or conditions. (Polanyi, 1975, p. 43)

By such training, too, can developing writers mutually establish increases in their abilities to appraise the value or meaning of certain objects, concepts or conditions of discussion or academic inquiry. The dialogue itself between two learners seeking similar aims forces both into moments of raised attention. By "straining their senses" can developing writers raise their awareness of the value, or precision, of the words they choose to represent their ideas, appraise the foremost ways in which they come to together to form complete or well crafted sentences. In descriptive writing, for example, if choosing a precise word is important and requires increasingly keener observations on the part of writers, a dialogue may consequently help them negotiate a word's potential for precision or economy. Elbow also takes a similar approach and argues for the significant role that dialogues play, suggesting that two heads are better than one as two heads can make conflicting material interact better than one head usually can. For him, this is

> ... why brainstorming works. I say something. You give a response and it constitutes some restructuring or reorienting of what I said. Then I see something new on the basis of your restructuring and so I, in turn, can restructure what I first said. The process provides a continual leverage or mechanical advantage: we each successively climb upon the shoulders of the other's restructuring, so that at each climbing up, we can see a little farther. (Elbow, 1998, p. 49)

Dialogue is essentially the sort of useful scaffolding over which more increasingly expedient writing techniques may be developed. How precisely, though, might dialogues assist in the construction of these skills? Another term that has appeared throughout this discussion and which the greater aims of this study focus on is *play*.

## 7.2 Playing in the Zone

From a pedagogical perspective, it would be hasty to pigeonhole play strictly in the narrowest slot: as a seemingly non-rational activity that merely measures out satisfying doses of free pleasure (Huizinga, 1939/1986, pp. 3-4). Vygotsky observes that other activities provide children with much more acute experiences of pleasure than play (1934/1978, p. 92), like sucking a pacifier when satiation is short-lived. Vygotsky sees play as the means by which humans satisfy certain needs throughout their development: "That which is of the greatest interest to the infant has almost ceased to interest the toddler" (1934/1978, p. 92). He believes that it is impossible to ignore the fact that children satisfy certain needs in play, and where one lacks an understanding of the special character of these needs, one cannot understand the uniqueness of play as a form of activity whose meaning and utility (to be elaborated on in Part 3) can be extended to adults coping with difficulties in generating sentence-level meaning in composition classrooms (1934/1978, p. 93).

Vygotsky further points out, for example, that no one encounters children under three years of age who want to do something a few days in the future—suggesting that the very young tend to gratify, or seek to gratify, their desires immediately, as in the very egocentric temper tantrum (1934/1978, p. 93). But, at preschool age, children begin exhibiting a growing interest in many unrealizable tendencies and desires. Play appears to be invented, Vygotsky reasons, when children are confronted by situations in which they want something but cannot immediately satisfy their desires. In his estimation, play creates a world of imagination within which children are offered a chance to realize the previously unattainable. It is worth noting, too, that imagination in children, Vygotsky argues, is "a new psychological process …, not present in the consciousness of the very young child, … totally absent in animals, and [representing] a specifically human form of conscious activity. Like all functions of consciousness, it originally arises from action" (1934/1978, p. 93).

This latter observation here appears much in line with what Polanyi claims about conscious activity and its direct connection to the shaping of personal knowledge. If play is imagination in action (1934/1978, p. 93) and if "our urge to understand or control our experience" (Polanyi, 1975, p. 42), as earlier noted, "causes us to rely on some parts of [this urge] subsidiarily in order to attend to our main objective," then play is a useful subsidiary way of shaping personal knowledge—offering an imaginative means by which to reach the main objective. Expressed another way, if the ultimate goal appears to be attainable but, nevertheless, realizable later than sooner, and if at times we cannot attain it straight away, play can then become a strategy for moving towards the objective by permitting the creative imagination to entertain the many possibilities of how best to proceed.

This is, perhaps, one principal reason why frustrated student writers mired in their apprehensions and unable to circumvent the rational rule-based strategies imposed upon them by academic structures report sometimes that effective written communication represents an often unattainable goal. For all of the creative possibilities offered to writers who resort to play strategies, play is not, however, an entirely unproblematic approach to achieving some academic objective. Johan Huizinga begins his critique of play's value by arguing that nature could have given

> … her children all those useful functions of discharging … abundant energy, relaxing after exertion, training for the demands of life,

> compensating for unfulfilled longings, etc., in the form of purely mechanical exercises and reactions. But …, she gave us play, with its tension, mirth and fun … [and] the fun of playing resists all analysis, all logical interpretation…. Here we have … an absolutely primary category of life, familiar to everybody … right down to the animal level…. Animals play so they must be more than merely mechanical things. We play and know that we play, so we must be more than merely rational beings, for play is irrational (1939/1986, pp. 3-4).

For Huizinga, play represents an open invitation to free and voluntary action undertaken for its own sake, and, though setting the stage for creative invention, is entirely unproductive and impractical. Those engaged in the temporary actions of play are bound by space and time and regulated by arbitrary, conditional rules and conventions. Huizinga points out that the fun that play engenders defies logical analysis. But, must the reasons behind the fun derived in play be necessarily explicated in order to interpret in some meaningful way the sometimes unintended positive outcomes gained through the acts of play itself? Similarly, Roger Caillois argues that play, in its many forms, is an "occasion of pure waste," ([1961] 2001, p. 16). He sees play as embodied experience, a testing of mental or physical limitations against other players or even the world at large, inviting both pleasure and pain. Play, for Caillois, can assume unstructured or highly disciplined forms occupying four principal categories.

Wherever competition (*agon*) governs action, players enjoy taking chances while striving toward artificially created goals. Wherever chance (*alea*) dominates, they permit fate to determine success or winning. In games where mimicry (*simulation*) governs action, players enjoy achievement in successfully assuming a different persona, that is passing as another person without the intention to deceive. In Caillois' last category, where games of vertigo (*ilinx*) prevail, players submit to states of dizziness or disarray, feeling the sensation of the embodied experience in heightened awareness or a rush of endorphins. Caillois' notion of competitive play seems to have value for students of composition who at times compete against one another for distinction and against their self-perceived linguistic shortcomings for self-expression. The "goals" set within the composition classroom may sometimes be artificial or merely academic exercises, but students struggling for intellectual growth or recognition are likely to see goals like these as legitimate and worthwhile.

In more recent years, other researchers have resisted the wholesale acceptance of Vygotsky's theory of play as it relates to cognitive and motor development. For example, in "Cultural Variation in Play: A Challenge to Piaget and Vygotsky," Suzanne Gaskins and Artin Göncü argue for the need of another theory set upon a better understanding of the "cultural origins of play" (1992, p. 34) and suggest that neither Piaget's theory "focused on the developmental origins" nor Vygotsky's "focused on the developmental outcomes" (1992, p. 31) can adequately account for the cultural differences and motivations behind play. In their critique, they certainly avoid committing what they appear to feel are the potentially fatal hasty generalizations that Piaget and Vygotsky had made by having failed to observe the import of culture upon play, but Gaskins and Göncü themselves restrict much too tightly, it seems, their own conclusions about the necessity of a new theory.

By citing what they feel are sharp differences in Mayan children and those observed by Vygotsky and Piaget, they reject inducing any universal conclusions about children, their development, and play as a means of hastening it. For them, a new and more expedient theory "… will not only allow [them] to understand more adequately the play of Mayan children …, but [as parents, they] will also gain a much more significant understanding of the play of [their] own children by realizing how their play reflects [their] own culture and prepares them to function in it" (1992, p. 34). While these are decent goals, they appear to presuppose that play "represents something fundamentally different for Mayan children" (1992, p. 32) than other western children because of differences in the cultural artifacts used during play, differences in the time Mayan children have to play, and the different attitudes and meaning that Mayan parents attach to play. Their concerns overlook a basic fact that children universally want and, despite the time constraints imposed on them by their culture, do find ways *to* play. In light of the tendencies toward play and the apparent parallel drawn to child development, however relative, this line of reasoning can be extended to adult behavior and learning even though the youthful forms of, say, mimicry or simulation no longer preoccupy the thoughts and behavior of adults as they do in children.

The word *play* is itself interesting here insofar as studies of language in general, and English composition in particular, are traditionally anything but playful. At the very least, what the word communicates implicitly is that the object of play—in this case writing—can be fun. Too often, though, writing in the context of a classroom seems to translate into institutionalized drudgery. Pedagogically and historically, academic writing in the North American tradition has typically been neither an engaging pursuit nor a very gratifying diversion from the often stultifying routines of formal schooling. If writing requires the production of words on paper, then play provides a lively means of generating the needed words, negotiating their uses in various contexts, and arranging them syntactically—inoculating participants from the stress of having to confront head on the academic task at hand and to cope with its many associated standard treatments for correctness.

What specific implications does play have in writing pedagogy and how could the skills developed in the midst of play serve as scaffolding for future abilities? A close reading and discussion of the following apt quotation may provide some insights. Piaget observes that "Logical activity isn't all there is to intelligence." And Vygotsky responds:

> Imagination is important for finding solutions to problems, but it does not take care of verification and proof, which the search for truth presupposes. The need to verify thought—that is, the need for logical activity—arises late. This lag is to be expected, says Piaget, since thought begins to serve immediate satisfaction much earlier than to seek truth; the most spontaneous form of thinking is play, or wishful imaginings that make the desired seem obtainable. Up to the age of seven or eight, play dominates in the child's thought to such an extent that it is very hard for the child to distinguish deliberate invention from fantasy that the child believes to be the truth. (1934/1978, p. 18)

As Piaget observes, if "… the most spontaneous form of thinking is play" (1932/1969, p. 201), then the opposite holds true: play serves as a way of thinking spontaneously. While indeed play does dominate children's thoughts, one could modify slightly and well extend Vygotsky's observation and apply it to adult learning and behavior. It appears that adults tend to modify their forms of play, usually, with what they feel to be more intellectually sophisticated or more monetarily expensive playthings. For example, trivial pursuits, such as board or beer drinking games, test intellectual reflexes in social settings that help participants confirm knowledge or abilities.

To further illustrate this point, the word *play* itself when used in relation to musical instruments is not arbitrarily chosen. This means that playing an instrument is not merely realizing a score but being able to imagine music and then perform the music you are imagining. If budding players are able to realize the music they are imagining, they are truly playing an instrument in the strictest sense of the word. This kind of realization is analogous to the qualities of creatureliness that Wallace Stevens called "the instinctive integration which is the reason for living" (quoted in Berry, 2002, p. 23). He writes that in our creatureliness "we forget the little or much that we know about the optic nerve and the light-sensitive cell, and *we see*; we forget whatever we know about the physiology of the brain, and *we think*; we forget what we know about anatomy, the nervous system, the gastrointestinal tract, and *we work, eat,* and *sleep*" (Stevens, in Berry, 2002, p. 23).

In play, we likewise forget the little or much we know about the subordinating conjunction and subordinate clause, and we communicate complex thoughts; we forget the little or much we know about conjunctive adverbs and comma splices, and we simply write. If play is elemental to certain adult behaviors, such as coping mechanisms, undertaking useful diversions or extending personal knowledge, resistance to academic forms of play can be met with a modest appeal to reason and reflection on the developmental courses that humans take in their walks through school.

## 8. Playing and Gestalts

> Do not use compulsion, but let early education be a sort of amusement; you will then be better able to find out the natural bent.
> —*Plato, Republic, Book VII*

In the midst of play, the child arranges circumstances and selects strategies (Matlin, 1998, p. 256) to gain greater forms of awareness when working out problems on his or her own or in collaboration with more clever peers (Piaget, 1974, p. 80). If, as Vygotsky argues in *Mind in Society*, play serves a crucial role in the development of thought and language, then certain forms of language play ought to precede a child's initial exposure to teaching strategies that encourage the development of meta-linguistic discourse and later, if the need eventually arises, skills in parsing. Vygotsky points out that in "play, a child is always a head taller than himself. As in the focus of a magnifying glass, play contains all developmental tendencies in a condensed form and is itself a major source of development" (1934/1978, p. 102). As the source of development, play alone is a social symbolic pastime, living depictions of cultural norms wherein participants learn the rules uninhibited by prying authorities.

To illustrate, as children discover in play how building blocks may best fit together to form what resembles a solid towering structure, how some blocks appear to give balance and symmetry to the whole structure while others do not, so too do children in classrooms find in their free inventions that designs of written thought build from discursive activities developed through experiment and marked by self-discovery. Such an observation rests upon what seems to be a rather fundamental predisposition in humans, a way of adapting to surroundings and seeking order amidst chaos (Roney & Trick, 2003). Aristotle's theory of form and art, for example, whether we agree with it or not must have its roots in a plain fact (Feldman, 1978, p. 152): humans are natural matchers, that is, they spontaneously compare what they see to what they have seen. According to Edmund Feldman, this is a basic mode of cognition without which we cannot know or recognize something except in relation to something else like it we already know (1978, p. 152).

As we absorb, categorize and catalogue the complex array of sensory elements that comprise even a seemingly simple experience, we can take comfort in the fact that simple decisions do not rearrange our lives, do not require days of deliberation to process. Gestalt theory may also provide a useful framework for understanding how we tend to create the harmony that we tacitly feel we need as we routinely seek organization while filtering order out of confusion (Matlin, 2002). The individual sensory elements that comprise an experience, whether one is playing with blocks, arranging words in sentences, or observing artwork are organized into units of a larger scale to form meaningful patterns (Jackendoff, 1994) so that we do not have to strive too terribly to understand each element as a separate event (Lakoff, 1994; Pinker 1994, 1997; Roney & Trick, 2003).

How people view or experience a painting, for instance, can serve as a metaphor for the Gestalt approach to perception (Matlin, 2002). When we gaze at van Gogh's "Starry Starry Night," for example, we do not immediately focus on a single splotch of orange here, some purple there, and fifty other splashes of color thrown about the canvas. Rather, we instantly see a night sky represented in a unique and utterly foreign way. Langer further clarifies this point by suggesting that

> ... visual forms—lines, colors, proportions, etc.—are just as capable of articulation, i.e. of complex combination, as words. But the laws that govern this sort of articulation are altogether different from the laws of syntax that govern language. The most radical difference is that visual forms are not discursive. They do not present their constituents successively, but simultaneously, so the relations determining a visual structure [such as van Gogh's rendering of a night sky] are grasped in one act of vision. (1979, p. 93)

This way of interpreting and, hence, perceiving the sky embodies the theme of Gestalt psychology that the whole (the Gestalt) is greater than the sum of its parts (Piaget, 1972, pp.46-7; Matlin, 2002). We, thus, absorb van Gogh's original impression of the night sky without much effort because the overall quality of the painting transcends each individual stroke of color. Similarly, in classrooms where sentence-level writing is the focus and play with phrase structures permitted, this approach to the construction of meanings may help students see more readily on paper (distally) what they already tend to do naturally in the mind (proximally). This natural tendency to organize "the sensory field into groups and patterns of sense-data, to perceive forms ... seems to be inherent" and deeply embedded "in our ... experience ... our power of perceiving and in the elementary functions of our eyes and ears and fingers" (Langer, 1979, p. 89).

## 8.1 The Gestalt of Meanings in Play

If syntax is the ordering of words (parts) in certain design sequences to represent or convey meaning (the whole) and is a naturally developing consequence of the mind, Gestalt theory could help explain how humans tend to design novel meanings with ease from rather disparate phrase structures. The tendency of humans to group or find patterns can be seen in a more abstract form of expression. Max Wertheimer's most enduring effect on design developed from his "Theory of Form" (1923) and is best illustrated in the so-called "dot essay" filled with abstract patterns of dots and lines. Wertheimer shows that "certain gestalts are enhanced by our innate tendencies to constellate, or to see as 'belonging together' elements that look alike (called 'similarity grouping'), are close together ('proximity grouping') or have structural economy ('good continuation')" (Behrens, 1998, p. 3). Although words and phrases themselves are not necessarily abstract figures arranged in arbitrary patterns, they are, effectively, symbolic language.

The close proximity of the sequenced symbols $c - a - t$, taken customarily, for example, to be a commonplace noun representing a feline mammal, can possess a wide range of antecedents represented in various regions of the mind. That is to say, a mind "that works primarily with meanings must have organs that supply it primarily with forms" (Langer, 1979, p. 90). Whether rooted in personal knowledge born of a history of taste, tactile, visual, olfactory, or auditory experience, the free associations "constellated" in the mind that converge on and reveal themselves through dialogues may work under the same principles outlined by Wertheimer.

That such tendencies to constellate, group and categorize are or, at least, might be inborn, not learned, is suggested by the cross-cultural effectiveness of sleight-of-hand magic and camouflage, both of which work by subverting the "laws" described in Wertheimer's paper (Behrens, 1998). Roy Behrens asserts that the construction of certain gestalts is aided by our natural tendencies as humans to see elements that look alike, are close together, or seem to complement one another as, in fact, belonging together.

Another example of our dynamic involvement in the subject matter can be found in art. By understanding the importance of implicitness, Japanese artists are also cited as prime examples of those who take advantage of the "active complicity" of their audience, recognizing that the members thereof would eliminate the insignificant while focusing on the more meaningful—a process that Gabriele Rico sees in reading, which, at its most fundamental level, is a constructive act of the imagination (1978, p. 33). Behrens continues by explaining the premise of these artists that "genuine beauty [can] be discovered only by those who mentally complete the incomplete" (1998, p. 6). In the case of students engaged in the search for new meanings during rhetorical play, this method also recognizes the active complicity of writers and their audience by encouraging students to experiment with phrase structures. That is to say, if most of us simplify the world to make it more manageable, whether we are taking in sights, sounds or sentences, our brains allow as much by ignoring countless details to help create useful gestalts (Cowley, 2003, p. 48).

Play offers the space and time wherein free opportunities permit the mind to perceive with interpretive efforts (Polanyi, 1966, p. 12) these connections while ignoring seemingly countless and conflicting prescriptive details that govern the stricter, or more academically rooted, uses of the language. Some approaches in the process school, as characterized by Canagarajah's table in Part 1, have encouraged anxious students otherwise hindered by writers block to ignore, say, the mechanics or the spelling of a word until drafting is complete and the approximated ideas have found their proper groupings onto paper.

Roney and Trick (2003) concur that organizing the world by grouping events or other phenomena is a functional behavior. Play creates free space and time wherein students may group phrases. In this way, they hypothesize, we integrate our experiences into a manageable and understandable construct, and therefore feel better able to predict future experiences. Gestalt psychology highlights the significance of unfinished situations. Because people choose to avoid situations that are stressful (like writing), a pedagogy that encourages students to employ some useful coping mechanism (like play) can guide them in arranging circumstances and selecting strategies to improve future cognitive performance" (Matlin, 1994, p. 256).

When the student is free to operate in play, to interact with peers while using the written symbols of thought, to readily and conveniently invent meanings and uncover unintended new ones, the gain of knowledge has the appearance of being natural and unforced by the grammarian's standard prescriptions. This perception of inherent self-discovery ought to lead, it seems, to much higher levels of confidence and to a deeper awareness of the self as an inventor, shaper, and communicator of novel meanings. "But how is it that meaning can be made from forms never before encountered?" asks Elliot Eisner (1978, p. 16). Though lengthy, his response to the rhetorical question is pivotal to the overall argument for play and creativity in composition. Eisner argues that when we

> … pick up a book, listen to a piece of music, observe another's behavior, that … book, piece of music, [and] … behavior, has never before been encountered. We cannot explain our ability to construct meaning from events that are new entirely on the basis of previously learned responses. While the use of repertoires of learned behaviors certainly contribute to the recovery or creation of meaning, something more must be added. [That something, to him] resides in [the human] ability to build a world

beyond the stimuli provided, to go beyond the information given, to use [the] imaginative capacity to construct pattern, to perceive implied meaning, to read between the lines, in short, to break free from the discrete, digital character of each separate stimulus in order to form wholes, patterns which carry meaning to consciousness. (1978, p. 16)

Immersed in the customary media of the traditional classroom with its abundance of textbooks, exercises, and other codified and structured ways of conducting academic business, our ability to rise above these fixed media we have at our disposal, to piece together what is discrete and separate, requires both an interest and inclination to treat emerging ideas in creative ways, to be both willing and able to play with these media or stimuli one meets so that they can be patterned, given form and meaning (Eisner, 1978, p. 16). The elemental acts of play, in effect, become precursors to higher levels of *know-how*, naturally reinforced knowledge and skills that point toward the desirable consequence, the willful construction of written meanings. If early forms of play in the young are precisely aimed at exploration, the search for possibilities that culminate in the discovery of patterns or forms that hold meaning (1978, p. 16), then play with rhetorical phrase structures in the older student of composition should serve as an expedient means of bridging gaps between abilities and inabilities, between merely having language *skills* and having a level of *know-how* that springs from individual creative action in meaning making.

## 8.2 A Method of Playing and Discovering Form

In *Women, Fire and Dangerous Things*, George Lakoff cites the work of Brent Berlin (1964), Eleanor Rosch (1978), Eugene Hunn (1977), Carolyn Mervis (1984), Barbara Tversky (1984) and others who have isolated a significant level of human interaction with the external environment (the basic level), characterized by gestalt perception, mental imagery, and motor movements. He notes that at this level, "people function most efficiently and successfully in dealing with discontinuities in the natural environment. It is at this level of physical experience that we accurately distinguish tigers from elephants, chairs from tables, roses from daffodils..." (Lakoff, 1987, p. 269). I shall extend and apply this observation of basic level interaction and perception to the notion of play as it relates to composition and the creation of meaning.

The teaching method for which I have been clearing the theoretical groundwork was applied in the context of a case study—discussions of which appear in Part 3. As participants engage in play with rhetorical structures, they apply the play theory in the most basic and practical sense. For example, two participants sit beside one another and peruse the pages of selected newsprint: magazines, tabloid, or any other sort of print media on hand. Textual play commences as the two writers begin searching for structures (phrases or clauses) that strike them as particularly vivid, interesting, or related to a common theme of their choosing. This act of moving beyond the media that confronts them ought to free them from feeling compelled to observe strictly the syntactic rules of a grammar while helping them focus more energy on extracting from existing texts useful images or turns of speech that aid in their reproduction of meanings.

In his monograph, "The Role of Imagery in Learning," Harry Broudy suggests that when we have "loosened the tie of symbol or sign to that for which it stands, we are free to combine images almost at will. The key to this power is the separability of the image or other symbol from the thing or, more technically, from its ordinary denotation" (1987, p. 14). Similarly, given the creative context of play, if simple words or rhetorical structures can call up images loaded with a range of denotations and connotations and can, thus, be treated as pieces of a larger puzzle, then developing writers can feel free to search for and select images (or structures) at will to recreate meanings. As they collaborate, they may also feel compelled either to focus on a particular subject and direction or to allow one of these to emerge naturally from the phrases they choose. While this approach is meant to allay participants' anxieties of having to initially focus on a specific direction and subject and to generate words that embody the subject, it also circumvents the pre-writing phase in the process school.

As play unfolds, participants identify by circling all structures in a given span of time, then in no particular order transcribe all they had marked for play onto a clean sheet of paper. Initially, the building of meaning may appear to mimic the building of poetic lines or stanzas in their initial stages. Since rhetorical structures contain the seeds of meaning in their condensed forms (noun and verb phrases), writers may begin to discover how the images or meanings represented in simple phrases relate, combine to form more precise or elaborate meanings, play on one another (pun unintended) and, when assembled, grow into complex strings of thought.

Having laid out all structures, participants may begin to expeditiously see and draw connections between them. One aim of the study remains somewhat concealed, the demonstration of how thought and word and image are interconnected and share relationships that must sometimes be spelled out explicitly through clear transitional expressions. One expected outcome is that participants become increasingly more sensitive to their own growing knowledge, that they are developing a more conscious or explicit awareness of the need for transitional expressions, and of the connections that ideas or images must take in accord with the concepts of coherence and unity. If, as Lakoff observes, humans function best at this basic level of perception, that is in dealing with discontinuities, then play with a disparate range of phrase structures should allow them the freedom and opportunity to move more readily toward the free and creative reconstruction of meaning, to discover that mere phrases can serve as linguistic seeds from which, say, complex sentences, whole contexts and rhetorical effects can develop.

The play exercise is unlike those found in traditional American composition courses where assignments typically require students individually to find a topic, narrow it to a manageable size, generate ideas about it, take a stand if need be, brainstorm, outline, draft, edit, and revise. In this context, students contend with a variety of difficulties, some interrelated. Some not. Students report that anxiety precipitates procrastination which, in turn, only further compounds anxiety. One result is "writer's block," the physical manifestation of anxiety. Anxiety may, also, take other forms such as preoccupations with correct word spelling, apostrophe, or commas use.

As discussed in Part 1, Section 3.2, some students also report that the prospect of writing for critique engenders debilitating forms of anxiety. If students perceive, as they commonly do, the red ink of hand-scrawled critiques or the voiced disapprovals of their writing as direct assaults on themselves as human beings who possess invaluable histories, then play is also meant to free the teacher by offering a useful means of circumventing the perceived necessity of dispensing prescriptions.

Pedagogies that emerge from the sorts of traditions described throughout this inquiry appear to rely upon a fairly specious assumption: human beings typically work alone and rarely consult with other perhaps more capable peers for potential suggestions and guidance. Neither the professional nor the apprentice, though, works, lives or writes in a complete vacuum. Everyone relies to some degree on references, whether inanimate or animate sources, to assist the generation of ideas, to inform the construction of meanings, to raise awareness of audience needs, and the pragmatic utility of words chosen for whatever subject, audience and purpose. Within the North American paradigm, composition studies often seem to dismiss the evidence that writers are not simply engaged in one-way communication with a computer screen or sheet of paper, but are being communicated to by all manner of external sensory input: the physical forces of the material world influence every act we engage ourselves in when in the process of turning abstract thoughts into the concrete sequenced symbols of language (Langer, 1979, p. 88).

If, therefore, one begins with the premise that composition students possess already a tacit awareness of their language, have already acquired a natural bent toward the consistent rules in the dialect (Labov, 1969, p. 179) of their native speech community, one need only concern oneself with the meanings embedded in phrase structures in order to address concerns about the appearance of peculiar turns of speech, the dialect expressions seeping in to an otherwise standard variety. Lev Vygotsky expands on these observations in *Thought and Language*:

> The child does have a command of the grammar of his native tongue long before he enters school, but it is unconscious, acquired in a purely structural way, like the phonetic composition of words. If you ask a young child to produce a combination of sounds, for example *sk*, you will find that its deliberate articulation is too hard for him; yet within a structure, as in the word *Moscow*, he pronounces the same sounds with ease. The same is true of grammar. The child will use the correct case or tense within a sentence, but cannot decline or conjugate a word on request. He may not acquire new grammatical or syntactic forms in school, but, thanks to instruction in grammar and writing, he does become aware of what he is doing and learns to use his skills consciously. (1934/1986, pp. 183-4)

Vygotsky's suggestion that a child "may not acquire new grammatical or syntactic forms in school" appears to rest upon an irrelevant preconception. It does not matter so much whether children do or do not become explicitly conscious of grammar. Regarding their potential to improve, that is to nurture their discourse styles, it matters whether they become conscious of their dialect expressions that give the impression of being unacceptable or incorrect constructions of grammar. Dialect varieties appear on the surface, ringing in the ears in speech or assaulting the eyes in words on paper, and these normative peculiarities only disguise a more important and unchanging fundamental: languages are naturally formed and abide by rules—whether codified in grammar texts or encoded in the minds of their users through their speech communities.

Since, perhaps, the needs or expectations of a writer's audience are not always obvious or clearly defined for the writer, the natural adjustments that speakers make to meet those needs or expectations do not always or easily translate into writing. Given the famous student refrain, "I write how I speak," what may not be so apparent to developing writers is their use of dialect expressions within their writing. It seems obvious, therefore, that the foremost concern of an instructor ought to be in nurturing a budding writer's level of awareness, to help turn the often tacit use of written language into the more explicit. To further illustrate the connection between conscious and non-conscious uses of language and their perceived dependence on grammar instruction, Vygotsky speaks of mental development and grammar as a tool in cultivating what the mind already does naturally:

> Grammar is a subject that seems to be of little practical use. Unlike other school subjects, it does not give the child new skills. He conjugates and declines before he enters school. The opinion has even been voiced that school instruction in grammar could be dispensed with. We can only reply that our analysis clearly showed the study of grammar to be of paramount importance for the mental development of the child. (1934/1986, p. 183)

For adult periphery students, though, bringing with them the full mental development absent in children but who are aiming, nonetheless, to acquire new means of written expression as adults, the prospect of play presents these students with a wide range of possibilities that can be freely explored while demonstrating that meanings are ubiquitous, can be found in many unexpected ways and places, and can be easily refined for precision or the writer's intended rhetorical effect. As students isolate certain phrases that they see fit for word play, these creative examinations of language frame the study of grammar in such a way that students forget that they are actually parsing sentences in ways that more traditional approaches have explored but with little positive returns. Phrase play appears to engender a fuller awareness of the writer's own active involvement in the construction and shaping of meaning.

As the results in the case study should show, Vygotsky's own theory of play in the development of knowledge and ability—despite "the study of grammar"—should prove to be more useful, at least initially, than many prevailing prescriptive approaches to grammar studies. That is, if Vygotsky and colleagues observe that grammar is important to the mental development of children, and if humans already bring significant tacit forms of knowledge of their language to the classroom, then language play should help shift emphasis away from obsessive concerns over correctness while naturally increasing knowledge of grammar and the limitations of language use.

# PART 3. THE PRACTICE OF PLAY

## 9. An Approach to Prose through Play with Phrases in Poetry

In light of the preceding discussions of attitudes about language uses and standards, of linguistic theories and their roles in shaping pedagogies, my intent here is to develop an argument for play in classrooms where composition is the principal study but where poetics is the means through which to encourage that study. Just as the explication of, say, painting is concerned with pictorial, or presentational, structures discussed by Langer (1979, p. 72-3), "poetics," according to Roman Jakobson, "deals with problems of verbal [or discursive] structures" (1960, p. 350). Moreover, "[s]ince linguistics is the global science of verbal structure," Jakobson points out that, "poetics may be regarded as an integral part of linguistics" (1960, p. 350).

In his discussion of the growth and direction that rhetoric has taken since the ancient Greeks, Richard Lanham points out that "rhetoric has always tended to outgrow its original concern with persuasive public speaking, or direct verbal communication, and to lend itself to written communication as well" (1991, p. 131). Lanham cites Cicero's observation that oratory serves three principal functions, that is to teach, to please, and to move, and he points out why the areas of communication they cover offer reasons why "rhetorical theory has so often in its history overlapped poetics" (1991, p. 132).

What do the linguistic and rhetorical underpinnings of poetics have to do with the development of writing skills? Joy Peyton and Pat Rigg identify the intrinsic value of poetry in language learning in the adult ESL classroom. This poetic utility can also be applied to classrooms where adult 'periphery' learners dealing with the difficulties of writing apprehension and self-doubt are experimenting with new forms of self-expression in composition. Whereas poetry is an immensely compressed form of communication, Peyton and Rigg observe that poetry provides adults with rich learning opportunities in language and content, and community building—a social action peculiar to "collaborative writing situations" (National Council of Teachers of English, 2004). The repetition of words and structures typifies poetry, and poetry encourages language play with rhythmic and rhyming devices. Poetic themes are often universal, at the same time giving insight into individuals' lives, cultures, beliefs, and practices. (Peyton & Rigg, 1999, ¶ 17).

The following discussion outlines the phases of a case study that includes play with phrases in the writing of poetry as a method of surreptitiously disarming students' apprehensions in the process of writing prose. My discussion will describe the strengths and weaknesses of this approach and the extent to which initial exposure to play with phrase structures seems to defer marginalized students' imminent worries over correctness in standard grammar or mechanics, a considerable obstacle to many apprehensive and overeager students engaged in generating and drafting ideas during text production.

## 9.1 Summary of Previous Observations

Based upon my fourteen years of informal observation in college composition classrooms with the University of Maryland University College, *Asia* in both Korea and Japan, it has appeared that merely modest amounts of value and emphasis are placed on the spontaneous and creative aspects of language and how these qualities of human nature could be better used to address the needs of periphery students in college-level English writing courses.

This observation may appear to suggest some institutional effort is afoot to suppress creativity among faculty. But, this is hardly the case. I have sensed also from my exchanges with faculty at stateside campuses that creativity is just as valued. So, it is worth clarifying again that my intent, here, is not to conflate creative classroom approaches to developing motivation in students with creative approaches to developing in students a greater awareness of their already existing linguistic abilities. This is not a matter of bad teachers, bad intent, or bad methods but a matter of too tight a focus on a general approach. The approach is largely prescriptive, and the focus on its value, no matter how creatively employed, fails to notice the vast amount of valuable rhetorical knowledge and skill already existing in students.

As far as could be determined from the literature that criticizes largely prescriptivist strategies so far discussed, popular approaches to composition yet appear to be influenced by this dated presumption that an increase in explicit knowledge of traditional grammar and associated meta-lingual terms remain the clearest signs of acceptable or valuable forms of knowledge. That is to say, these forms of explicit knowledge presuppose that student writers are capable of performing at higher levels of competency.

Beneath what appears to be growing approval of exclusively expressivist approaches to composition in the North American paradigm there lies a residual belief in prescriptivist orthodoxies. In his article, "Reforming English Language Arts," Edgar Schuster recounts an experience with a teacher who insisted on forcing students to memorize and recite the parts of speech in drills but finds little success in the exercise (1999, p. 518). Interestingly, these forms of knowledge that Schuster calls into question have not fully aided students in their efforts toward improved writing. Significant numbers of successful student writers have demonstrated through the years, for example, their virtually complete ignorance of the parts of speech, whether in or out of the context of writing classrooms. Identifying a prepositional phrase as a dangling modifier would be, to them, more difficult than identifying a single snowflake in a snowstorm.

It has seemed more likely that those who could commit to memory the parts of speech, dissect and diagram a complex sentence into its constituent parts had become successful in submitting to the rather long-held tradition of standard grammar indoctrination—to be trained by another person to abide by standards that are, as Brodkey expresses it, "anything but standardized" (1996, p. 45). She argues that instruction in composition

> ... appears to have succeeded best at establishing in most people a lifelong aversion to writing. They have learned to associate a desire to write with a set of punishing exercises called writing in school: printing, penmanship, spelling, punctuation, themes, book reports, and library research papers in college preparatory and advanced placement courses. It is probably worth wondering whether the most successful students are not those who learn early on that writing assignments are occasions for students to display and teachers to correct errors, and not, as one might think, invitations for students to write about and teachers to respond to ideas. (1996, pp. 135-6)

Moreover, according to Robert de Beaugrande, decades of research in the phenomenon of text production has yielded little understanding of the complex processes at work in humans engaged in the act of writing. In *Text Production: Toward a Science of Composition*

(1984), de Beaugrande cites a range of experiments conducted from 1929 to the present to measure or assess the physiological, psychological and social phenomena present in or perceived by writers. Galvanic skin response, palm sweat, eye-blink rate, pupil dilation, sensory deprivation, room temperature, noise distraction, self-consciousness scales, test anxiety scales, isolation measures, audience sensitivity measures, etc. were all clinically designed and tested to better apprehend the range of challenges facing students of composition. De Beaugrande argues that while such a battery of measures may seem impracticable, time-consuming and exaggerated, researchers cannot tell in advance and independently of experience which factors might be relevant for language performance (1984, p. 89).

Bizzell sees the problem of writing instruction as much more complex than simply "helping—or requiring—students to learn Standard English" (1992, p. 164). She argues that students' awareness of their own non-standard "dialect expressions" (p. 165), their ignorance of acceptable academic "discourse forms" (p. 165), and their "ways of thinking" (p. 166) are complicated by the ongoing debate among academics who tend to concentrate on one form of prescription, such as surface features, while ignoring or overlooking another, such as discourse conventions or ways of thinking. She sees the problem as the result of too "narrow a focus" (p. 167) and argues for a remedy that requires teachers to fundamentally alter their views of language, by seeing language users as engaged in a discourse community that "coheres because of common language-using practices" (p. 167).

Beyond the noble efforts of compositionists since Bizzell's observations, the increasing authority of the expressivist school, and the range of creative pedagogies now on offer, a complete theory of composition must consider too the immense often unexploited value of language play emerging from a natural tacit awareness of language itself.

## 9.2 Hypothesis

If writing is a skill like other abilities that humans develop, if play helps hone skills and if it represents a safe means of experimenting with and exploring meanings, students, whether peripheral or mainstream, can use play to develop naturally as writers, discovering in themselves their abilities to locate, generate, and refine to recreate meanings while overcoming writing apprehensions.

## 9.3 Method Description and Aims

Behind this case study, I have examined current pedagogies in light of research in linguistics and psychology and assessed ways in which popular attitudes about language and use shape language policies and teaching practices. Although my proposed method draws on work from diverging areas of inquiry, the marriage of Vygotsky's theory with a common rhetorical exercise and its application in the context of a composition classroom represents a new way of addressing a rather old and persistent problem.

Implicit in this approach comes the opportunity for a fundamentally different way of analyzing student writing: instead of prescribing supposedly standard remedies of correctness, the instructor is free to shift his or her focus on the problem away from his or her traditional perspective and set out to describe the many ways in which students may search for and build meaning with phrases. The act of describing becomes a model for students and how they themselves may experiment freely with the rhetorical structures they mark out for play. That is to say, it contrasts with contemporary methods that typically have at their center the teacher holding to the persistent belief that prescriptions of correctness are best dispensed from an authority figure.

While the "process school" (Elbow, 1998) compels students to initially generate their own thoughts, this method encourages students to locate fragments of thoughts, so to speak, to use as tools for play in their search for new meanings—an act that mimics the play of, say, a dozen children who find their way towards a common solution in games of make-believe. So, the phrase, like a chisel in the hands of a student sculptor, can be a tool whose repeated handling will yield ever-increasing adeptness in the search for more meaningful forms of expression.

The method encourages play with the following phrase structures: (a) noun, (b) verb, (c) prepositional and (d) infinitive. While each phrase forms a grammatical unit, each lacks a finite verb and a subject-predicate structure (Richards, 1999, p. 53). Nevertheless, although each phrase lacks this structure, a student can easily modify simultaneously or separately any of the four phrases to suit coherence on either of two levels: the syntactic and/or the semantic. The following examples expand on Chomsky's well known observation (1957, p. 14) and serve to illustrate my point.

> a. Colorless green ideas were in the pool yesterday evening sleeping furiously.

In *a.*, if a student identifies *Colorless green ideas* as an NP, *in the pool* as a PP, *yesterday evening* as an NP, and *were sleeping furiously* as a non-contiguous VP, the student thus recognizes a number of constituents and is free to rearrange each in new combinations to represent a new meaning or grammar.

> b. Pooling in a furious sleep yesterday evening were colorless green ideas.

In *b.*, the student has morphed a single word, *pool*, modified its syntactic position and, thus, drastically altered the 'meaning' of the sentence. This method of play on a larger scale permits the apprehensive writer to separate two complex tasks often merged during drafting: the working out of a coherent syntax and the search for a coherent semantics. Was the student's tacit knowledge of the language and of the necessary morphological changes enough to help the student create a new meaning with a new grammar? Was an explicit knowledge of a meta-language necessary for the student to modify existing phrases to produce new syntactic structures and semantic relationships? The exercises taken up by students throughout the case study are intended to provide some possible answers.

Another aim of the play exercises is for students to increase their knowledge of the significant versatility of phrases. This initial approach towards furthering this sort of knowledge may come through identification. It may come through the mere handling of phrases. Identifying and labeling the constituent parts of a sentence does not, however, come without potential problems for students. Although some students are likely to mis-recognize and mislabel these phrases early on, their creative efforts in play remain more valuable to the greater aims of composition.

If, for example, a student mis-recognizes a subordinate clause (*since she arrived*) for a verb phrase (*arrived for dinner*) or prepositional phrases (*from dried okra to baked beans*) for infinitive phrases (*to make a full pot to take to the party*), his or her *knowing how* (Ryle, 1949) to handle these phrases to create new meanings remains, nevertheless, intact. *Knowing that* (Ryle, 1949) *for dinner* is a PP attached to the verb *arrived* is useful, but not as useful as *knowing how*, despite the potential grammatical overlap, to use the entire phrase to create a coherent grammar or meaning. Successful plays with phrases do not hinge upon the student's *knowing that* one phrase is a prepositional and another is an infinitive. Success depends principally upon the student's own creative powers, tacit awareness of the necessary coherence, and a naturally unfolding sense of *knowing how* to use these phrases, despite their meta-linguistic labels, to create meaning.

From the traditional grammarian's perspective, drills such as identifying and labeling various de-contextualized phrases as one of several types presents certain syntactic ambiguities and, thus, meta-lingual uncertainties. Superimposing a syntactic perspective upon a fairly inconsequential act promotes the kind of writing anxiety many teachers try to avoid creating. Nevertheless, the resultant confusion, as Daly and Miller (1975) observed, is part and parcel of the writing apprehension that significant numbers of students must contend with.

## 9.4 Case Study

Initially, my principal aim in this research and case study was to investigate the strengths and limitations of Vygotsky's theory of play and its use to the development of writing skills. To help illustrate this significance, it was profitable to draw on an exercise in poetics known as *found poetry* (Peyton & Rigg, 1999, ¶ 15). Originally, I had estimated that liberal play with phrase structures could be a useful means of helping students raise their awareness of diction's effect on message or tone, awakening in them any unrealized sensitivities to creativity, subduing their apprehensions, and exciting in them a wider appreciation for language. Other aims were to illustrate, at least implicitly, the extent to which present traditional methods in composition studies engender feelings of exclusion, alienation from the norm, or general anxiety about communicating with others.

## 9.5 Soliciting Participation

In order to avoid any conflicts of interest or potential abuses of power, I solicited participation outside the university community in which I work. I was able to identify and select participants who felt that they had been labeled as deficient writers or who had perceived themselves to be inarticulate or in need of repair as communicators.

Well before the commencement of the first workshop, I had originally conceived that I would encourage students to experiment with two modes of composition. I would then closely compare their work to another group's work: either samples of anonymous work from previous students who had received traditional lectures or published samples drawn from academic journals (such as *College Composition and Communication*, *College English*, *Phi Delta Kappan* and *TESOL Quarterly*), or anthologies. I had intended to focus my comparisons on narration and description, since these forms typically underpin many other basic modes of composition, require introspection as well as keen observation, and represent many of the general difficulties students encounter in expressive writing.

However, as the aims and motivations of the participants in the experimental group workshops differed dramatically from those of students who attend typical college composition courses, I realized that attempts to draw parallels between these two groups would be inherently skewed. Typical standard measurements of quality university composition could not possibly be applied to any sample of writing generated in the experimental group workshops. Apart from my initial exuberance to compare the work generated in these workshops with other published work and my initial miscalculations of the effectiveness of play to this end, I did come to realize, perhaps more importantly, that the exercises in play with phrase structures appeared to be much more useful in bridging wider gaps between generating an idea and not being able to, between responding to language and not wanting to, between wanting to experiment and not caring to. Distinguishing between the process and the product, participants appeared to ultimately conceive of 'essay' as work in progress.

## 9.6 Participant Profiles in Experimental Group Workshops

The term "participant" appearing throughout this discussion refers to any student who involved him- or herself through mutual cooperation in the research project. A single group of participants was assessed in terms of their personal observations of and experiences with English composition throughout their secondary and tertiary schooling. The term "experimental group workshop" was chosen to describe the setting in which students who responded to public solicitations to participate in the study could engage with one another in playful creative experiments with rhetorical structures.

Eight people initially responded to an advertisement posted in local community newspapers. A short telephone interview with each student about the potential responsibilities of those who would like to participate narrowed the final number to seven. While one potential participant could not meet for all of the workshop gatherings and opted out, four males and three females offered their time and energy in the experimental group workshops (*workshops* hereafter).

Although the sampling of students was relatively small, the participants represented three categories fundamental to the overall study: (a) age (b) ethnicity and (c) socio-economic status. The following table illustrates these details peculiar to each participant. The six text boxes that contain figures represent the number of participants per age category as well as the approximate socio-economic status to which the participants reported they had belonged during their schooling. As six of the seven participants did not see themselves situated squarely in the middle class, it was reasonable to assume, therefore, that the majority of students had not enjoyed the sort of equal access to resources that students coming from a higher—middle or upper—class typically do. Thus, in accordance with Mike Rose's similar conception of the marginalized student (1990, p. 128), their participation was appropriate.

Table 8

*Participant Profiles*

| class \ age | White | | | Black | | | Hispanic | | | Other ESL | | |
|---|---|---|---|---|---|---|---|---|---|---|---|---|
| | up'r | mid- | low- | up'r | mid- | low- | up'r | mid- | low- | up'r | mid- | low- |
| 20s | | 2 | | | | | | | | | | |
| 30s | | | 1 | | 1 | | | 1 | | | | 1 |
| 40s | | | | | | 1 | | | | | | |

The majority as well as the two leading minority ethnic groups, Hispanic and African-American, were represented. It should be noted that the only Hispanic participant was multilingual, born in Spain of American and Spanish parents, but nevertheless felt that her more dominant language was English. Additionally, the participant noted in the "Other" category was born in France but had immigrated to the United States at the age of twelve. He initially felt unsure what his dominant language was yet later admitted that perhaps he was more precisely seen as an ESL student, despite his apparent verbal fluency and absence of any obvious French accent.

Notwithstanding the range of ages included in this study (mid-twenties to mid-forties), the participants had likely experienced some measures of the effects of approaches peculiar to the CTP, such as those discussed throughout Part 1, Section 3. The fact that the participants agreed to be part of the study suggests that they were dealing with the sorts of writing apprehensions and related difficulties outlined in the announcement itself. Subsequent discussions throughout the case study confirmed this observation: certain impressions and attitudes expressed by teachers and peers combined with their experiences both inside and outside of classrooms had given shape to the participants' perceptions of their own skills.

All participants except two were undergraduates, i.e. still working towards their initial college degree. One was a graduate student coping with various "indefinable difficulties" in the writing of his thesis and the other was a teacher, a self-described lifelong apprehensive writer, in the "Reading Recovery Program" at a local elementary school.

As it was a primary goal to sample a fair cross-section of adult American college students who typically appear in introductory composition courses, subsequent discussions of them and their levels of participation will be confined to group references. Wherever essential for clarification of a point about linguistic bigotry, stereotypes, or other perceived relationships between class status and accent, I will refer to individual students.

## 9.7 Workshops

I met the participants on six Saturday mornings in 6 x 1.5-hour sessions. Although contact hours were spread over six meetings and represented much less time than students normally spend in typical composition courses, I had expected that the proposed method should operate independently of institutional time constraints, student gender, and participant age group.

Despite their differences in age, socioeconomic and linguistic background as well as differing experience with composition as a study, all of the participants shared two clear and unambiguous aims, to put to rest their vexing anxieties about writing and to enlarge their skills as practicing writers. All participants were unequivocal about the problems they saw and still see in English as a study, yet all were equally willing to learn new ways in which they could achieve greater awareness of their voice or the message they felt was not being heard or communicated clearly enough on paper.

## 9.8 Research Methods Rationale

The kinds of questions I had designed and posed to student participants throughout the workshops had been intended to elicit extended and meaningful discussions that would expose certain details about their previous experiences with American English as a study. My purpose had been to develop questions that would encourage participants to reflect and to open up and feel entirely uninhibited about telling the stories of their experiences. This approach was effective when useful verbal responses were at stake. The participants appeared much less enthusiastic, though, when written responses, such as initial and final diagnostic essays, were required. However well intentioned I was in this aim, it was, nevertheless, easy to arouse in all workshop participants an eagerness to recall their experiences and give voice to those aspects of writing that remained, from their perspective, vexing or over-burdening.

Rather than simply accepting as a given the vast research in sociolinguistics tracing the traditions of complaining about declining standards and attitudes expressed by these widely perceived linguistic phenomena, I had sought to underscore the weight of the arguments taken up by previous scholars, to determine the extent to which these traditions affect academic discourses presently and in the immediate past, and therefore to offer further examples of the effects that these practices have on the growth of skills in developing writers. Apart from this aim, the extemporaneous method of question and answer proved useful in allowing a number of insightful responses to the research questions and to the greater aims of the study.

## 9.9 Methods

In view of the entire case study, I used an inductive approach to data collection and a phenomenological approach to data analysis, the goal of which was a synthesis of participant comments and reactions not for internal comparison but awareness of and reflection on potential commonalities. The wide variety of responses to my research questions (see Part 3, Section 10.2 below) were largely responsible for helping me to recognize general patterns in attitudes about English composition as a study, about language uses and perceived abuses, and about the overall usefulness of the teaching method.

Since I had developed the case study around a certain set of assumptions about the generalities I would likely find, these approaches to data collection and analysis allowed me to determine more readily the trends I had anticipated, but to also be surprised when unexpected discoveries emerged in participants' expressed attitudes and behaviors within the writing process.

This perspective is drawn from Michael Quinn's discussions in *Qualitative Evaluation and Research Methods*. Quinn observes that such approaches to data evaluation are inductive to the extent that the researcher attempts to make sense of the situation without imposing preexisting expectations on the phenomenon or setting under study. Inductive analysis begins with specific observations and builds toward general patterns (2002 p. 44). Given my initial estimations, though, I had anticipated that these general patterns would reveal themselves throughout the case study. The participants would exhibit two important responses to the method of phrase play: (a) increased eagerness to embrace composition as a study and a precipitous drop in "writing apprehension" (Daly & Miller, 1975, p. 242)—the components of anxiety present in evaluation, stress and product apprehension; and (b) increased awareness of phrase structures, how they can be used to understand grammar in lieu of parsing exercises and how the structures can be easily handled to create new meanings initially at the sentence level.

## 9.10 Epistemological Assumptions

The teaching method investigated here finds its origins in the epistemological assumption that humans are foremost social creatures, that our beliefs and behaviors are continually shaped and reshaped by our social experiences and biological predispositions, as well as informed by our complex histories. Given this viewpoint, it remains important to acknowledge that much in keeping with an inductive approach to data collection and analysis that any insights culled from the case study are not hermetically sealed from or impervious to any personal expectations to see the method work.

Admittedly, I had hoped to see that the method for which I am building an argument is valid and useful to composition studies. I had imagined that if I involved myself in the social dynamic of drafting and placing myself as a genuinely interested observer/participant among the subjects that I would be performing three notable actions crucial to my gathering data:

1. I would not presume that I could gain a level of absolute objectivity, a level at which hard scientists ordinarily try to place themselves to observe controls and experiments at a distance, so as not to contaminate or bias results. Typical teachers of composition, even the most ardently prescriptive, maintain at least some measure of social contact with their subjects—even if that contact is implicitly dominant.

2. I would be better able to understand the phenomenon of play as it relates to the practice of writing, to gather more subtle and nuanced messages conveyed within the case study, that is, if I could convince my subjects that I could empathize with them and better appreciate

their challenges. Since participants' nonverbal cues might be potentially useful forms of response, this method would allow sufficient opportunity for me to witness more keenly what useful insights could be noted from their reactions to the exercises and topics of discussion.

3. I would be better able to draw a more comprehensive picture of the study, to better describe the dynamic while it is occurring. If I want my observations and conclusions to be accurate, this position also forces me to remain open to new ways of knowing, in spite of the initial expectations I have of the participants' own abilities and attitudes.

While I acknowledge that my research methods may likely allow a measure of subjectivity to color my own conclusions, I submit that a much earlier pilot study has tentatively confirmed that the method and its theoretical underpinnings have practical and rather surprising positive uses. The following discussions taken up in Part 3, Sections 10 to 10.5, represent the case study's corpus, which expands on what I mean by "practical and surprising uses" and which includes critical analyses of participants' progress and success with the proposed method.

## 10. Meeting 1

The first workshop was meant to acquaint participants with the overall goals of the study, and to explain the parameters of play with phrase structures. A brief discussion of the usefulness of phrases and descriptions of four phrase structures (prepositional, infinitive, verb, and noun) was followed by an actual exercise wherein all participants were able to cooperate and see very early on the surprising effects of play. One principal aim of the overall study had been to recognize explicitly the usefulness of dramatically reducing, if not eliminating, references to meta-linguistic terms peculiar to grammar studies or, as Canagarajah (1999, p. 148) notes, the Current Traditional Paradigm (CTP), and then drastically limiting their uses in the workshops. I, thus, clarified to participants the effort to achieve a forum in which these kinds of reductions could be realized without fundamentally undermining the potential for quality instruction and gratifying play.

I arranged students randomly in groups of two and distributed to each group four to five pages of tabloid newsprint.

Negotiating levels of vividness in phrases.

As a means of reinforcing their knowledge of phrases, I asked participants to identify and mark two phrases that they found interesting, unusual, or appealing in some way. After five minutes of searching the articles, a student from each group then came forward and marked the blackboard with the chosen two phrases with the stipulation that he or she attempt, at first, to achieve a level of incoherence. That is, they were encouraged, for example, to place one phrase in the center of the board and the other anywhere else so that no apparent syntactic or semantic relationship appeared to play between them. It wasn't long, though, when a noticeable level of merriment broke out amongst the participants as they had evidently begun seeing very soon some surprising semantic connections between the phrases, how explicit or implicit meanings in one phrase would mysteriously begin to play on the meanings in another.

Creating unlikely connections among phrases for new meanings

There appeared shortly thereafter an apparent necessity to also extend the definition of *transitional expression*: the participants had had knowledge of transitionals, but only in the strictest sense outlined by grammar reference texts already familiar to them, such as *Evergreen* and *The Little, Brown Handbook* discussed in Part 1, Section 3.2. For the purposes of the workshops, I found that I would have to slightly expand the description to include any single word, phrase, or clause that helped participants achieve a syntactic or semantic link between two or more phrase structures.

This link was to be independent of their usual conceptions of cohesion where writers attempt to adhere to the needs of unity on multiple levels: verb tenses, topical discussions, metaphorical references, tone, chronological concerns, etc. That is to say, coherence or, as M. A. K. Halliday and Ruqaiya Hasan describe it, "cohesion does not concern what a text means [but] … how the text is constructed as a semantic edifice" (1976, p. 26). To Halliday and

Hasan, cohesive relationships among words and sentences can help readers recognize the unit beyond a sentence.

Similarly, Martha Kolln's later discussion describes cohesion as the grammatical, lexical and semantic connections between sentences (1996, p. 19). These connections are furnished by pronouns that have antecedents in previous sentences, by adverbial connections, by known information, and by knowledge shared by the reader (Kolln, 1994, p. 394). Kolln's notion of "cohesion" finds no distinction between both the unity of ideas within a text itself and the unity that readers themselves sense with the text. To her, the terms *cohesion* and *coherence* are interchangeable and are also treated in the same way below.

Perhaps the best alternative is the definition put forward by linguists Richard Roberts and Roger Kreuz. To them, since researchers "… have avoided the problem of defining *what* coherence is in favor of establishing *when* it occurs," Roberts and Kreuz remind their readers that "… discourse has been considered coherent when the purpose of the discourse is shared by all participants" (1993, p. 451-2 [authors' emphases]).

The exercise began with students randomly recording their two favorite phrases on the board. As predicted, their limited knowledge of the four phrase structures discussed earlier produced a wide range of structures. The following table illustrates the arbitrary order in which they appeared.

Table 9

Initial experiment with phrases

| Order | Expression – Construed as Phrase by Workshop Group |
|---|---|
| 1 | going ape over new CD |
| 2 | gladder than a herd of elephants in a room full of peanuts |
| 3 | their worst nightmare |
| 4 | fear of peanut butter in their mouths as |
| 5 | fills holes for the doughnut maker |
| 6 | Jose wears |
| 7 | the same underwear |
| 8 | like a prize hog |
| 9 | as all of his neighbor's gawk |
| 10 | can't see past anyone's hips |
| 11 | dwarfed that guy |
| 12 | with her head |
| 13 | rips a child's arm right off |
| 14 | go nuts for donuts |

*Note.* Each participant recorded two phrases on the board.

The following table illustrates their initial experiments with transitions and coherence. Whereas initially the board was filled with a mix of phrases that appeared at first glance to be entirely unrelated, students very quickly began to see humorous or meaningful connections. While Table 9 contains the list of phrases in a random series, Table 10 contains the phrases sequenced with (underlined) transitions that the participants invented themselves. In order to begin recognizing coherence on either a syntactic or semantic level, they simply connected the randomly scatter phrases on the board with lines and arrows.

Table 10

Subsequent experiment with phrases

| Order | Expression – Construed as Phrase by Workshop Group |
|---|---|
| 3 | their worst nightmare is the |
| 4 | fear of peanut butter in their mouths as |
| 6 & 8 | Jose, like a prize hog, wears |
| 7 | the same underwear |
| 10 | and they can't see past anyone's hips |
| 1 | everyone's going ape over Jose's new CD |
| 9 | as all of his neighbor's gawk |
| 2 | he is gladder than a herd of elephants in a room full of peanuts |
| 11 | dwarfed by that guy |
| 13 | who ripped a child's arm right off |
| 12 | who cried, "off with her head," |
| 14 | everyone's going nuts for donuts |
| 5 | as love fills holes for the doughnut maker, Jose just sings |

*Note.* Each participant took a turn in connecting one structure to another

The scattered phrase structures appearing in Table 9 became, it seems, a sort of puzzle that would serve as a problem in coherence. As I transferred each structure, *phrase* hereafter, onto the board, it became clear to me that this exercise seemed to encourage the participants to make, in the words of Wilhelm von Humbolt, "infinite use of finite means" (quoted in Chomsky, 1965, p. 8). Their experiments in Table 9 demonstrate, at least, a vast or indefinite number of possibilities with a set of finite phrases. Given the number of underlined passages, participants saw the invention of transitions as not only necessary, but also "pleasing or moving" (Lanham, 1991) on some level.

After reflecting on what it actually meant as I witnessed their almost immediate explorations with the potential meanings hidden in these disparate phrases, the exercise seemed to me to be akin to gestalt making. The pursuit of coherence in the midst of what seemed to be at first glance a completely incoherent field of phrases became a kind of gestalt building wherein a form, shape or organization could be found not in a picture (Elbow 1998, p. 167), but in a range of words nested in various phrases that called up vivid images, unusual sounds or connotations when in close proximity to one another. The following image illustrates this initial exposure to phrase structures.

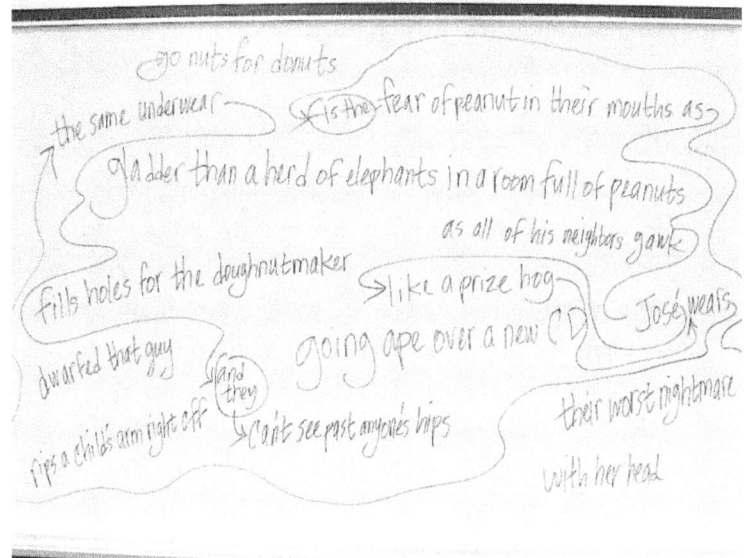

Initial connections among phrases located and drawn by students.

Witnessing firsthand the unlikely collocation of phrases with vastly different connotations gave students the opportunity to find a way to creatively fit them all together. Put another way was Ulrich Neisser's observation that "the act of seeing seems ... an act of construction that makes wholes out of fragments" (quoted in Elbow, 1998, p. 167). What they may have seen was a wide range of possibilities in terms of play with grammar or meaning. As discussed in preceding sections, this early discovery became a kind of metaphor for the entire process of play with phrases.

In following discussions, students appeared drawn towards the act of constructing wholes from fragments. With these the sorts of tendencies (discussed in Peter Elbow's *Writing without Teachers* (1998, p. 167)), students became, in effect, gestalt-making machines.

Apart from these interesting findings, I also asked students to produce and submit an initial sample of writing as a way of establishing a record of their current ability. The initial narrative essay was meant for students to reflect on and describe in the essay some previous significant experience with English composition in school. The free and reflective nature of the narrative was intended to represent a break from more popular writer-focused approaches that conceive of composition as having distinctly different categories of genre. Where any discussions seemed to need some measure of brevity, I synthesized each self-analysis and had aimed toward a narrative summary of their written responses. If some of the participants raised concerns verbally about the extreme emphasis traditionally placed on, say, correct spelling and punctuation, many more of them further demonstrated some awkwardness with these aspects of writing in their initial extemporaneous essay.

In keeping with Hudson's discussion of linguistic insecurity in *Sociolinguistics* (1996, p. 210-1), one participant lamented that he had believed he was "going to need a great deal of training to bring [him]self into the full realm of the English lanugage [*sic*]," as if to suggest, perhaps, that proper English is some ethereal kingdom entered only by a baptism of correctness in spelling and standard grammars. Despite having earned "two bachelors degrees" and finished a "graduate degree in Information Systems," he wrote a relatively short paragraph that featured the recurring "lanugage" for "language;" "acheive" for "achieve;" "achedimic" for "academic," and "nineth" for "ninth." Apart from his occasional alternative spellings of words, he intimated in the essay a steadfast belief that he was nonetheless lacking a "fundamental foundation in reading and writing" and these were to cause him "unimaginable stress" when he was asked to write in the workplace. The remedy, he felt, would come in the form of some sort of "serious intervention." For all of the times that the spellchecker had betrayed him in the workplace, his impromptu essay, though, revealed no evidence of the serious sorts of problems he had felt he was facing as a writer.

Another participant who had confessed his complete ignorance of English writing, from mechanics to metaphor, saw the academic essay as an "intimidating stress monster that could only be tamed by hours of massaging, re-writing, re-thinking and constant re-evaluation of [his] ideas." Despite this apparent irony and the seriousness with which he discussed the problems of institutionalized forms of "inciting fright and fear" in students, writing assignments, to him, had usually led to "immeasurable uncertainties about proper sentence structure—starting with subjects and ending with whatever English structures do end with." Throughout the years of "learning and unlearning so many rules and exceptions to rules about prepositions ending sentences or infinitives being split by one thing or another thing, it all became another way of learning new reasons why not to write in order to avoid the old monster."

A graduate student in the local counseling program felt that "learning occurs in stages and is relative to the emotional and intellectual age of the learner." His experiences in the subjects he had been taught throughout his primary and secondary schooling, as well as in college, have told him that his conclusions are valid. He believed that this "view holds true for all subject areas except for one—English." His grades in many disciplines have shown that he is a capable learner, yet English composition has defied his "desire to see improvements." Worth noting is his confession in later meetings that he had come to see academic rule over this discipline as a metaphor for "legitimized emotional caning" meted out to those who could never quite "memorize and recite to a class the conjugation of an action verb or all of the forms of *be*." Standing in place of explicit definitions of excellent or acceptable writing were often vague hand-scrawled assessments in the requisite red ink. Throughout the years, he could not find connections between "the methods and the madness," the games that he and his schoolmates played during class to win points for devising the longest sentences and the essays that he and his mates later wrote to see those same points deducted. He had often been curious about the significance of constructing single sentences so long in classroom exercises and what their relationship was to constructing a string of coherent meanings in the context of full essays.

Another student's "earliest recollections of handling the English language came from middle school" where "most of [her] memories [were] of reading … rather than writing." She pointed out that writing was not a requirement until college where she has since learned quickly that the dialect she had "handled" while growing up in a New York City borough furthered her skill in using the most contemptible conventions of discourse in her academic essays. She recalled a vivid experience of receiving an essay she'd submitted for a grade so marked in "blood-red ink that the white bond paper appeared to be blotted out." What had once been her long-abiding fascination with human language became a much deeper mistrust of her own voice as a speaker and writer. Perhaps her repeated use of "handling" connotes, herein, the feelings she has since developed in college about the extreme care required in using English.

In all, a comprehensive re-examination of the essays exposed a general trend in anxiety over uses of minor marks of punctuation and spelling. Despite some of their periodic problems in syntax and semantics, their concerns over these aspects of written communication appeared to take a back seat in their drive toward the more visible and realizable goal of correctness in mechanics, an element of composition harped on by many of their teachers.

## 10.1 Meeting 2

The second gathering included two exercises in labeling and analysis. I had estimated that it might be somewhat useful initially to assess participants' explicit knowledge of the parts of speech since significant emphasis is still sometimes placed on obliging students to commit various words and their associated labels to long-term memory. Just as importantly, I had wanted to gauge their reactions to the prospect of confronting a task that was, to them, anything but playful, an assignment that stood in stark contrast to their preconceptions about the sort of fun or enjoyable work ahead of them. Although this exercise featured deliberately de-contextualized terms and is, perhaps, the most extreme example of a form-focused approach to teaching, it, nevertheless, reflects some very similar kinds of labeling exercises still practiced and still found in grammar texts such as those discussed in Section 3.2.

In later meetings, when a series of research questions would come into play, I had imagined that as they would reflect on this particular task that their responses alone could be potentially honest and revealing. That is, since so much time seems to be spent in some classrooms on these sorts of labeling exercises, this particular exercise could represent a discernable gap between knowledge of meta-linguistic terms and a writer's sensitivity to other more important features of composition, such as attending to aspects of clarity or precision. The following table is an adaptation of the exercise given to each student:

Table 11

DIRECTIONS: Label each word with its respective part of speech.

| running | smack    | skunk   | herb     | if     |
| or      | built    | flavor  | lover    | slow   |
| black   | has      | very    | lovely   | burnt  |
| liver   | me       | thought | sanctify | then   |
| olive   | between  | however | flying   | refuse |

*Note.* Borrowed from a UMUC colleague.

    Perhaps much more revealing than the labels they assigned to each word were the surprised and disgusted personae they donned when they initially recognized the exercise as another "familiar stupid chore." The following responses at the bottom of each exercise illustrated clearly their level of disgust. They felt "betrayed," and that the exercise was a "useless use of hand, finger, and wrist muscles." It seemed to immediately build "apprehension" and "frustration." It certainly heightened "anxiety" and compelled them to express how "uncomfortable [they felt] with rules they only half remembered." Since I had merely aimed to determine the presence of apprehension or aversion, I was not able to ascertain precisely why they responded in the way they had. Even so, in light of their general reactions here, my much earlier suspicions of the disconnection between explicit knowledge of these terms and effective uses of the language were later justified in the workshops (described in Meetings 4, 5 & 6) as students were able to set aside their apprehensions and produce a level of creative writing that far surpassed my initial expectations and likely theirs.

    Given the list of obviously de-contextualized words, analysis of the labels that students assigned to the words reveals only partial successes. Three of the seven participants neglected to respond to half of the words. The four participants who did label each word were successful with only half of the list, supplying accurate names to slightly more than 50 percent of the words. Only two participants appeared to be sensitive to the possibilities of the words assuming more than one label e.g. the word *thought* was both a verb and a noun, applicable to at least eleven of the twenty-five. As the products of their later play with language in prose and poetry should illustrate, their marginal success here belied their more significant success in later meetings.

After the participants reluctantly submitted their responses, I introduced another exercise that would serve as a means of assessing their own attitudes towards style and usage. This exercise contained an excerpt of Joan Didion's essay, *Many Mansions*, that Richard Leahy had explicated in an article titled, "Style Matters: Helping Students Develop Good Style." In his critique, Leahy observes that various passages throughout Didion's work are "a tour de force of rhetorical devices" (1996, p. 7). His analysis is cogent and useful as it illustrates, at least implicitly, how well defined prevailing attitudes are toward supposedly standardized uses of diction cast in stylistically superior rhetorical schemes.

These rhetorical schemes represent the sorts of sensitivities to valued prose styles that students are encouraged to develop an ear for and are in keeping with what Kathryn Fitzgerald refers to as "discourses of power" (2001, p. 225). The following excerpt illustrates that sort of linguistic power.

Table 12
_____

DIRECTIONS: Read the following passage then comment on its effectiveness.
_____

This is the twelve-thousand-square-foot house that Ronald and Nancy Reagan built. This is the sixteen-room house in which Jerry Brown declined to live. This is the vacant house which cost the state of California one-million-four, not including the property.... All day at this empty house, three maintenance men try to bulletproof windows clean and the cobwebs swept and the wild grass green and the rattle snakes down by the river and away from the thirty-five exterior wood and glass doors. All night at this empty house, the lights stay on behind the eight-foot chain link fence and the guard dogs lie at bay and the telephone, when it rings, startles by the fact that it works. "Governor's residence," the guards answer, their voices laconic, matter-of-fact, quite as if there were some phantom governor to connect. Wild grass grows where the tennis court was to have been. Wild grass grows where the pool and sauna were to have been.
_____

*Note.* Adapted from an analysis of Joan Didion's essay by Leahy (1996).

    Leahy had aimed his analysis at an academic audience employed in the field of composition and rhetoric. He argues skillfully that our conceptions of good writing, as writing teachers, are typically framed by our often unarticulated preferences for certain intelligent and intentional uses of rhetorical schemes (Leahy, 1996, p. 8; Bourdieu & Passeron, 1977, p. 73). In the case of the excerpt of Joan Didion's work, these appear in the form of ancient Greco-Roman rhetorical schema. Leahy points out that Didion had employed six of these masterfully, such as syllepsis, ellipsis, anaphora, isocolon, etc., and that these kinds of schemes often serve as a basis for analyzing college compositions and distinguishing between good and excellent skill or scholarship. Leahy puts his finger on the precise qualities of excellence that typical writing teachers implicitly seek but rarely explicitly teach. These schemes rooted in ancient forms of western rhetoric, he suggests, compose some of the prized aspects of composition that winnow the academic wheat from chaff.

    On the surface, his observations appear justified. But, they don't seem to fully account for the wide-ranging uses of diction that students draw on and which apparently elicit some of the most extreme negative reactions. Beyond the slightly more objective and testable qualities of writing, like mechanics and spelling, semantics is perhaps the most transparent aspect of composition which often excites the most impassioned irrational responses. Leahy focused mostly on the ways in which style helps convey meaning (1996, p. 7), as if to suggest that awareness of stylistic schema, as much as awareness of semantics, weighs on the meanings that a writer intends to communicate.

His message seems to insinuate traces of another kind of institutionalized linguistic exclusion, a fairly myopic focus on acceptable uses of diction cast in the appropriate molds of tradition and hand-crafted by classical Greek rhetoricians. Since knowledge of these forms is drawn on such a highly prized history in the Western academy, it is, possibly, this direct lineage to ancient tradition, the long narrative of scholastic excellence that overshadows our better discerning the qualities of contemporary academic merit, or for the presence of potential excellence. If our present-day customs of complaining about falling standards unite with the long-cherished niceties of ancient rhetorical traditions, we may more likely risk recycling and reemphasizing, it seems, the long-held myth that languages are stagnant immovable mechanisms of human communication (O'Conner, 1996, pp. ix-xii).

As an attempt to clarify these points, I rendered Didion's work into African-American vernacular English (AAVE)—a variety marked by semantic choices that historically have been least likely to engender positive reactions from the public in general and from academics in particular. If Leahy's suggestions were entirely valid, both renderings, I had anticipated, ought to receive nearly equal responses irrespective of audience expectations. Discussions of participant responses follow.

Table 13

DIRECTIONS: Read the following passage then comment on its effectiveness.

Dis here's da twenty-by-twenty foot space dat Jo Jo cleared out for us. Dis here's da so-called cramped cubicle in which Puffy had declined to chill. Dis here's da once-abandoned room among a hundred others which cost the city of Crooklyn one-million-ten, not including the playgrounds where da other peddlers and pushers like us hang. All day at dis here once-empty crib, three of us hommies try to keep da crack pipes clean and water bongs filled and green bud bagged and da rival Bloods away from da eight-foot high metal, wood, and glass front door. All night at dis here once-empty crib, da brothers stay lit and sit slumped behind da thick wall and da pit bulls lie at bay and da beepers, when they buzz, startle cause they actually work. "The flat of da New Lords of Flatbush," the beeper reads, da line terse, liquid crystal, plain as day, quite as if there was some phantom homeboy to answer. Wild homeboys roam free where da 5th Precinct was gonna be. Wild homeboys roam free where da local youth center and da new white bread church was gonna be.

*Note.* As with Table 11, participants were also asked to write a few sentences to serve as responses.

A cursory glance at this rendering will show that I have employed all of the rhetorical schemes that Leahy lauds yet replaced the more widely accepted lexical items with those more typical of periphery urban American varieties. This piece was useful in gauging reactions to non-standard usage and to reveal the existence of unspoken prejudices toward periphery varieties—to show, essentially, that a propensity to thoroughly scrutinize written forms continues to pervade many levels of society, that even potential modest advances in developing, say, a keener ear for style, may be delayed by obsessive concerns over acceptability. In other words, I aimed to see, here, whether these participants who had been seeking radically different approaches to practicing writing actually engaged in the sorts of obsessive practices that they themselves had protested so strongly against and if their protests influenced their own progress as writers.

As their reports generally indicate, complaining appears to be a rather customary practice among those who seek to distance themselves from the very traditions they appear to question or feel contempt for. Most surprising about participant responses were the largely negative comments expressed toward both pieces. Some responses bordered on vitriol while other critiques were somewhat less venomous. Sometimes, too, the author's name alone, despite the quality or lack of quality in his or her creative work, engenders blind or hasty assessments. So, perhaps it was their ignorance of the author of the *Many Mansions* excerpt, as a generally regarded master of prose style, that enabled participants to respond with such unambiguous reproof. Point to point contrasts amongst their rejoinders reveal that the tendencies to condemn certain uses of the language appear evident, nonetheless, even in those who condemn such customs.

Only one participant weighed in with a positive response, labeling Didion's work as "extremely nice and effective, a clearly acceptable form of writing." She was just as forgiving of the form rendered in AAVE, calling it an "effective use of non-standard English." In stark contrast to her kindness were various other critiques leveled against both pieces.

One student exclaimed that Didion's work is "too simple and dull, ... not at all an impressive piece that provides any kind of essential visual impact!" To the piece set in AAVE, she asked about the "the extent to which we should go before we judge whether English is or isn't English." Furthermore, she "would love to find a newspaper written in this style, including the neighborhood where it's understood," contemptuously implying, it seems, that such a style could never pass for legitimate communication. She suggested that this sort of "spoken English would never pass the standardized test that our schools require."

Another participant remarked that Didion's work was "much too choppy to be fully understood." "The run-on sentences and dangling modifiers"—wherever he thought they appeared—"distracted [him] entirely and forced [him] to re-read two or three times." He likewise saw the other piece in a similar light, as "non-acceptable, non-effective, nonsense!" yet didn't see the irony in his own choices of diction.

Other participants weighed in and responded to both pieces with a range of similar comparatives and superlatives: too repetitive, too long, too simplified, too passive and incomplete, too hard to follow, too regional to communicate; and the most incomprehensible street language, the worst inner-city jargon alive, the most imprecise and incoherent slang, the most ambiguous urban chatter in print. Apart from their impassioned critiques, the participants displayed, all the same, a nearly complete ignorance of the stylistic devices that Leahy celebrates.

Given their mainly negative commentaries, it appears that awareness of and appreciation for these sorts of rhetorical schemes may be more a matter of concern for the initiated. In light of participants' experiences in the North American paradigm, their terse remarks multiplied by the exclamation points appearing periodically throughout seem to punctuate, perhaps justifiably, a range of irrational feelings about various uses of language, implying that acceptability in speech and writing remains in their eyes a tightly restricted standard.

## 10.2 Meeting 3

I had planned for the third meeting to be occupied by discussions of the difficulties that arise for participants during the process of writing. I had wanted to encourage them to reflect on their own previous experiences with writing and to tease out of them some of the reasons for the generating, drafting, and revising difficulties that had, for so long, traditionally vexed them. My discussions with students, therefore, focused mainly on discovering some the causes of writer's block. I asked them to reflect on the ways in which they had traditionally attempted to turn their thoughts into words on paper and to attempt to attach names to certain difficulties that confronted them when engaged in the act of drafting—the tendencies or behaviors or thoughts that had preoccupied their minds or had prevented them in some way from bringing forth the words they had intended to.

As suggested by Connelly and Clandinin (1990), the research questions posed were meant to elicit extended and explicit responses, to encourage participants to convey stories of their experiences. I posed some of the following kinds of questions to the members of the *experimental group workshop*. What I found in their responses were many surprising details about their notions of correctness and fluency, of English education, and of feeling connected or disconnected to the mainstream because of the way they speak or write. Although each participant had opportunities throughout the workshops to offer commentary, some chose not to or chose to contribute so little verbally that including their input would have been inconsequential to the underlying aims of the study. What follows, therefore, sometimes synthesizes and condenses, and sometimes directly quotes what I had felt would be useful to understanding the sorts of attitudes and apprehensions that students generally bring to the task of writing.

In the interpretations of my field notes and audio taping, it was always a principal goal of mine to remain true to the spirit and letter of their responses. Paraphrased summaries of their verbal feedback, nonverbal reactions, and my discussions of those responses follow each question.

1. *Can you describe some of your early experiences with English composition in school?*

"English composition in the early 1990s was really just English where we'd learn how to disassemble sentences," one participant remarked with a barely distinguishable Texas drawl. He submitted that he had never wanted anything to do with writing because of his speaking. As a Texan transplanted during his teenage years to Northern California, writing and speaking in many English classes became something to avoid at all costs. Introducing, for example, the "y'all" variation of "you," even in casual conversations, would elicit jeers from so-called friends and other forms of reprisal from academic authority figures. When asked how he was presently able to conceal his Texas accent, he said that folks in California had been so good at mocking his drawl that he decided to reject being an object of ridicule and do all he could to hide his regional verbal peculiarities.

As he recalled quite clearly, there had been for many years an explicit effort to suppress certain varieties spoken at his public middle and high schools, beginning with mildly painful forms of corporal punishment, such as when a wooden ruler in the hands of an authority figure would meet his knuckles, or moderately excruciating forms of humiliation, such as when a small yellow circle drawn on the chalkboard would serve as a meeting point for the tip of some rule breaker's nose. Undesirable accents mixed with strange written varieties were clearly, in his view, a way of separating or labeling those in need of remedial forms of physical and mental encouragement. How were these verbal peculiarities to translate into writing peculiarities? The regional idioms of the spoken Texas variety carried into classrooms in the Northwest were incredibly difficult for him to expunge from the academic practice of written communication.

Another participant added that, year after year, English classes had often been reduced to learning and reviewing the basic rules that governed the uses of the apostrophe and comma, reviewing the "correct" spellings and pronunciations, and learning the ways in which to identify and label the types of sentences (declarative, interrogative etc.) and how to diagram them. In statewide exams, students would endure a grueling testing cycle to demonstrate their ability to observe these sorts of standards or they would risk failing the grade.

None of his peers ever seemed to know if the term *failure* had been merely part of an elaborate idle threat or a real and potential effect, yet they all sensed that the risk that loomed before them remained too great to ignore. As a natural consequence of the emphasis on learning rules, he and his peers felt that writing had always been a strange activity. The academic essay was a completely foreign concern to him until he went to college. Despite the many years of being drilled with exercises in labeling the parts of speech and diagramming sentences, he admitted that he still remains a bit unsure about how best to spot a sentence subject. So far as he could establish, the art of placing a comma in its correct position was much more of a concern for English teachers than the art of constructing ideas in words on a page.

*2. How did your perceptions of correctness at home differ from your perceptions of correctness at school?*

One participant added that the contraction *ain't* in school and at home was reduced to a level of contempt reserved typically for vulgarities. On any occasion that *ain't* slipped out of the mouth of an unsuspecting pupil, one might see in a teacher's face a start of surprise and hear accompanied by it a startled gasp in response. This participant wanted to be certain that I emphasized what still seems to him to have been rather odd behavior, even if it was popular in the late 1980s. In his estimation, his parents and teachers were all equally saddled with ultraconservative concerns for youngsters resisting authority and testing the limits of acceptable speech. As he reflected on this sort of behavior, he admitted that it was perhaps the ever-present fear of children, like him, remaining forever mired in the socio-economic depressions of his small coal-mining community that enabled local self-appointed experts, or what Pinker terms "language mavens" (1994, p. 373), to comment on and correct the linguistic abuses that any child would dare commit. In her book *Outcomes in Process: Setting Standards for Language Use*, Roseanne DeFabio addresses these sorts of attitudes:

> Local communities can no longer set standards for their graduates based on the particular needs of that community; can no longer assumes that their children will stay on in that community to continue its economic, political, and social traditions; and can no longer even expect that those economic, political,

and social traditions will continue to exist as they know them. (1994, p. xi)

Notwithstanding these realities, neither academic nor social settings in the community at large would dissuade anyone with authority from encouraging others to strive toward developing better verbal communication skills. In apparently well-coordinated efforts to maintain conformity, all tax-paying citizens, it seemed to him, were vigilant and encouraging in that regard. From speech to writing, he came to believe as a young man that the long campaign for proper language use became the best means by which to "train up the [children] in the ways [they] would go" (Proverbs 22:6), to liberate the less privileged provincials from their financial and societal ruts. He was somehow later able to attribute this kind of vigorous indoctrination to observing rules of linguistic correctness to a virtual community-wide obsession with maintaining correct production quotas and schedules at the coal mine, a veritable lifeblood of the community, and preserving the general social and religious balance so tied to their identity.

3. *Did your parents' talk of proper speech contrast with your teachers' talk?*

Most participants admitted that they could neither identify any noticeable differences in discussions of acceptable speech, nor did they appear to care very much about what styles of discourse were acceptable in or out of school. Nobody appeared to take notice.

One participant, though, announced that she had become more aware of "sharp differences in the way teachers and parents in [her] community communicated." The differences were so obvious and plain that they had not really registered in her mind until she was forced to reflect on her experiences while growing up. She reckoned that differences in their conceptions of correctness were more often made visible by marked essays returned to her by her ever-alert teachers. The red ink became sort of symbolic of the blood streaming from the tear ducts of her wounded readers for her sinful uses of

English. No student probably ever heard a parent cry over misplaced or dangling modifiers. But, by the same token, no pupil probably ever wrote an essay for his or her parents. Therefore, in her mind, disparities in the kinds of expectations that these different audiences had were not entirely apparent to her until she herself was encouraged to reflect on her whole historical communication experience as a member of the community.

What did these differences mean to her? She came to see writing, especially the academic variety that prepares students for the professional world, as the best way in which to identify those who lacked a "proper education." Writing, to her, was speech set in stone, which became clear and concrete evidence of intellectual achievement and the potential for economic gain.

4. *In your mind, which students seemed to have excelled best in English?*

One participant pointed out that her school district was clearly divided along racial boundaries, that kids like her from K through 12 in a much poorer section of the city were bused to a nearby suburban district to take part, in her view, in a sad experiment that only further highlighted the "differences between the 'haves' and the 'have-nots.'" Perhaps the government decision-makers who had designed such a grand scheme had had benevolent intentions, but the contrasts in discourse styles were so great that those who had the power in classrooms could not help but naturally alienate themselves from their far lesser articulate pupils. To her, the obviously different discourse conventions of the more privileged only further clarified the already existing socio-economic disparities, points outlined by Bourdieu and Passeron in their discussions of "cultural capital" (1977, p. 118). She saw *proper* speech as a sort of metaphor for social position and academic power.

Those students who were able to adjust and speak the regional dialect more akin to the variety used by those who held the institutional power to judge, it seemed to her, were far more academically successful. Yet, classroom communication never came without certain amounts of real risk. For those in her peer group who were brave enough and could adapt well and use the acceptable forms, these students were castigated in social situations outside the school gates yet rewarded in academic ones inside.

While attempting to keep concealed from her peers her intentions to prevail academically in the end, she found that language use alone became a complex and vital game, which everyone in her peer group had to play, a way of pretending both in and out of class that she did not really want to act like the very people whose ancestors had historically oppressed hers. Interestingly, Rachel Jones (1982) reflected on a very similar observation she had made as an adolescent in school. She found that when she used discourse styles typically associated with the speech of white folks that she used these styles at her own peril. The dangers were very real to her as she recalled being threatened occasionally by some of her black peers.

In spite of trying hard to adapt and overcome the obvious verbal obstacles, this participant was able to perceive implicit questions circulating for years in her school district about "who could and could not speak English," and, of course as the conventional wisdom goes, since speaking was just a more dynamic form of writing, then composition studies became just another way of drawing more graphically even further attention to the already existing socio-economic inequalities. Since neither she nor any of her peers could ever ascertain who had given birth to these sorts of peculiar suspicions, there seemed to be an ever-present undercurrent of contempt for those students, like her, who could never quite take command of the more desirable varieties. Was it skin color or an occasional slip in the accepted diction that was the wedge separating one class from another? Was it both? She felt that she never could learn what it was precisely.

Perhaps, when normative judgments like these become so pervasive, it becomes all the more difficult to pin down precise instances of linguistic bigotry, a feat nearly matched in difficulty when attempting to isolate, with an untrained ear, one specific note in a symphony.

5. *Since your primary or secondary education, how have you come to perceive your own uses of language? substandard? non-standard? different? correct?*

One participant exclaimed that "[he was] convinced [he couldn't] even speak English, so how [could he] expect to write it!" He cited newspaper columnists and political pundits weighing in with their commentary about the abuses of English and the decline of standards, and he asked, "Who speaks and writes correctly?" It can't be the powerful and wealthy since even George W. Bush can't escape from the occasional comments of some amateur linguistic authority, a position also echoed by Steven Pinker (2000) in his article, "Decoding the Candidate." In it, Pinker comments on what seems to have become the commonplace pastime in America of criticizing so-called verbal peculiarities, where attacks on speech are a way of lumping the politically well-connected into a solitary mass of corrupt and ignorant language abusers.

As this participant seemed to indicate, this sort of behavior exists on such a massive scale that even he, despite his best efforts to resist, cannot escape its pull. The very notion of free speech draws the citizen towards an often irresistible tendency to speak out, yet, paradoxically, "free" speech itself comes at a great cost—the speaker's risk of public or private humiliation. Confused by the contradictions in public and political discourse and the past comments of his teachers, professors, friends and parents, he had come to believe that nobody really knows what is correct or unacceptable, standard or nonstandard. In their relentless search for language abuses, no nitpicking commentators, in his view, seem to ever consider the actual contexts in which one typical listener or reader naturally accommodates a native speaker's or writer's supposed imperfections. Standards of correctness, it seemed reasonable to him, depend upon the extent to which the members of an audience can actually apprehend the meanings communicated in the message.

6. *To what extent were your uses of language stigmatized either in or out of classroom settings?*

"Teachers," responded one participant, "appeared routinely to take great joy in making light of someone's use of *ain't* and berating him or her in front of the class." It was not uncommon for teachers to respond to uses of *ain't* and *y'all* with explicit derision. When these words appeared in writing, the students who dared use them were subjected to mild insults. In her school among her peers, a word like *ain't* became a kind of symbol of resisting the extreme methods used in civilizing the inarticulate masses of youngsters that appeared in classrooms. One student recalled the details of a ten-year high school reunion that buzzed with decade-old tales of the extreme measures taken by a few ardent teachers to extinguish all forms of linguistic corruption.

Not until years later, in the real world of business and taxes and personal finance, did they realize how necessary it was to drastically modify their choices of diction to suit the needs and expectations of their audience, but how unnecessary it was to publicly castigate a child for using so-called improper language. All agreed that the prevailing classroom methods never seemed justifiable.

7. *To what extent did you or do you feel excluded or alienated from the mainstream because of the ways in which you spoke or speak?*

Feelings of alienation or exclusion, one student suggested, appear over time and can develop even from rather simple reactions, like the subtle expressions that some people seem to wear on their faces when they hear other supposedly ignorant people speak. Having been reared "in the deep South," he found that this seemed generally to hold true whenever he had to "speak in front of a bunch of

Yankees." To underscore the relevance of this student's observation, Rosina Lippi-Green points out in her chapter, "Hillbillies, rednecks, and southern belles," that it is "primarily on the basis of intellect linked to education that northerners try hardest to convince southerners that their language is deficient" (1997, p. 212). Hence, there remained his conviction that stereotypes, such as those in the "Speaker Evaluation Paradigm" discussed by Giles and Coupland in Part 1, Section 1.2, are often partly responsible for giving rise to the negative attitudes that help feed into the sorts of behaviors that tend to alienate one person from another.

Another student immediately responded with a statement of support, saying that she was not at all surprised about the extent to which stereotypes affect people's attitudes regarding language uses, whether written or spoken. In her position as a receptionist for an American university, she had often heard many different languages spoken by foreign students who would enter her office area. When Hispanics who had had no knowledge of her bilingual ability would adjust and periodically comment in Spanish on her buxom and vivacious appearance, they couldn't help but react with great astonishment when she would adjust from English and respond to their comments in a "perfect Castilian variety." Born and reared in a town just outside of Valencia, Spain, she had moved to the United States as a child where she, consequently, "picked up a rather thick Southern accent," peculiar to the Blue Ridge Mountain region of North Carolina. She could recount many personal instances growing up when the language coming from her mouth wouldn't meet the expectations that others had prematurely imposed upon her and her appearance.

She further discussed some of the expectations that most people seem to generally have of others and the styles of discourse that others should use. She cited, for example, an occasion when a certain black woman whom she had known of had had a phone interview for a job. By this woman's account, she had done well because she was asked to come to the office to sign a letter of intent.

When she appeared at the personnel office to sign, though, she was "immediately and mysteriously denied the offer."

Rachel Jones also reflects on a very similar experience she'd had while "apartment hunting in Evanston, Illinois." In the winter of that year, she had "gotten many leads over the phone, was immediately invited over, and immediately turned away" (1982, p. 55). It wasn't long before she was able to recognize the pattern—that despite her "white voice," her "black skin" betrayed her ability to secure confidence in a prospective landlord and thus a place to live. She suggested that she'd once held on as a child to an idealized view of the world wherein her supposed "white" uses of English would be overshadowed by her genuine desire to be an informed citizen able to participate fully. Yet, she had come as an adult to "realize the depressing reality that for many blacks, standard English is not only unfamiliar, it is socially unacceptable" (1982, p. 54).

8. *To what extent does your speech affect the way in which you write?*

One participant suggested that since we usually write the way we speak, a view challenged by Elbow (1985, pp. 299-300), then our speech is bound to have some influence on our writing. If we're socialized in school to believe that we don't even know how to speak correctly, how we can expect to write correctly? To her, this seemed analogous to the *rubbish in, rubbish out* principle. She found that many English teachers throughout her four years of secondary schooling in the South would make allowances for her in slightly patronizing ways for the Puerto Rican Bronx accent she had developed as an adolescent in the New York City borough and, subsequently, brought to classroom discussions.

Even casual conversations would not be complete, it often seemed to her, without some occasional acknowledgements from her peers about the "foreign" influence on her speaking and from educators about those same influences on her writing. While "folks in [her] neck of the woods in the Bronx would, for example, 'stand on line', folks in Florida would rather 'stand in line.'" This single difference in her choice of prepositions for the idiomatic expression highlighted by her strange foreign Yankee accent, as well as a few other regional New England constructions, was for her the cause of countless embarrassing situations.

9. *To what extent do you believe the dialect you use in speech impedes your ability to articulate on paper precisely what you mean to? That is, do you feel impeded by your own preoccupations with "correct" forms that you are unable to write naturally, or even "correctly"?*

All participants were unequivocal about the various difficulties they felt that they must confront each day. Codes of correctness, to them, were as plentiful as oxygen molecules. "As speakers and writers," one student remarked, "how can we not be influenced by the expectations that audiences have of us?" He complained that split infinitives, for example, have given him since the sixth grade countless headaches just as he would set his hands to the task of writing. What he perceived to be the constant cleaning up of his diction and usage at home and in school by strict teachers was to suppress otherwise perfectly good thoughts he often felt should be expressed but could not be. He submitted that each time he presently feels compelled to reach for the infinitive marker, *to*, he "must re-interrupt the act of drafting and over-analyze the words that follow, *to*, and ask whether [he] has grossly split one thing or another thing." Drafting had become a truly painstaking act of analysis. He felt that the ideas "buzzing about" in his head would "often disappear" before he could command them to "reappear" through his fingertips working at the keyboard.

Another participant immediately responded to his remarks with her own empathetic tales of writing woe. Drawing on her high-school knowledge of grammar and style, and the lectures she had received from a well-respected grammarian, she was entirely convinced that conjunctions could never begin sentences. So much as she was concerned with correct diction and usage, conjunctions such as *because*, *although*, *and*, or *but* were off limits as opening words for clauses. When I asked her if she could produce the details of some prescription or prohibition outlined in any authoritative text, she felt that it was only necessary to cite the guidance of her beloved English teacher from high school. Yet, despite her staunch convictions, her response was not altogether surprising—given the hundreds of students I have seen in my own composition courses who have relied on tales like these throughout their years of primary and secondary schooling.

As I have reflected on these sorts of tendencies of students to pass on stories about purportedly correct uses of diction and the accepted conventions of style, perhaps some prime reasons why teachers may feel compelled to devise these kinds of sweeping generalizations is that these maxims are simple. Even the most ardently prescriptive approach, it seems, must rely on a few primary remedies that can be easily taught and retained by students and recalled in their times of editing.

Moreover, to launch into discussions of the many niceties of usage is to further belabor students with still more prescriptions. Notwithstanding the best efforts of teachers to attempt to standardize the language through the centuries, prescriptions such as these simplify the complexities of usage, but do nothing to promote abiding truths about languages and the syntactic rules that underpin their uses. Recent scholars (e.g., Aitchison, 1991; O'Conner, 1996; Bauer, 1998) have pointed to an early period in the development of English when their ancient predecessors revealed a nearly "slavish devotion to Latin" when it seemed useful to superimpose certain Latin rules on English grammar. Earlier attempts to Latinize an entirely different language, in this case English, have since distorted modern thought, it seems, about contemporary usage.

Given the responses of those participants who offered answers to question number nine as well as the comments of other English composition students throughout previous years, it is clear that confusion reigns and that remarks about these prescriptions arise from a range of contradictions and other assorted curious institutional customs.

10. *Describe in a word or two your anxiety for producing writing, especially the kind that will be assessed.*

None of the participants saw the prospect of writing as a kind of catharsis, nor even practiced writing simply for the intellectual passions that the act itself had the potential to stir. When they imagined themselves engaged, instead, in the process of drafting an essay for review, all of them saw writing and all of its requirements as a significant obstacle to building or achieving any level of self-confidence. Whatever confidences they had had as students in general, those feelings were too often displaced, it seemed, by ever-growing doubts as student writers. With this open invitation to respond, they all appeared to feel moved to offer little more than a series of negative descriptions of themselves.

After some reflection, one participant gave voice to her belief that she had been implicitly encouraged as a child to sharpen her skills in postponing work in the English courses she had taken throughout her youth and became, as a young adult, a "highly skilled professional procrastinator in college." She felt that she had been able to devise rather clever ways by which to delay the inevitable, not because she "hated English particularly" but because of the ways in which she had been "schooled" about her "simply dreadful uses of the comma." So, images and feelings of English composition to her had always been entangled, it seemed, in a set of contradictory institutional goals of feeling forced to accept humiliation on one hand while seeking knowledge on the other. Avoiding English altogether in later years became her personal motto. Besides her attempt to evade the writing requirements inherent in a liberal arts education, other participants listed and discussed some of the reasons behind their general anxieties.

One participant wasted little time weighing in on what he saw as "an ancient verbal caste system designed to exclude those who can't speak properly." His words seemed to hang uneasily in the air for a few moments while everyone present appeared to interpret their connotations. Of particular interest, though, was the resultant class chemistry that soon developed into a mildly playful form of inquisition aimed halfway at me as a double agent acting on behalf of the kind of institution impeding their advances. As the meanings of the "verbal caste system" metaphor sunk in, those very words, it appeared to me, elicited resounding assent from all those gathered.

A fellow participant promptly agreed but suggested that it would seem reasonable to order a society as such, to set up barriers that can challenge or slow the relative progress of pretenders to social or economic prosperity, just as attorneys might feel obliged to protect the arcane rites of their profession with difficult and mysterious jargon. Neither was it so difficult to sense in the tone of their voices a kind of ever-growing irritation with how the entire, from kindergarten to university, seems inherently to frustrate more than encourage the genuinely curious learner. What they perceived to be built-in barriers of institutionalized linguistic intimidation were, in my estimation, the very methods meant to emphasize the incorrectness of their speech or writing. Intimidated, anxious, frustrated, stressed, these were the sorts of unanimously pessimistic responses they felt needed to be communicated.

## 10.3 Meetings 4 & 5

Returning once again to play with phrases, I initially administered an exercise (Appendix A) featuring a mosaic of various phrase structures in order to reinforce their earlier knowledge of simply identifying the four phrases types. No additional reminders of the various meta-linguistic labels these phrases assumed were needed. A 5-min "warm up" with this exercise was followed by a longer exercise with tabloid print media. Meetings 4 & 5 were, subsequently, occupied by plays with phrases and presentations of their poems. Appendices C, D and E feature poems constructed with approximately 25 minutes of searching for and playing with the various combinations of phrase structures. Any underlined passages appearing throughout the poems indicate transitions that participants had felt the need to invent.

Perhaps most surprising of all was the level and quality of experimentation with rhetorical schemes and tropes. The initial goal of play with phrases had been merely to examine the consequence of tacit knowledge on the syntactic and semantic construction of prose and poesy. From this small group in its entirety developed quite unexpected exuberance of testing the limitations of the language, of their own creative powers to produce not only grammatically sound but artistically pleasing verse. It may be worth noting, though, that their exuberance may have developed more from the sheer novelty of the exercise.

For example, *Kindergarten Cop* (Appendix B) features experiments with parallelism in the opening two lines with a simile (like funeral mourners) used as a parenthetical in the third. In apposition to line six (the blond bombshell) stands Eve. Lines nine (out in public and) and ten (in the background) feature a sort of play on antithesis. Participants also played on the word *hit* in line seventeen. Expecting the American idiom *with a lawsuit*, readers find in the following line *with friends and a family*.

From the title, *Beautiful Beginnings* (also Appendix B), to the third line, this poem features fairly clever uses of alliteration. The fourth line (the gladiator roustabouts) works as an object for the *blowsy blonde*, as an appositive for *burly bozos*, and also as the subject for a verb phrase in line eight (trotted out their nasty damage) separated by a series of parallel verb phrases in lines five through seven (drinking, brawling and bad behaving). Parallel structures follow in lines nine and ten (intensifying their intentions and reinforcing their positions).

Poems appearing in Appendices C and D also feature a variety of clever uses of schemes and tropes. The authors of *How About Dinner?* experiment skillfully with alliteration in line six (a heaping mound of Hershey's molten mojo), with rhyme in line fourteen (sexy junk in the trunk) and with assonance and alliteration in lines twenty and twenty-one (gnaw away / at all). The *Alibi of Pussy and Russell* also includes plays with alliteration in line seven (wild wet weather) and invented parallel structures in lines fourteen (who had suggested) and eighteen (but who neglected).

*Miami Beach Bar Monty's* (Appendix D) opens with a use of asyndeton (conspicuous absence of conjunctions) in a series of parallel adjectives (bumping, pushing, pulling, pawing) for the subject (medicine woman). A poetical parenthetical (tamed by tiger love) interrupts the verb phrase (lets go of her rage). In lines four and five, it was difficult to know if the authors had intended to use a sylleptic[13] verb phrase (lets go) for both (her rage) and (her dreaded two-headed twins), but interesting to note their efforts in playing with alliteration and assonance. Highly inventive verses evoking images of the sensual and sensuous follow in lines fifteen through twenty, where *juiced up dudes search for ecstasy and body heat dipped in sugar.*

Perhaps the most experimental of all was *Scandal Meter*. This somewhat long poem begins with a clever and poetical use of synæsthesia (mixing one type of sensory input with another in an impossible way). *Serenaded by the sounds of the moving melodic medicine* seems an intended use of this trope, given their deliberate choice of *medicine*. This kind of trope appears also in later passages (lines twenty-two and twenty-four) as if *pink mixed elixirs* could actually *ear* the *complaints* of *patrons*. The *ear* appears, here, to be an anthimeric (using a different part of speech to act as another) play on *hear* or *listen*.

---

[13] Use of a single word in such a way that it is syntactically related to two or more words elsewhere in a sentence but has a different meaning in relation to each of the other words
(http://www.sil.org/linguistics/GlossaryOfLinguisticTerms/contents.htm).

Parallelism appears in lines seventeen and eighteen (though crabby and cranky / though left with a left hand). In nineteen, there also seems a catachrestic (completely impossible figure of speech) play on a *left hand* that is *gnarled by industrial strength topical scalp solution*. Clever uses of alliteration and assonance also close up this poem: *worried housewives wondering whether they'll ever reach another sale on patent leather stiletto heels*.

Although it would be difficult, if not impossible, to extract fully unified and coherent meanings from any of the poems, it should be noted that the level of creativity and invention would seem to far surpass any similar efforts that typical students might make without the creative crutch of play. As with any creative endeavor, the creator must feel beforehand a sense of freedom from the constraints of convention and truly feel the impulse to invent. These exercises with tabloid newsprint, so far, appeared to engender significant interest in rhetorical schemes and tropes and to invite wide experimentation.

## 10.4 Meeting 6

The final workshop featured a basic shift in expressive modes of communication, a leap from poetry to prose. The movement from one form to another had been characterized all along as an important step in the process of writing, a fundamental change from highly creative and free forms of expression to a fairly more coherent and developed form. Appendices F through H feature their experiments with phrase types in prose, none of which were given titles. As in their earlier experiments with poetry, I asked participants to underline all of their invented transitions to encourage them to reflect on the ways in which they felt that they had achieved some measure of cohesion.

What was most readily apparent about their trials with prose were the sheer number and variety of transitions they incorporated. From single-word transitions, such as *despite*, to complex, multi-word clauses, such as *yesterday evening while I sat underneath*, all of the participants were now clearly bent on inventing more coherent and meaningful works, even while trying to remain close to the original goals of the exercise.

The experiment appearing in Appendix E reads like the exquisitely incoherent babble of a female superhero who is both denying and lamenting her diminishing popularity and power but who is slowly slipping into an oriental wine-induced reverie of the past. In the final few lines of this short piece, the superhero appears to be coming to a stark reality: despite her super strength, she can sadly not withstand the damaging effects of excessive alcohol intake.

Appendix F features another highly inventive piece. In the opening line, the author seemed to aim for a catachrestic play on *uncertainty*, as though it could *ignite the flames of an inspiring tale*. She followed this with a play for assonance and alliteration in *treacherous creatures … triggering a wave of heat and hate*. The author creates a strange mixture of fantasy (the almost-human creatures) and reality (the Marines, patrolling the area). She concludes the piece with another catachrestic play on an *intimate evening*, as if it could *teem with thousands of fabulous panoramic views*.

Compared to all other creative efforts, the work appearing in Appendix G was the most developed and perhaps the most cohesive and creative. Efforts made in the invention of a true tale appear quite evident throughout the entire sketch. Three aspects of composition figured prominently: cohesiveness, rhetorical schemes and tropes.

Firstly, the author was able to create an almost apologetic tone for his narrator, whom readers might empathize with as a real character with a complex past and a troubled present. The full narrative seems to border strangely yet realistically on fragmented war story telling and the agitated ramblings of a past war hero suffering the slight effects of post traumatic stress disorder.

Secondly, on a rhetorical level, the author appears to have developed this character trait in a play for meiosis or litotes in *Just a flesh wound*. Such an obviously invented play, here, is perhaps in keeping with anyone recalling past accounts of barbarous behavior on the battlefield and who would, thus, feel emotionally unmoved by seeing a *head explode* as the main character admits to the deed of using a *.44 Magnum* on one *suspicious prisoner* who had been caught *slipping something into the sole of his right shoe*. Allusions to Richard Reid (a.k.a. Shoe Bomber) and to the JFK assassination, *take the body to Dallas*, appearing in the latter section, seem to shade the passage with a tinge of conspiracy. The writer also seemed to play for syllepsis in *living <u>on</u> fairly frozen meals and <u>under</u> the strictest orders*…. The appearance of <u>*schooled in sniffing out suspicious prisoners*</u> seems an intended play for alliteration.

The author's sketch appearing in Appendix H was the least developed. He found a number of what appeared to him to be quite useful phrases, but after many minutes of staring blankly at the mix of them on his page, he was unable to construct a passage of what he felt to be substantial length. When I later asked him to try and name the difficulty that he felt had confronted him, he admitted that he simply could not begin. He couldn't isolate any phrase to use as a subject for the passage, at least one that he felt could be explored. After surveying the significantly dissimilar themes represented by the nouns and verbs in the phrases he'd chosen, I asked him if he saw any hope of achieving some sort of coherence or development, given what he had to work with. A few moments of reflection on his part revealed that his difficulties had arisen because of his initial desire to locate very early on some semblance of coherence, to construct unified meanings more than to simply play with the phrases in combinations and to be surprised by whatever meanings or interesting rhetorical effects that might emerge.

Despite the author's much earlier expressions of grief for never having come to truly understand metaphor, the last sentence in this piece represents significant improvements in his implicit knowledge of metaphor. Likening <u>foot soldiers</u> to <u>hermit crabs</u>, he was not able to pinpoint precisely where the metaphor was but, nevertheless, sensed something interesting about the passage. When asked on several occasions, throughout the case study, what "metaphor" means, he would typically shrug his shoulders and admit to having no idea. He was clearly experimenting, though, all along with various forms of figurative language. Relying on the *war is a disease* metaphor, he described how *soldiers rise out of the crystal blue sea* and *spray a spectacular epidemic of dense metal projectiles*. Despite the brevity of his piece, the images that emerged from it are certainly quite remarkably vivid.

## 10.5 Discussion of Case Study

While we routinely rely upon our tacit knowledge of the pragmatic, semantic, syntactic, lexical, and phonemic features of language to help us communicate a message verbally, writing, though, presents an added complication. As Vygotsky observes, writing represents a double abstraction: an abstraction from the sound of speech and ... from [an] interlocutor" (1934/1978, p. 181). That is to say, in speech, the key communicative shift from the "I-you" (rhetorical) or the "I-it" (referential) relationships inherent in the act itself withdraw in the writing act to a fundamentally different kind of communication—that with a blank sheet of paper (Moffett, 1983, p. 18). Such a complication, apart from the other concerns of performance, competence and about attitudes discussed earlier, can amplify apprehension in a writer (Daly & Miller, 1975) and diminish a writer's ability by affecting his or her sense of confidence in communicating.

Play with phrases in the creation of new meanings appeared to dramatically alleviate or even annihilate the sorts of anxieties that can distract the writer attempting to concentrate on the message but who feels entangled or encumbered by the other linguistic aspects of text production. Liberal play with phrases has shown to dramatically simplify the task. If bricks were building material cooperating in meaningful ways with carefully placed mortar holding the material into the form of a wall, then the phrases students played with collaborated in meaningful ways with carefully chosen transitions for cohesion.

By the close of Meeting 6, I came to realize clearly that explicit discussions of the narrative and descriptive modes of exposition, so typical of freshman composition courses, would have been much too ambitious in the span of six relatively short meetings where the principal aims were maximum exposure to plays with phrase types. I realized too that such a discussion could have been counterproductive and certainly counter to my original thesis. It was, perhaps, also ironic and fortuitous to have discovered this condition, for the participants appeared by then to be naturally predisposed to assuming the personas of clever storytellers set on concocting the most unusual narratives.

Certainly worth noting were both the attitudes of everyone involved and the extensive, creative uses of figurative language. The freedom they sensed to invent seemed itself to create the ideal impetus needed for radically adjusting their own negative attitudes about the various language varieties brought into classrooms. Also, any hint of apprehension about writing for assessment appeared to vanish, a significant but clear contrast to the visible apprehensions some participants exhibited during the first two meetings. Where plays with rhetorical schemes and tropes appeared most dramatic was in these latter workshops, the fifth meeting in plays with poetry and the last meeting in plays with prose.

When we began the last meeting, all participants appeared to expect one last play with phrase structures and seemed quite content, too, with seeing the last encounter as a sort of literary grand finalé. I encouraged them all the more, therefore, to satisfy their appetites for creativity. As in the workshops with poetics, the last meeting clearly became a rather competitive game of which small group of two could best the others in the production of outrageous prose refined by determined searches for fresh expressions. Thus, it seemed to me that any formal or explicit lectures about how to assume a point of view in narrative situations, for example, how to achieve a desired tone, or how to develop vivid descriptions could have potentially stifled the sense of freedom that participants felt they had, or had come to expect, in their plays to achieve certain rhetorical effects.

Apart from what the participants produced in the final meeting, I should submit that what I had fully intended to address and what actually occurred diverged in some ways. I had initially envisioned that part of the final meeting would be occupied by a re-evaluation of the participants, to determine what particular aspects of the method they had found most useful. It had been my early intention to assess their level of ability by taking a final sample of their writing, a writing task that would encourage them to reflect on the overall *workshop* experience. What I received in written response was a rather disappointing mix of half-hearted, half-developed comments.

Notwithstanding either their lack of confidence or effort on this front, I was able to discover that play does indeed appear to offer writers the theoretical space and time enough to distance themselves from the immediate difficulties of actually having to generate words. Play with the phrase structures of existing texts certainly allayed their anxieties and feelings of indecision more than the prospect of facing a blank page, therefore permitting students more opportunities to search for, uncover and shape their own traces of meaning. Play with phrases was both truly experimental and experiential and offered a new way of giving shape to new meanings and drawing connections between those meanings.

Also, since the conclusion of the case study, I have found that, quite apart from my initial speculations, this method appears to address a considerable difficulty that beginning writers face. Play with phrase structures helped partition three tasks critical to the making and articulation of meaning but which students typically conflate as they draft—their search for a coherent standard grammar, a clear and coherent message reflected in the semantics, and the coherent use of punctuation. The data have shown, thus far, that play initially liberates the writer from having to deal immediately with these three principal concerns and allows the writer to simply respond to the mix of phrases and the possibilities for creating new meanings without the responsibility or pressure of generating those meanings. Later, as they played, they also appeared naturally to gain interest in finding and refining meanings as well as playing with surface structures. That is to say, they appeared to shift their concerns from taking delight in finding syntactic connections between structures to actually locating coherence in meaning.

In the case study workshops, students stood on the pre-writing scaffolding (Cazden, 1983, pp. 3-6), so to speak, and played with the surface of the rhetorical building, manipulating surface structures for the sake of semantic or syntactic coherence. This sort of scaffolding appeared to permit and further encourage liberal play with phrases, removing the writer from the immediate concerns of working out the problems of a precise and finished piece of writing. Phrase play also located the activity closer to the student and was, therefore, more empowering and less threatening. As a consequence, it appears as though play can render subjective judgments of writing moot as play seems to subdue such compulsions to judge. Assumptions about syntactic or semantic correctness or precision fade to the background, since the participants possess different expectations of themselves than students in other more traditional composition courses.

Data culled from workshops certainly appeared to undermine Chomsky's distinction (1965, p. 11) between acceptability and grammaticalness, where the scales of one do not coincide with the other. Indeed, his distinctions appeared to collapse during play. During the workshops, the students themselves demonstrated that their free explorations toward coherence in one aspect of writing (the syntactic) did not need to immediately or simultaneously hinge upon their explorations for coherence in another aspect of writing (the semantics). These students certainly appeared to feel, in the words of John Trimbur, "…released into the activity of interpretation, of discovering and formulating meanings, whether of personal or textual experience" (2000, p. 193).

Their work illustrated very clearly the theoretical lines that Chomsky (1957, p. 15) had drawn between the grammatical and the meaningful. That is, they became clearly much more comfortable with problems in semantics because problems in connecting phrase structures syntactically appeared, to them, to be much more easily manageable. Their heightened desire to respond initially to these surface structures and to engage in the search for coherence in one or the other aspect of written expression seemed also to further their desire to experiment—or play—all the more with semantics and syntax.

This level of awareness and willingness to engage with the text marked a significant milestone for them. Their creative plays and laughter-laced responses to their own experiments were, in the words of T. R. Johnson, like "renegade rhetorics,… which offer a shiny renewal, a transfusion of fresh [rhetorical] vitality" (2001, p. 631). This way of conceiving of writing, Johnson explains, "offers students [some] space for a particular sort of laughter, laughter that proceeds as a critical intervention against any structure that would prove more limiting than liberating" (p. 637).

He notes that this sort of laughter counters what he calls the "… naïve idealism that would cast academic discourse as a pristine vehicle for the realization of a rationalist utopia and … to the modernist hope that we can reconstitute any such reliable foolproof foundation that … we lost" (p. 637). What organizing principles typically underpin North American academic discourses in the composition classroom? Johnson suggests that instead of

> … organizing ourselves around a central, transcendent ideal of 'academic discourse' as that which names, masters, and controls reality, we need to sensitize ourselves and our students to the openings, cracks, and fissures in every discursive act, the holes …through which the play, laughter, and general slippage of meaning flows. (p. 637)

If the playful approach to writing taken throughout the workshops drew more attention to the typically overlooked subversive dimensions of writing, it also highlighted the immense but often unexpressed creative powers at work in individuals groping toward more meaningful and expedient ways of self-expression.

# *Conclusion*

The principal aim of this inquiry was to determine how adult peripheral learners in American community colleges could be better assisted in formal classroom settings to overcome their writing apprehensions and to solve common sentence-level problems in composition. It was necessary, therefore, to draw upon knowledge in divergent areas of scholarship, to learn where these areas intersect to produce a philosophically sound and expedient method that reflects more accurately and considers more fully the natural linguistic abilities and behaviors that adult periphery learners tend to bring to classrooms.

The development of an appropriate and useful alternative also required answers to a few secondary concerns. To understand from a sociolinguistic viewpoint what tends to shape the writing apprehensions of learners, a critical examination of the attitudes at work behind the prevailing standard language ideology in North American public and academic discourses today was critical.

Another concern was to understand the literacy schooling context that adult learners today had typically been exposed to as youths during the 1960s and 1970s. It was, thus, useful to ground discussions of contemporary language norms in a brief history of the concept of standardization and to connect this concept to present concerns about the perceived decline of the language itself and of the teaching of English writing.

Also, since a critical examination of the major schools of thought in North American composition studies would help form the basis of a new alternative, it was essential to assess the dominant paradigms of literacy education that these students had likely experienced.

Finally, in keeping with the assumption outlined in the introduction, that play is an inherent tendency that prefigures human intellectual and motor development, it was therefore natural to ask what could be achieved through play in the composition classroom.

## Major Findings

### The mislabeled

Nine hours of discussion and shared experimentation in the workshops revealed that my initial understanding of the term "periphery" as well as my borrowing and adaptation of it to represent those students who possess the less desirable social and/or linguistic capital was too simplistic and narrow. Though having emerged largely from the lower-middle class, according to their own perceptions, the participants simply did not have access to the kinds of economic resources and social connections that students of the middle and upper class enjoy.

I include this fact as a major finding as it illustrates the ambiguity of popular labels such as "periphery" or "marginalized." A student, for example, with unlimited access to the sorts of resources described above may as easily, though not always likely, be set at the margins of the academic center as the student emerging from periphery speech communities. This realization had become merely a reflection of the sort that Mike Rose had experienced as he tells his readers in *Lives on the Boundary* that these students are not poor but simply adrift in academic conventions they do not adequately understand. They tend to memorize what and when they should scrutinize, resist what and when they should risk, embrace what and when they should oppose. These sorts of errors, Rose argues, mark "the place[s] where education begins" (1990, p. 189).

Given the range of immigrants beyond Hispanic groups and the ways in which these groups perceive their status, perhaps what are needed are more expedient terms to describe what appears to be an increasing multiplicity of students that this proposed method could best assist. That is to say, a term that embodies not only the ways in which educators perceive and evaluate the needs of students from the socioeconomic periphery but the needs of the "educationally underprepared" (1990, p. 3).

## Workshops

In light of Vygotsky's theory of play, the workshops alone demonstrated clearly and early on the enormous and often unexploited possibilities afforded to students through playful experiential learning in English composition classrooms. Conversely, in light of Vygotsky's argument for the value of formal grammar instruction, indeed, its necessity to the development of written language (1983, p. 7) the workshops appeared contravene this purported necessity. Certainly, the term *workshop* itself appeared to mean to the participants a kind of liberty and freedom to invent new personal ways of working out sentence-level syntactic and semantic difficulties typically unrealizable in traditional grammar lectures where parsing or drilling exercises would typically dominate.

If the concept of *workshop* had initially provided for participants the psychological space necessary to experiment freely, the literal workshop demonstrated that play with phrase structures works well as a kind of scaffolding that developing writers were able to stand on, so to speak, while dealing with difficulties that the complex task of writing itself presented. During the workshops, as the participants played in small groups, they appeared increasingly more aware of the need for sentence-level experimentation to capture more precisely intended rhetorical effects and how these needs could easily be achieved through their own dialogues and liberal plays with phrase structures. According to Gordon Wells (1999, p. 127), this sort of group play is consistent with those activities peculiar to scaffolding: (a) the essentially dialogic nature of the discourse in which new knowledge is co-constructed, (b) the significance of the kind of activity in which knowing is embedded and (c) the role of artifacts (in this case a *pen*, some *paper* and *phrases* (Cole, 1997; Vygotsky, 1982) that mediate knowing.

Play also appeared quite effective in disarming apprehensions while encouraging students to engage directly with some of the problems of writing, such as generating, organizing and dealing with syntactic and semantic difficulties. The workshop exercises generated substantial enthusiasm, sustained, it seemed, by the participants' desire to increase knowledge while increasing their search for new ways of creating meaning. In light of the rather long history of prescriptive approaches to assessing the quality of writing, not once was it necessary to intervene with linguistic prescriptions and encumber the creative process and the participants' progress in sentence-level experimentation. Their propensity to naturally seek cohesion and meaning appeared to circumvent the need for explicitly teaching them something about language, composition and audience. That is, their very own acts of trying to make sense of things subsumed other issues about language and composing.

As the participants played with phrase structures to invent new meanings, they appeared to realize, too, the need for coherence on multiple levels to help communicate a much clearer message or to create some intended rhetorical effect. That is, they were able to discern more readily three distinctly different concerns that naturally arise in sentence-level writing: a coherent syntax, a precise semantics and correct punctuation. Play merely appeared to provide the freedom of opportunity for students to separate and confront what many tend to conflate and, thus, confuse. More importantly, they were able to see more readily the distinct separation of these three primary tasks of drafting. As one participant worked out any difficulties in grammar, the other tended to work out the meaning expressed through the grammar. Any questions about the need for punctuation and placement were addressed after syntactic and semantic solutions were at hand.

Since play involved two people in small groups and since it replaced one concrete interlocutor with what Vygotsky (1934/1978, p. 181) sees as a "double abstraction" (addressed earlier in Part 2, Section 1.3) in writing, the exercise appeared to dramatically simplify for them the task of generating and organizing new meanings. Worth noting here is Mei-Yu Lu's observation that "writing ... is a sociocultural, generative, and developmental process and that students acquire written language as they actively explore various forms and functions and interact with other more competent writers in their community" (2000, ¶ 10). More importantly, she notes that children also play with written language and weave it into activities such as drawing, speech and play. It is through the various and rich literacy experiences that children become competent and increasingly creative members of a literate society (2000, ¶ 10). Lu's argument is supported by the research of Sanches and Kirshenblatt conducted three decades earlier. They note that speech play is instrumental to the acquisition of adult verbal art and which is supported by two facts:

> (a) ... children's ordinary discourse does not exhibit the same of disciplined formal patterning as do their speech play productions; and (b) that when analyzed closely children's speech play does exhibit many of the rhetorical figures appropriate to adult eloquence and codified in the rhetoric handbooks (1976, p. 106).

Although dealing with more written than verbal forms, participants' plays with phrase structures during the workshops demonstrated the validity of Sanches and Kirshenblatt's earlier research, the accuracy of

Lu's argument, and how relevant and useful play is to adult learners coping with rhetorical problems.

## Prescriptivism

Rather than accepting in advance and independently of my own experience the potential connection between prescriptive behavior in the public discourse and prescriptive approaches to teaching English composition, I had imagined that an accurate depiction and critical discussion of the present state of North American composition studies would include not only the necessary review of academic literature but an assessment of the popular attitudes that may give shape to the literature. While deconstructing various traditional approaches to teaching writing, I was encouraged to learn further about the influences that had apparently given those methods their form. If there were certain negative attitudes or beliefs present beneath the mix of linguistic interactions among speakers in the public discourse, those attitudes also seemed to elucidate some of the motivations that influenced certain popular approaches to composition studies.

Anecdotal observations made during the past five years of this study, especially in discussions with case study participants, verify what scholars have critiqued and called attention to for at least the past fifty: language varieties are like gates that can open or close off access to the promise of future socioeconomic power. Perhaps, there is little wonder why many Americans, having endured these practices at such young ages, may feel naturally inclined to clean up the language they hear their brethren use in routine daily interactions. Certainly, the case study participants, the majority, i.e., not all of whom were adult learners of the periphery, communicated clearly their own disregard for discourse styles outside the mainstream.

These sorts of attitudes and practices seem to pervade all levels of the mainstream culture, from concerned parents of the working class who forbid their children from using *ain't* at the dinner table through good-hearted members of the intelligentsia who publicly encourage their colleagues to avoid splitting infinitives at academic conferences.[14] One citizen will invariably inform another that double negatives are undesirable, or some such appalling use of the language, and so "language maintenance traditions" (Cheshire & Milroy, 1993) such as these continue propagating new generations of amateur or professional commentators intent on dispensing what they feel are fitting linguistic prescriptions for the continued survival and purity of English.

Missing what an extraordinary instrument of cognition it is, commentators of this kind narrow the definition of language and restrict the versatile roles it plays in the lives of humans. It is, perhaps, the common preoccupation with the maintenance of a standard language ideology that bespeaks the kind of distractions necessary for misrecognizing or overlooking the inherent creative strengths with which students already enter classrooms. What remains, nevertheless, is a popular belief that somewhere those teachers and professors in the position to do so are not upholding standards, that standards are directly connected to test scores which are connected to true knowledge which is, in turn, connected to ultimate socioeconomic success.

## Limitations of findings

Of course, play with phrases is not and was not intended to be a panacea for all the difficulties that apprehensive periphery students of writing, irrespective of age, tend to confront. This somewhat self-directed approach to writing allows considerable

---

[14] A colleague of mine was publicly berated by a political science professor at an "Effective Teaching Methods Conference" in 2002 as he "split" a number of infinitives while delivering an essay on the art of persuasion in political discourse.

freedom yet, perhaps, not enough of the necessary guided constraints for learning explicitly how to construct, say, complex or compound sentences. In this respect, play might appear at first glance to oversimplify the process of writing. While students were able to realize for themselves some surprising gains in their ability to express intended meanings, phrase play does not come without its inadequacies. It seems that this method has limitations in three principal areas of composition and just as well raises questions in another related area of inquiry.

Firstly, liberal play with phrase structures does not appear to help raise explicit awareness of mechanics. While it may not teach students about the accepted conventions of comma placement, uses of hyphens, dashes, apostrophes, semicolons, etc., play with phrases in poetry does seem to help raise their awareness of the connection between a thought, a pause for effect, and the break of a poetic line. That is, their experiments in poetry certainly seem to suggest that their sensitivities to the natural rhythms in the spoken language can be reflected in critical breaks in verse, a step away from prose.

Secondly, play with phrases does not appear to lend itself well as a method of raising awareness of the other more academic modes of exposition, such as definition, critical analysis, or cause and effect which are typically associated with the Genre School discussed in Part 1, Section 3.1. One related positive byproduct of play, though, is the development of a greater awareness of metaphor and other tropes sometimes used in critical analysis to expand on or clarify certain abstract or arcane concepts. As an example, students should see benefits in drafting, say, a critique of present-day concepts of democracy and, thus, use their greater awareness of and deftness with figurative language gained in play to capitalize on their development of an illustration or analogy that might better embody this abstraction.

Thirdly, while participants did play with a range of rhetorical schemes in poetry and prose, it was difficult to know what level of awareness they were tapping into during their experiments. Given their apprehensions and their somewhat limited and mostly negative experiences, historically, with composition studies, traditional classroom approaches cannot fully account for their highly inventive and clever uses of language expressed in poetry and their consequent experiments with prose. That is, the level of creativity brought to text production in the case study cannot be explained away as explicit knowledge increased in traditional institutional settings.

A few worthwhile questions that lead into related areas of inquiry, nevertheless, remain. Were they merely in-built mechanisms of cognition and consciousness connected to their experiences with the language that equipped participants with such remarkable creative facility with rhetorical schema? It certainly appeared as though their liberal experiments with the language demonstrated a level of competence that belied their own self-effacing beliefs in their skills and abilities.

Was play with a wide range of phrase structures one of Gestalt perception, a way of naturally giving order or form to what, at first, seemed a disparate and quite chaotic mess of meanings cast in a series of phrases? If so, it would be useful to ask where the human drive for and fascination with pattern, form, symmetry, sound and syncopation crosses paths with cognition and the perception of meaning and whether these concepts of the mind and body are rooted in a social tradition. As Polanyi observes, expertise or *competence*, is not a "… property but a relation between individual actors and a social system of rules. A person is an expert within a tradition: in a competent mental act, the agent does not do as he pleases, but compels himself forcibly to act as he believes he must" (1975, p. 4).

Furthermore, if culture influences how we think and how we believe we must act in light of norms, and it shapes our attitudes, and thus, personal biases, then the experiences of culture are integral to perception and the interpretation of meaning. To what extent, though, does culture and tradition influence our tacit powers of perceiving and interpreting meaning in the discursive and presentational forms of communication?

Are the discursive and presentational forms of communication discussed by Langer (1979, p. 81-2) polar opposites and so different that they will invariably invite entirely different ways of perceiving or interpreting the meanings communicated in them? Lastly, to what extent do the inherent interpretative acts of the observer brought to the task of perceiving meaning in the written signs figure in the meaning humans make of the world's other communication phenomena?

Given the long history of "verbal hygiene" (Cameron, 1995) in western discourse and the various attitudes that tend to underpin these behaviors, it certainly seems as though culture heavily influences our ability to interpret and perceive meaning much more than we might like to admit. Perhaps this is one principal reason why some speakers tend to develop such ingrained irrational biases and are more apt to hastily judge linguistic output negatively more than attempt to meet other communicators halfway.

## New Research Issues and Directions

Who precisely might well benefit from this Vygotskyan approach to writing pedagogy? Apart from the high apprehensive adult learner experiencing writer's block, composition students of all grade levels, despite their cultural capital, must contend, generally, with a wide range of difficulties in the generation of ideas, their organization, and the use of rhetorical structures. Workshops have shown that this approach to rhetorical play may be easily adjusted to fit the needs of any student, despite difficulties, such as the pressure to perform, he or she carries into a composition classroom. Exercises, such as those appearing in Appendix A, can be adjusted to the emotional or intellectual level, or the cultural cues of the developing writer. Besides the successes that L1 speakers realized during workshop sessions, L2 speakers in collaboration with their L1 peers also showed remarkable promise.

Unlike in traditional tertiary English composition classrooms in North America, phrase play creates a radically different context in which experiments conducted in the shared search for meaning and coherence can lead to very surprising rhetorical discoveries any student would feel empowered to make. Play helps students gain two kinds of distance from codified rules: (a) it allows for the emotional space to widen between apprehensive peripheral actors and the sentence-level difficulties they often feel they must immediately attend to in syntax, semantics or mechanics, and (b) it also allows for the intellectual space to widen between old ways of creating meaning informed by rigid academic conventions and new self-realized ways guided by creativity, curiosity and the student's own tacit knowledge of the language. Students' nearly immediate success with the exercises combined with the creative level of their work seem to testify clearly that their own tacit knowledge of English is already sufficient for an important kind of success in composition—the implications of which may invariably lead to other important questions.

For example, in *Philosophy in the Flesh* (2004), Lakoff reminds readers of the common conceptualization of the human mind limited by a category as narrow as a machine. But, is this frame a necessarily useful one through which to understand the strange mix of curiosity, creative exuberance and control brought to the task of written expression? If the human mind were a machine wired with parts ready to perceive and process the fuel of lived experience by "turning out ideas at a great rate," then to what extent do humans maintain the control over their linguistic output representing their experiences? (Lakoff & Johnson, 2004, p. 247). This examination of play has shown that students of composition have control over not only their explicit knowledge of the names of certain linguistic components, but can control with great deftness the course and reshaping of meanings. In light of what the participants were able to accomplish personally and rhetorically during the case study, the popular mind-is-a-machine metaphor seems only partly to embody the process and progress observed in the case study.

The workshops demonstrate that "exerting this [high] level of explicit control over language" (Cameron, 1995, p. 219) is not entirely necessary for success in composition—at least the sort of success that can supplant debilitating forms of writing apprehension. Imposing the sorts of excessive or superfluous explicit knowledge of the language upon a natural human urge to give order and structure to ideas seems unnecessarily to belabor—in the initial stages—the complex and creative cognitive processes and energies brought to bear in generating, drafting and revising. The supports for popular prescriptive approaches having been further weakened by success seen in the case study, a practical task now would be an even more detailed explication of what liberal rhetorical play can do for students of composition experiencing difficulties well beyond the sentence level.

Follow-up studies of a more representative group of North American college students would be rather useful for furthering an understanding of phrase play and its long-term effects on apprehension as well as on tracking the growth of skills. Apart from the participants in this case study that largely represented dialect speech communities, an unpublished review of an earlier draft of this book notes that ESL students currently comprise the largest and most pressing problem that compositionists face (G. L. Rico, November 16, 2006).

A subsequent case study with a much more diverse group of participants than those cited here could certainly help uncover details about the pervasiveness of problems that students have in text production. Such a study could enlist only non-native speakers of English to test the limitations of Chomskyan traditions in Universal Grammars. What specific sorts of interferences, for example, prevent ESL students from acquiring through phrase play a more complete, more explicit knowledge of phrases and their impact on coherence, meaning and grammar? The following image illustrates uses of this approach in exclusively ESL writing instruction.

Japanese students finding and experimenting with phrases structures (2006).

Another limitation of the study was that nine 'contact' hours did not adequately approximate the time that students in typical college composition courses enjoy. Extending the case study over a full semester, or multiple ones, would certainly create an even more detailed and useful depiction of phrase play's pedagogical effectiveness as well as allow practitioners to develop further classroom strategies with this sort of play. Presently, Japanese students in our freshman writing program enjoy an entire semester of phrase play and have been shown to produce significantly improved work in poetry and prose production.

At last, if Leahy's arguments, referenced earlier, for the value implicitly placed on the kinds of rhetorical features he had outlined in his paper are valid, a new case study adopting a quantitative approach to rhetorical analysis could be launched. Such a study could further interrogate Leahy's claims about the intrinsic academic merit added to students and writing that demonstrates their awareness and use of the more valued rhetorical schemes. The primary argument that Leahy defends is that teachers of writing naturally reward competence at the sort of level Leahy himself had described, so a study that aims to reveal in more quantifiable ways these connections would offer another valuable layer of understanding of what we judge, how we judge and, perhaps, why.

# APPENDICES

Clearing a Vygotskyan Path

Appendix A

DIRECTIONS: Identify only the phrases you like and then use them to construct a poem on a new page. Try to create something meaningful and/or grammatical.

a common house pet   coping with an addiction to cake   sad funeral mourners   using the cell phone as a weapon   back at the house   by the door under the musty heavy wool blanket   kindergarten, crayons and coloring books   about dinner   beautiful new beginnings   their best positions   averted a disagreeable situation   just wanting some cool water   a very beautiful blonde bombshell   after his job bad interview   sucking up their courage   for a dead garden   near the tall waiter with his hands   in his back pockets   the rude cab driver   behaving badly with fancy friends   their very nasty deeds   living alone at last   weighed the moldy musk melons   in the bed   out-of-control preteen behavior   blowing out two very thin candles   the drunken sailors   dreamed of escape   surrounded by enemies on all sides   the gladiator bullies   surrounded by a boatload of rare Roma beauties   a rather tragic situation   with the entire family   living the life of Sally's brother   eating very bad sushi rolls   a near-death experience   Miami Beach midnight bash   drinking gin with Thelma and Louise   a dumb cop   brawling all night   attributing to the flash flood   a sudden burst of rain   smashed by a large blue truck   tamed by a love for cherries   medicine woman Jane   bumping and grinding pushing pulling and pawing   for one low price   serenaded by the soothing music   the little lady next door   selfish and crazed   in the background   lets go of her rage   her two-headed twins   in a pair of high heels   a sexy seamstress   just beyond the door reunites lost lovers   eating grapes   ignored the obvious dangers   their wildest dreams displayed the contents   patent leather stilettos   half-past 7:00 A.M.   happily divorced his nasty deeds   of their dangerous damaged minds   intensifying their good intentions talked of lasting love   in her past lifetime   to live on the lamb   paying for a past crime on time   seemingly unaware of the monster   potty-mouthed Rosie   queen of big bootie disco   plundered and raped   saved from the grip of drugs   from the deck of the aircraft carrier   paying space aliens   camping in the Navajo National Forest   sporting a new crew cut and sideburns   wandering in the wilderness   slid back in   for a two-week holiday   two very long years in the jungle   eating under the shade tree out back because of their good work   a secret agent   a hopeless correctional institute inmate feeling like a neglected stepchild   hoping to rob a Family Mart with a spoon   busted the coffee table in half   with her sexy short shorts and tight tee   a star-studded evening with Brad Pitt and his mistress   the psychotic shopaholic   fashion goofball accessory   with Uncle Joey   suggesting they move to Tokyo   onto the ice rink for dancing   throwing a party for the neighbors   a strait jacket for any kind of intruder   to tax all auto imports from Canada   in an outpouring of anguish   to slip it back in place   the portly celebrity   on land and in the air   before spring thaw melts Fuji-san's ice going incognito at night   publicly question the tax increase   a brand new fashion phenomenon sweeping England   New York style cheesecake   guessing the weight of her hefty aunt   attracting more prey than she'd wanted   paint a very disturbing image dangerously linked to another crime   to slap a quick lawsuit on her ex-husband permanently etched into the minds of those who witnessed the murder   display true impatience   the correctional institute inmate   to cross over the red Golden Gate Bridge   a total solar eclipse   of the moon   a rather hungry sloth   longer than the others   a show of support   only for dark chocolate   to run in the family   hot foods and very young dudes   to dress up in jeans and boots   her adoring fans excited about the new adventure   playing house with Sissy Spacek   rubbed the back of her leg raw

## Appendix B

| *Kindergarten Cop* | *Beautiful Beginnings* |
|---|---|
| chambermaids, bellhops | the blowsy blonde |
| and busboys | blew two |
| like funeral mourners | burly bozos |
| weighed the consequences | the gladiator roustabouts |
| of death. | drinking, brawling |
| the blonde bombshell | and bad behaving |
| Eve | trotted out their nasty |
| ignored the obvious dangers, | damage intensifying their |
| out in public and | intentions |
| in the background. | reinforcing their positions |
| insiders attribute the | they dreamed of escape |
| performer's out-of-control | sucking up their courage |
| behavior | they averted a |
| to the Iranians. | disagreeable situation |
| After her stint | surrounded by a |
| on the Cosby Show | bevy of beauties |
| she was hit | cookin' up their |
| with <u>friends and a family</u> | wildest dreams |
| until | |
| a dumb COP | |
| busted her | |
| in the no-holds-barred | |
| starr-studded | |
| Friars Club | |
| with a dozen kids. | |

## Appendix C

| *How About Dinner?* | *The Alibi of Pussy and Russell* |
|---|---|
| half-past dead | happily married |
| potty-mouthed Rosie | Pussy and Russell Polgren |
| queen of big disco bootie | plundered and appropriated |
| saved from drug hell | from others |
| 5    pays friendly space aliens | 5    while camping in the |
| a <u>heaping mound</u> of | wilderness for |
| hershey's molten mojo | two weeks of <u>wild</u> wet |
| <u>while</u> sporting her skimpy | weather <u>and</u> |
| gas eater underwear | because of their |
| 10    her correctional institute | 10    good deeds |
| inmate <u>persona</u> the | in past lifetimes |
| liberated psychotic lesbian | they were confident |
| <u>with</u> | in Mr. Fish |
| sexy junk in the trunk | who <u>had</u> suggested as penance |
| 15    uses only the best | 15    for their dastardly deeds they |
| straitjackets for her kids | move their piano onto the ice |
| for stamping out | for a winter-long public party |
| <u>any</u> juvenile insurrections | <u>but who neglected</u> |
| any outpourings of anguish | to tell them |
| 20    <u>that</u> might gnaw away | 20    to slide it back |
| <u>at all</u> <u>of her</u> | on land |
| fancy iconic incognito | before spring thaw |
| dance club status | |

## Appendix D

*Miami Beach Bar Monty's*

```
     bumping, pushing, pulling, pawing
     for fame, medicine woman
     tamed by tiger love
     lets go of her rage
5    of her dreaded two-headed twins
     who seemingly seem so unaware
     of a disturbing painted picture made public
     linking them to a dangerous
     correctional institute inmate
10   at one low price
     even as
     other similarly hungry individuals
     strut their stuff
     at a chocolate show
15   with candies, foods and dudes
     who are all juiced up
     and looking for ecstasy with
     body heat
     dipped in
20   sugar and dancing which
     runs a whopping $1000
     and which makes a pretty penny
     reselling plastic Gucci purses
     due to an overwhelming response
25   at a shoot 'em up free for all
```

Appendix E

*Scandal Meter*

    serenaded by the sounds
    of the moving melodic <u>medicine</u>
    the girl next door
    sex-crazed, selfish
5   and cruel
    in a pair of sexy <u>sharp</u> stilettos
    reunited long lost lovers
    permanently with super glue
    while nearby prostitutes
10  crossed a solar-Pluto conjunction
    and displayed their impatience
    with the others
    intent on attracting the kind
    of prey
15  <u>that</u> runs in the family
    the gifted love specialist
    <u>though</u> crabby and cranky
    <u>though left</u> with a left hand
20  gnarled by industrial strength
    topical scalp solution
    begged Pee Wee Herman
    for a pink <u>mixed</u> elixir
    advertised to
25  <u>ear</u> intently
    to all of the complaints
    of WalMart patrons
    <u>to all of</u> the worried housewives
    wondering whether
    they'll ever reach another
30  sale on
    patent leather stiletto heels

Appendix F

Yesterday evening while I sat underneath pink cherry blossoms gulping sake', munching snacks, and belting out a tune or two, the buzz over my superhero image came to mind. But, firing up tigers in the depths of the jungle and deep sea giants all makes me feel a little vertigo. Watching clouds of blue flowers, with decreased anxiety and increased relaxation, I thought to myself, "I am rich and famous, from my Porsche to my model boyfriend, I am the Queen of Tarts." Two weeks ago, I was depicting rogue lawyers as vultures in their spirals of greed and looming financial disasters. Today, I honestly can't tell a daffodil from a daisy. I ought to marry, have kids and spend my days at the country club until the devil finally enters with his hotshot lawyer Beelzebub offering me tons of money. Although many will quiver at the sight of him and his accomplice and have since ancient times, I will probably spend months swapping fisticuffs with them from my chair at the local alcohol rehab center.

## Appendix G

<u>Despite</u> the apparent sea power of spectacular ocean dwellers, an unsettling uncertainty ignited the flames <u>of</u> an inspiring and incredible tale. Underused and inefficient, <u>the treacherous creatures were able, nevertheless</u>, to penetrate the dense thicket of seaweed, triggering a wave of heat <u>and hate</u>. Defying every one of us to stay away and breaking the chains of gravity, they once again raided <u>our</u> important underwater sanctuary of lush tropical gardens, as <u>the almost-human creatures</u> concocted a scrumptious treat <u>for</u> our fervor and feverish imaginings. On condition of anonymity, the Marines, <u>patrolling the area</u>, expressed their love <u>of the unexpected</u>. Reluctant to divulge the source of our creation, we exerted our utmost efforts to <u>convincingly</u> indicate our aspirations <u>to join them in their endeavor</u> to fan the flames of love for the intruders of our undersea world. Teeming with thousands of fabulous panoramic views, our intimate evening expanded the experience <u>of our dwelling</u> amidst the wetlands below the surface of the sea.

## Appendix H

Before the March mating season, when life was a little more simple, I was just another eight-to-five, barely-getting-by postal worker. Before I continue, allow me to explain some history. I used to battle enemies in backyards across America. My foes, who fell without choice from the powerful blows of my bloody bayonet, would yell, scream, and ask for help. Those who didn't perish were treated for severe fungal infections and were imprisoned in Captain Dick's musty basement, living on fairly frozen meals and under the strictest of orders to hide in a back bedroom should the sirens sound. Though I was a hero in Captain Dick's army, I also had to perform menial tasks, such as guard duty and licking boots. It was an early Sunday morning and the sunlight just started to throw its life-giving rays through the windows cross-hatched with rusty iron bars. Looking over at prisoner 134M, I noticed that he was slipping something into the sole of his right shoe. Since I'd been schooled in sniffing out suspicious prisoners, I could sense that he was looking for something that would get him out of this boxy basement and would enable him to fly. Pulling out my .44 Magnum, I aimed at his forehead and fired one deadly round. His head exploded. Just a flesh wound. I yelled for the private standing outside the door, "Put this body in the armored car and take it to Dallas!"

Appendix I

Between military intervention <u>and</u> the hubs of socialization <u>lays the soldiers</u>. Rising out of the crystal blue sea and running across sand, <u>they</u> unleash a spectacular epidemic of dense metal projectiles. With <u>military</u> rucksacks strapped on their backs, and heads covered with kevlars, <u>these foot soldiers</u> are hermit crabs on jungle promenades seeking nourishment from hapless victims <u>of war</u>.

## WORKS CONSULTED

Adger, C. T. (1997a). Language policy and public knowledge. *Center for Applied Linguistics*. Retrieved September 10, 2003, from CAL database at http://www.cal.org/ebonics/eboped.html.

Adger, C. T. (1997b). Dialect education: Not only for Oakland. *Center for Applied Linguistics*. Retrieved October 2, 2003, from CAL database at http://www.cal.org/ericcll/News/9703Dialect.html.

Aitchison, J. (1991). *Language change: Process or decay?* Cambridge: Cambridge University Press.

Ansalone, G. (2003). Poverty, tracking, and the social construction of failure: International perspectives on tracking. *Journal of Children and Poverty, 9*(1), 3-20.

Ansalone, G. (2004). Elementary school teachers' perceptions and attitudes to the educational structure of tracking. *Education, 125*(2), 249-58.

Barker, V., & Giles, H. (2004). English-only policies: Perceived support and social limitation. *Language and Communication, 24*(1), 77-95.

Barthes, R. (1999). *Elements of semiology* (A. Lavers & C. Smith, Trans.). New York: Hill and Wang. (Original work published 1964)

Baron, D. (2000). Ebonics and the politics of English. *World Englishes, 19*(1), 5-19.

Bauer, L. (1998). You shouldn't say 'it is me' because 'me' is accusative. In L. Bauer & P. Trudgill (Eds.), *Language myths* (pp. 132-138). London: Penguin.

Baugh, J. (1999). *Out of the mouths of slaves: African American language and educational malpractice*. Austin, TX: The University of Texas Press.

Behrens, R. R. (1998, August 12). Art, design and gestalt theory. *Leonardo on-line. 31*(4), 299-304. Retrieved March 3, 2004, from http://mitpress2.mit.edu/e-journals/Leonardo/isast/articles/

behrens.html.

Berk, L. E., & Winsler, A. (1995). Scaffolding children's learning: Vygotsky and early childhood education. Washington, D.C.: NAEYC.

Berlin, J. (1988). Rhetoric and ideology in the writing classroom. *College English*, 50(5), 477-494.

Bernstein, B. (1975). Class, codes and control: Theoretical studies towards a sociology of language. New York: Schocken.

Berry, W. (2002, November 14). Two minds. *The Progressive, 66*(11), 21-29.

Bickerton, D. (1996). *Language and human behavior*. Seattle, WA: Washington University Press.

Bishop, W. (1999). Places to stand: The reflective writer-teacher-writer in composition. *College Composition and Communication, 51*(1), 9-31.

Bizzell, P. (1992). *Academic discourse and critical consciousness*. Pittsburgh, PA: The University of Pittsburgh Press.

Blakeston, R. (2002, November 21). Why do Britons Waive the Rules? Retrieved March 10, 2003, from *Guardian Unlimited* database at http://education.guardian.co.uk/tefl/story/0,,843970,00.html

Blumenthal, J. C. (1998). *English 2600: A programmed course in grammar and usage* (6th ed.). Boston: Heinle & Heinle.

Bolinger, D. (1980). *Language: The loaded weapon: The use & abuse of language today*. New York: Longman Group.

Booth, W. C. (1963). Boring from within: The art of the freshman essay. In L. H. Peterson, J. C. Brereton, & J. E. Hartman (Eds.), *The Norton reader*, (10th ed.). (pp. 247-257). New York: W. W. Norton & Co. (2000)

Bourdieu, P., & Passeron, J. C. (1977). *Reproduction in education, society and culture* (L. J. D. Wacquant, Trans.). London: Sage Publications.

Brodkey, L. (1996). *Writing permitted in designated areas only*. Minneapolis, MN: University of Minnesota Press.

Broudy, H. (1987). *The role of imagery in learning.* University of Illinois, Urbana, IL: The Getty Education Institute for the Arts.

Buscemi, S., (2000). *The basics: A rhetoric and handbook.* Boston: McGraw Hill.

Bush, G. W. (2001). Address to a joint session of Congress and the American people. United States Capitol, Washington, D.C. Retrieved May 5, 2003, from http://www.whitehouse.gov/news/releases/2001/09/20010920-8.html

Caillois, R. (2001). *Man, play and games.* Chicago: University of Illinois Press.

Calderon, M. E. (1999). *Promoting language proficiency and academic achievement through cooperation.* Washington, DC: National Clearinghouse on Languages and Linguistics. (ERIC Document Reproduction Service No. ED436983), Retrieved May 10, 2003, from ERIC Digest database at http://www.ericdigests.org/2000-3/language.htm

Cameron, D. (1995). *Verbal hygiene.* London: Routledge.

Canagarajah, S. A. (1999). *Resisting linguistic imperialism in English teaching.* Oxford: Oxford University Press.

Cavallo, B., & Woolridge, F. (2003, November 19). American politicians serving foreign constituents. Retrieved December 20, 2003, from Michnews.com at http://www.frostywoolridge.com/articles/art_american_politicans_serving_foreign_2003.html

Cazden, C. (1983). Adult assistance to language development: Scaffolds, models, and direct instruction. In R. Parker & F. Davis (Eds.), *Developing literacy: Young children's use of language* (pp. 3-18). Newark, DE: International Reading Association.

Chambers, J. W., & Bond, J. (Eds.) (1983). *Black English: Educational equity and the law.* Ann Arbor, MI: Karoma Publishers.

Cheng, Y. S., Horwitz, E. K., & Shallert, D. L. (1999). Language anxiety:

Differentiating writing and speaking components. *Language Learning, 49*(3), 417-446.

Cheshire, J., & Milroy, J. (1993). Syntactic variation in non-standard dialects: Background issues. In J. Milroy & L. Milroy (Eds.), *Real English: The grammar of English dialects in the British Isles* (pp. 3-32). London: Longman Group.

Cheshire, J. (1998). Double negative are illogical. In L. Bauer & P. Trudgill (Eds.), *Language myths* (pp. 113-122). London: Penguin.

Chomsky, N. (1957). *Syntactic structures*. The Hague: Mouton & Co., B.V., Publishers.

Chomsky, N. (1965). *Aspects of the theory of syntax*. Cambridge: The MIT Press.

Chomsky, N. (1972). *Language and mind*, (enlarged edition). New York: Harcourt Brace Jovanovich.

Chomsky, N. (2001). Solidarity. In D. Barsamian (Ed.), *Propaganda and the public mind: Interviews with Noam Chomsky* (pp. 203-23). Cambridge: South End Press.

Christian, D. (1987). *Vernacular dialects in U.S. schools*. Washington, DC: National Clearinghouse on Languages and Linguistics (ERIC Document Reproduction Service No. ED289364), Retrieved April 11, 2003, from ERIC Digest database at http://www.thememoryhole.org/edu/eric/ed289364.html

Claiborne, R. (1983). *Our marvelous native tongue: The life and times of the English language*. New York: Times Books.

Cole, M. (1997). *Cultural psychology: A once and future discipline*. Cambridge: The Belknap Press of Harvard University.

Combs, C. E. (2001). Accessing institutional planning through accreditation and assessment. *Theatre Topics, 11*(1), 81-87.

Connelly, M., & Clandinin, D. (1990). Stories of experience and narrative inquiry. *Educational Researcher, 19*(5), 2-14.

Cowley, G. (2003, September 8). Girls, boys and autism. *Newsweek*, 42-50.

Crawford, J. (Ed.) (1992). *Language loyalties: A source book on the official English controversy*. Chicago: The University of Chicago Press.

Crawford, J., & Lyons, J. (1998/1999). California referendum mandates 'English-only. Rethinking Schools. *12*(3). Retrieved January 20, 2001, from http://www.rethinkingschools.org/archive/12_03/langmn.shtml

Crawford, J. (2000a). *At war with diversity: US language policy in an age of anxiety*. Clevedon, U. K.: Multilingual Matters Ltd.

Crawford, J. (2000b). Anatomy of the English-Only Movement. Presentation. Retrieved June 15, 2002, from http://ourworld.compuserve.com/hompages/JWCRAWFORD/anatomy.htm

Crawford, J. (2000/2001). Bilingual education: Strike two. Rethinking Schools. *15*(2). Retrieved June 15, 2002, from http://ourworld.compuserve.com/homepages/JWCRAWFORD/RS-az.htm

Crowley, T. (1989). The Politics of discourse: The standard language question in British cultural debates. London: McMillan.

Daly, J. A., & Miller, M. D. (1975). The empirical development of an instrument to measure writing apprehension. *Research in the Teaching of English 9*(12): 242-49.

De Beaugrande, R. (1984). Text production: Toward a science of composition. Norwood, NJ: Ablex Publishing Corporation.

DeFabio, R. Y. (1994). *Outcomes in process: Setting standards for language use*. Portsmouth, VA: Boynton Cook Publishers.

Dicker, S. (1996). *Languages in America: A pluralist view*. Clevedon, UK: Multilingual Matters Ltd.

Donato, R. (1998). Collective scaffolding in second language learning. In J. P. Lantolf & G. Appel (Eds.), *Vygotskian approaches to second language research* (pp. 33-56). Norwood, NJ: Ablex Publishing Corp.

Doughty, P. et al. (Eds.) (1971). *Language in use*. London: Edward Arnold.

Eagan, O. (2003). Baseball, apple pie and English: Lessons from a losing campaign against an 'English-only' ballot measure – case study. Retrieved December 12, 2003, from http://www.findarticles.com/cf_0/m2519/10_24/110813303/pl/article.jhtml.

Eisner, E. W. (1978). Reading and the creation of meaning. In E. W. Eisner (Ed.), *Reading, the Arts and the Creation of Meaning* (pp. 13-31). Reston, VA: The National Art Education Association.

Elbow, P. (1985). The shifting relationships between speech and writing. *College Composition and Communication, 36*(3), 290-1.

Elbow, P. (1986). *Embracing contraries: Explorations in learning and teaching*. New York: Oxford University Press.

Elbow, P. (1991). Reflections on academic discourse: How it relates to freshmen colleagues. *College English, 53*(2), 135-55.

Elbow, P. (1998). *Writing without teachers*. Oxford: Oxford University Press.

Fairclough, N. (1989). *Language and power*. London: Longman.

Farr Whiteman, M. (Ed.) (1980). *Reactions to Ann Arbor: Vernacular black English and education*. Washington, DC: Center for Applied Linguistics.

Fawcett, S., & Sandberg, A. (2004). *Evergreen: A guide to writing with readings* (7th ed.). Boston: Houghton Mifflin Co.

Feldman, E. B. (1978). Art, criticism, reading. In E. W. Eisner (Ed.), *Reading, the arts and the creation of meaning.* (pp. 141-157). Reston, VA: The National Art Education Association.

Fillmore, C. J. (1997). A linguist looks at the Ebonics debate. *Center for Applied Linguistics*. Retrieved May 5, 2002, from CAL database at http://www.cal.org/ebonics/ ebfillmo.html

Fish, S. (2002, June 21). Say it ain't so. *The chronicle of higher education, Chronicle careers.* Retrieved July 31, 2002, from http://chronicle.com/jobs/2002/06/2002062101c.htm

Fitzgerald, K. (2001). A rediscovered tradition: European pedagogy and composition in nineteenth-century Midwestern normal schools. *College Composition and Communication, 53*(2), 224-250.

Fowler, H. W. (1965). *A dictionary of modern English usage.* London: Oxford University Press.

Fowler, R. H. et al. (2001). *The Little, Brown handbook* (8th ed.). New York: Longman.

Fulkerson, R. (2005). Composition at the turn of the twenty-first century. *College Composition and Communication, 56*(4), 654-687.

Gaskins, S., & Göncü, A. (1992). Cultural variation in play: A challenge to Piaget and Vygotsky. *The Quarterly Newsletter of the Laboratory of Comparative Human Cognition, 14*(2), 15-46.

Giles, H. & Coupland, N. (1991). *Language: Contexts and consequences.* Pacific Grove, CA: Brooks and Cole Publishing.

Hairston, M. (1981). *Successful writing: A rhetoric for advanced composition.* New York: W. W. Norton & Co.

Hairston, M. (1982). The winds of change: Thomas Kuhn and the revolution in the teaching of writing. *College Composition and Communication, 33*(1), 76-88.

Halliday, M. A. K., & Hasan, R. (1976).*Cohesion in English.* London: Longman.

Halliday, M. A. K., (1987). Spoken and written modes of meaning. In R. Horowitz & S. J. Samuels (Eds.), *Comprehending oral and written language.* New York: Academic Press.

Halliday, M. A. K. (1989). *Spoken and written language.* Oxford: Oxford University Press.

Haussamen, B. et al., (2003). *Grammar alive! A guide for teachers.* Urbana, IL:

National Council of Teachers of English.

Hirst, P. H. (1965). Liberal education and the nature of knowledge. In *Knowledge and the curriculum: A collection of philosophical papers* (pp. 30-53). London: Routledge & Kegan Paul. (1974)

Hirst, P. H. (1973). The forms of knowledge revisited. In *Knowledge and the curriculum: A collection of philosophical papers* (pp. 84-100). London: Routledge & Kegan Paul. (1974)

Holt, J. (1967). How teachers make children hate reading. In L. H. Peterson, J. C. Brereton, & J. E. Hartman (Eds.), *The Norton reader* (10th ed.). (pp. 228-236). New York: W. W. Norton & Co. (2000)

Horner, B. (2001). 'Students'right,' English only, and re-imagining the politics of language. *College English*, 63(6), 741-758.

Horner, B. & Trimbur, J. (2002). English only and US college composition. *College Composition and Communication, 53*(4), 594-630.

Hornick, K. (1986). Teaching writing to linguistically diverse students. New York: National Clearinghouse on Urban Education (ERIC Document Reproduction No. ED275792) Retrieved June 01, 2002, from ERIC Digest database at http://www.ericdigests.org/pre-924/diverse.htm

Hudson, R. A. (1996). *Sociolinguistics*. Cambridge: Cambridge University Press.

Huizinga, J. (1986). *Homo ludens: A study of the play-element in culture*. New York: Beacon Press (Original work published 1939).

Hurn, C. J. (1993). *The limits and possibilities of schooling: An introduction to the sociology of education*. Boston: Allyn and Bacon.

Isserlis, J. (1998). This is only a test. *Adventures in Assessment.* System for adult basic Education Support, Massachusetts Department of Education. Retrieved September 11, 2005, from SABES database at http://www.sabes.org/resources/adventures/vol11/11isserlis.htm

Jackendoff, R. (1994). *Patterns in the mind: Language and human nature*. New York: Basic Books.

Jakobson, R. (1960). Closing statement: Linguistics and poetics. In T. A. Sebeok (Ed.), *Style in language*, (pp. 350-77). Cambridge: The MIT Press.

Johnson, T. R. (2001). School sucks. *College Composition and Communication*, *52*(4), 620-650.

John-Steiner, V. P. & Meehan, T. M. (2000). Creativity and collaboration in knowledge construction. In C. D. Lee & P. Smagorinsky (Eds.), *Vygotskian perspectives on literacy research: Constructing meaning through collaborative inquiry* (pp. 31-48). Cambridge: Cambridge University Press.

Jones, R. (1982). What's wrong with black English? In L. H. Peterson, J. C. Brereton, & J. E. Hartman (Eds.), *The Norton reader*, (9th ed.). (pp. 303-306). New York: W. W. Norton & Co. (1996)

Kamler, B. R. (2001). *Relocating the personal: A critical writing pedagogy*. Albany, NY: State University of New York Press.

Koch, C., & Brazil, J. M., (1978). *Strategies for teaching the composition process*. Urbana, Ill: National Council for Teachers of English.

Kolln, M. (1994). *Understanding English grammar* (4th ed.). Boston: Macmillan Publishing Co.

Kolln, M. (1996). *Rhetorical grammar* (2nd ed.). Boston: Allyn and Bacon.

Labov, W. (1969). The logic of nonstandard English. [Monograph]. *Georgetown Monographs on Language and Linguistics*, *22*, 1-31.

Lakoff, G. (1987). *Women, fire and dangerous things*. Chicago. The University of Chicago Press.

Lakoff, G. (1996). *Moral politics: What conservatives know that liberals don't*. Chicago: The University of Chicago Press.

Lakoff, G., & Johnson, M. (2004). *Philosophy in the flesh: The embodied mind and its challenge to western thought*. New York: Basic Books.

Lakoff, R. (1997). Remarks on Ebonics. Berkeley, CA: The American Cultures Archive, The University of California at Berkeley.

Langer, S. K. (1979). *Philosophy in a new key: A study in the symbolism of reason, rite, and art.* Cambridge: Harvard University Press.

Lantolf, J. P., & Appel, G. (1998). Theoretical framework: An introduction to Vygotskian approaches to second language research. In J. P. Lantolf & G. Appel (Eds.), *Vygotskian approaches to second language research* (pp. 1-32). New Jersey: Ablex Publishing Corp.

Leahy, R. (1996). Style matters: Helping students develop good style. *College Teaching. 43*(1), 7-12.

Leo, J. (1997, April 21). The answer is 45 cents. *U.S. News & World Report*, 14-15.

Lightbown P. M., & Spada, N. (1993). *How languages are learned.* Oxford: Oxford University Press.

Lin, A. M. Y. (1999). Doing-English-lessons in the reproduction or transformation of social worlds? *TESOL Quarterly, 33*(3), 393-412.

Lippi-Green, R. (1997). *English with an accent: Language, ideology, and discrimination in the United States.* London: Routledge.

Liu-Gale, X. (1997). The stranger in communication: Race, class, and conflict in a basic writing class. *JAC: A Journal of Composition Theory, 17*(1), 54-67.

Lu, M. Y. (2000). Writing development. Bloomington, IN: National Clearinghouse on Reading English and Communication (ERIC Document Reproduction No. ED446341) Retrieved May 10, 2003, from ERIC Digest database at http://www.ericdigests.org/2001-3/development.htm

Matlin, M. (1998). *Cognition.* Fort Worth, TX: Harcourt Brace & Co..

McCrum, R. et al. (1986). *The story of English.* New York: Viking Penguin Inc.

McKenzie, J. (1998). Forms of knowledge and forms of discussion. *Educational Philosophy and Theory, 30*(1), 27-49.

McWhorter, J. (2003). *Doing our own thing: The degradation of language and music and why we should, like, care*. New York: Penguin Group.

Miller, C., & Swift, K. (1990). Who's in charge of the English language? In L. H. Peterson, J. C. Brereton, & J. E. Hartman (Eds.), *The Norton reader* (10th ed.). (pp. 289-294). New York: W. W. Norton & Co. (2000)

Miller, S. (1998). *Assuming the positions: Cultural politics and the politics of commonplace writing*. Pittsburgh, PA: The University of Pittsburgh Press.

Milroy, J. (1998). Children can't speak or write properly anymore. In L. Bauer & P. Trudgill (Eds.), *Language myths*. (pp. 58-65). London: Penguin Books.

Moffett, J. (1983). *Teaching the universe of discourse*. Portsmouth, NH: Boynton Cook.

Murray, D. M. (1980). Writing as a process: How writing finds its own meaning. In T. R. Donovan & W. McClelland (Eds.), *Eight approaches to the teaching of composition*. Chicago: National Council of Teachers of English.

Murray, J. A. H., Bradley, H., Craigie, W. A., & Onion, C. T., (Eds.). (1970). *The Oxford English dictionary* (Vol. 1). Oxford: The Clarendon Press.

National Council of Teachers of English. (2004 November). NCTE Beliefs about the Teaching of Writing Retrieved from NCTE website at http://www.ncte.org/about/policy/guidelines/118876.htm

Neisser, U. (1967). Cognitive psychology. New York: Appleton-Century-Crofts.

O'Conner, P. T. (1996). *Woe is I: The grammarphobe's guide to English in plain English*. New York: Grosset Putnam.

Orwell, G. (1949). Politics and the English language. In L. H. Peterson, J. C. Brereton, & J. E. Hartman (Eds.), *The Norton reader*, (10th ed.). (pp. 304-313). New York: W. W. Norton & Co. (2000)

Owocki, G. M. & Goodman, Y. M. (1997). The teaching of writing. In V. Edwards & D. Corson (Eds.), *Encyclopedia of language and education, Vol. 2: Literacy*, (pp. 77-85). Netherlands: Kluwer Publishers.

Paglia, C. (2004). The magic of images: Word and picture in a media age. *Arion. 11*(3), 1-22. Retrieved December 30, 2004, from http://www.bu.edu/arion/ Camille%20Paglia/%20The%20 Magic%20of%20Images.pdf

Patton, M. Q. (2002). *Qualitative evaluation and research methods*. Thousand Oaks, CA: Sage Publications.

Peyton, J., & Rigg, P. (1999). Poetry in the Adult ESL Classroom. Washington, DC: National Clearinghouse for ESL Literacy Education (ERIC Document Reproduction No. ED439626) Retrieved Dec 09, 2004, from ERIC Digest database at http://www.ericdigests.org/2000-4/poetry.htm

Piaget, J. (1969). *Judgment and reasoning in the child* (M. Gabain, Trans.). London: Routledge and Kegan Paul. (Original work published 1932).

Piaget, J. (1972). Psychology and epistemology: Towards a theory of knowledge. (P. A. Wells, Trans.). London: Penguin University Books.

Piaget, J. (1974). *The language and thought of the child* (M. Gabain, Trans.). New York: Meridian. (Original work published 1955).

Pinker, S. (1994). *The language instinct: How the mind creates language*. New York: Harper Perennial.

Pinker, S. (1999). *Words and rules: The ingredients of language*. New York: Basic Books.

Pinker, S. (2000, October 31). Decoding the candidates [Letter to the editor]. *The New York Times*, p. 27.

Polanyi, M. (1958). *Personal knowledge: Towards a post-critical philosophy*. Chicago: University of Chicago Press.

Polanyi, M. (1967). *The tacit dimension*. New York: Anchor Books.

Polanyi, M., & Prosch, H. (1975). *Meaning*. Chicago: University of Chicago Press.

Pyles, T. (1971). *The origins and development of the English language*. New York: Harcourt Brace Jovanovich, Inc.

Quinn, M. (2002). *Qualitative evaluation and research methods*. Thousand Oaks, CA: Sage Publications Inc.

Reed, F. (2004). Random thoughts on the decline of English: Bile, vitriol, and lost clauses. Retrieved January 5, 2003, from http://www.FredOnEverything.net

Richards, J. C., Platt, J. & Platt, H. (Eds.). (1999). *Dictionary of language teaching & applied linguistics*. Oxford: Longman.

Rico, G. L. (1978). Reading for non-literal meaning. In E. W. Eisner (Ed.), *Reading, the arts and the creation of meaning* (pp. 33-53). Reston, VA: The National Art Education Association.

Roberts, R. M., & Kreuz, R. J. (1993). Nonstandard discourse and its coherence. *Discourse Processes*. Memphis, TN: Ablex Publishing Corporation.

Rolf, B. (1995). Profession, tradition och tyst kunskap. Nora: Nya Doxa.

Rose, M. (1990). Lives on the Boundary: A Moving Account of the Struggles and Achievements of America's Educationally Underprepared: New York: Free Press.

Rosenthal, R., & Jacobson, L. (1968). *Pygmalion in the classroom*. New York: Holt, Rinehart, and Winston.

Roney, C. J. R., & Trick, L. M. (2003). Grouping and gambling: A gestalt approach to understanding the gambler's fallacy. *Canadian journal of experimental psychology*, *57*(2), pp. 69-75.

Royster, J. J. (1989). [Review of the article Lives on the boundary: The struggle and achievements of America's underdeveloped]. *College Composition and Communication*, *40*(3), 349-350.

Ryle, G. (1949). *The concept of mind*. Chicago: The University of Chicago Press.

Sanches, M., & Kirshenblatt-Gimblett, B. (1976). Children's traditional speech play. In B. Kirshenblatt-Gimblett (Ed.), *Speech play: Research and resources for the study of linguistic creativity* (pp. 65-110). Philadelphia, PA: University of Pennsylvania Press.

Schaff, A. (Ed. Robert A. Cohen) (1964). *Language and cognition.* New York: McGraw-Hill.

Schuster, E. (1999). Reforming the English language arts: Let's trash the tradition, *Phi Delta Kappan, 80*(7), (pp. 518-24).

Schuster, E. (2003). *Breaking the rules: Liberating writers through innovative grammar instruction.* Portsmouth, NH: Heinemann.

Searle, J. R. (1969). Speech acts: An essay in the philosophy of language. Cambridge: Cambridge University Press.

Shafer, R. E. (1999). English teaching in USA. In *Concise encyclopedia of educational linguistics* (pp. 381-84). Oxford: Elsevier.

Simpson, P. (2000). A short history of the standard language question in England, *Okinawa International University Review, 29.*

Smith, C. B. (2000). Writing instruction: Current practices in the classroom. Bloomington, IN: National Clearinghouse on Reading English and Communication (ERIC Document Reproduction Center No. ED446338), Retrieved May 12, 2003, from ERIC Digest database at http://www.ericdigests.org/2001-3/writing.htm

Stanley, J., & Williamson, T. (2001). Knowing how. *The Journal of Philosophy, 98*(8), 411-444.

Strunk, W., Jr., & White, E. B. (1979). *The elements of style.* New York: Macmillan.

Sveiby, K. E. (1997, December 31). Tacit knowledge. Retrieved December 29, 2003, from Sveiby Knowledge Associates database at http://www.sveiby.com/articles/Polanyi.html

Tomasello, M. (2003). *Constructing a language: A usage-based theory of language acquisition.* Cambridge: Harvard University Press.

Toonkel, R. (2003, March 31). U.S. English supports introduction of English language unity act of 2003. Retrieved May 1, 2004, from U.S. English, Inc. database at http://www.us-english.org/inc/news/preleases/ viewRelease.asp?ID=14

Trimbur, J. (2000). Composition and the circulation of writing. *College Composition and Communication, 52*(2), 188-219.

Trudgill, P. (1998). Review of language is power. *Journal of Sociolinguistics, 2*(3), 457-461.

van Essen, A. (1997). Language awareness and knowledge about language: An overview. In L. Van Lier & D. Corson (Eds.), *Encyclopedia of language and education, Vol. 6: Knowledge about language*, (pp. 1-9). Netherlands: Kluwer Publishers.

Vygotsky, L. S. (1978). *Mind in society: The development of higher psychological processes*. (M. Cole, Vera John-Steiner, Sylvia Scribner, & Ellen Souberman Eds.). Cambridge: Harvard University Press. (Original work published 1934)

Vygotsky, L. S. (1983). From the notebooks of L.S. Vygotsky (M. Vale, Trans.). In A.A. Puzyrei (Ed.), *Soviet Psychology, 21*(3), 3-17. (Original work published 1934)

Vygotsky, L. S. (1986). *Thought and language* (A. Kozulin, Ed. & Trans.). Cambridge: The M.I.T. Press. (Original work published in 1934)

Wartchow, K., & Gustavson, L. (1999, June). The art of the writer: An aesthetic look at the teaching of writing. Paper presented at the Annual Meeting of the American Educational Research Association, Montreal, Canada.

Weaver, C. (1996). Teaching grammar in context. Portmouth, NH: Heinemann.

Wells, G. (1999). *Dialogic inquiry: Towards a sociocultural practice and theory of education*. New York: Cambridge University Press.

Wells, G. (2000). Dialogic inquiry in education: Building on the legacy of

Vygotsky. In C. D. Lee & P. Smagorinsky (Eds.) (2000), *Vygotskian perspectives on literacy research: Constructing meaning through collaborative inquiry.* (pp. 51-85). Cambridge: Cambridge University Press.

Wertheimer, M. (1924). Gestalt theory. Retrieved November 30, 2003 from Society for Gestalt Theory and its Applications database at http://www.gestalttheory.net

Williams, F. (1976). *Explorations of the linguistic attitudes of teachers.* Rowley, MA: Newbury House Publishers.

Williams, R. (1976). *Keywords: A vocabulary of culture and society.* (cited from Flamingo edition, 1981) Cambridge: Oxford University Press.

Wood, D., Bruner, J. S. & Ross, G. (1976). The role of tutoring in problem-solving. *Journal of Child Psychology and Psychiatry, 17,* 89-100.

Ziegahn, L. (2001). Considering culture in the selection of teaching approaches for adults. Washington, DC: National Clearinghouse on Adult, Career, and Vocational Education (ERIC Document Reproduction Center No. ED459325), Retrieved August 3, 2003, from ERIC Digest database at http://www.cete.org/acve/docgen.asp?tbl=digests&ID=116

# INDEX

## A

accent, 13, 32, 147, 148, 172, 179, 180, 181

acceptability, 8, 13, 14, 77, 78, 168, 170, 193

acceptance, 12, 26, 57, 94, 117

acculturation, 33

Adger, Carolyn, 32, 44, 81, 84, 221

ad populum, 82

African American Vernacular English (AAVE), 31, 167, 169

Aitchison, Jean, 182, 221

alliteration, 21, 185-189

anaphora 166

Ansalone, George, 30, 221

assonance, 186-188

antithesis, 185

anxiety, 130, 140, 144, 150, 162, 164, 183, 217, 223

Appel, Gabriele, (see Lantolf)

apprehension(s), 2, 26, 61, 63, 115, 137, 141, 144, 148, 150, 164, 171, 190, 191 196, 199, 203, 207

asyndeton, 21, 186

Asian, 34

attitude(s), 1-5, 8, 9, 13, 14, 17, 18, 22, 24, 26-30, 36, 47, 49, 52, 53, 58, 76, 78, 80, 88, 118, 136, 141, 148-152 165, 171, 178, 179, 190, 191 196, 201, 204, 205

awareness, 3, 71, 81, 90, 91, 95, 96-100, 102, 113, 117, 121, 126, 129-133, 138, 140, 143, 144, 149, 150, 167, 170, 194, 203, 209

## B

bandwagon, 34

Barker, Valerie, 19, 221

Barthes, Roland, 15, 221

Baron, Dennis, 84, 87, 221

Bauer, Laurie, 67, 182, 221, 224, 321

Baugh, John, 25, 35, 36, 221

Behrens, Roy R., 124, 125, 221

Berlin, James, 39, 57, 127, 222

Berk, Laura, E., 112, 222

Bernstein, Basil, 28, 65, 222

Berry, Wendell, 119, 120, 222

Bickerton, Derek, 83-87, 222

Bishop, Wendy, 56, 222

Bizzell, Patricia, 38, 42, 43, 61, 106, 140, 222

Blakeston, Rodney, 16-18, 222

Blumenthal, Joseph C., 60, 222

Bolinger, Dwight, 4, 31, 222

Booth, Wayne C., 65, 222

Bourdieu, Pierre, 24-28, 50, 73, 166, 175, 222

brainstorming, 6, 113

Brazil, James, M., (see Koch)

British Broadcasting Corporation (BBC), 13, 69

Brockenbrough, Martha, 15

Brodkey, Linda, 46, 48, 50, 139, 222

Broudy, Harry, 128, 223

Buscemi, Santi, V., 71, 223

Bush, George, W., 68, 177, 223

C

Caillois, Roger, 116, 117, 223

Calderon, Margarita E., 223

Cameron, Deborah, 25, 36, 42, 44, 71, 74, 79, 205, 207, 223

Canagarajah, Suresh, 6, 17, 27, 31, 39-43, 45-47, 49, 51, 52, 62, 63, 125, 153, 223

Cazden, Courtney, 112, 193, 223

Chambers, John, W., 29, 223

Cheng, Y. L., 36, 223

Chomsky, Noam, 1, 15, 41, 45, 78, 98, 142, 158, 193, 194, 207, 224

Cheshire, Jenny, 3, 8, 10, 11, 12, 22, 27, 31, 49, 53, 55, 59, 67-69, 74, 75, 78, 202, 224

Christian, Donna, 29, 224

codification, 12, 59, 75

coherence, 88, 129, 142, 143, 154-158, 189, 193, 194, 199, 206, 207

cohesion, 155, 156, 187, 191, 199

cognitive...
  activity, 45
  deficit, 27, 29
  development, 105, 117
  experience, 109
  performance, 98, 101, 126
  process theory, 41, 45
  processes, 58, 98, 206
  strategy, 45, 47

Cole, Michael, 199, 224, 235

Combs, C. 53, 224

community colleges, 2, 196

complaint tradition, 8

complement(s), 43, 65, 71, 125

composition theory, 4, 38, 49, 52, 63, 230

connection(s)...
  adverbial, 156
  attitude / identity, 5
  conscious / non-conscious, 107, 132
  conscious activity / personal knowledge, 115
  cultural / linguistic complexity, 82
  grammatical, 129
  ideas / images, 129
  lexical, 129
  meaningful, 157
  semantic, 129, 154-156
  social, 196
  symbolic, 44
  syntactic, 192
  thought / word, 103

Connelly, Michael, 171, 224

conservative, 20, 23, 32, 58, 76, 173

content, 21, 41, 47, 52, 61, 63, 75, 137

correctness, 13-16, 24, 26, 42, 47, 51, 56, 76-78, 87, 118, 133, 137, 141, 160, 162, 171, 173, 174, 177, 181, 193

Coupland, Nikolas, (See Giles)

Clandinin, D., Jean, 171, 224

Claiborne, Robert, 8, 224

Cowley, Geoffrey, 125, 224

Crawford, James, 23, 24, 34, 35, 225

Crowley, Terry, 10, 225

cultural capital, 22-25, 28, 47, 73, 77, 175, 205

Current Traditional Paradigm (CTP), 38, 42, 43, 52, 69, 72, 88, 147, 153

D

Daly, John, A., 4, 144, 155, 190, 225

de Beaugrande, Robert, 139, 140, 225

de-contextualized, 61, 143, 163, 164

DeFabio, Roseanne, Y., 173, 225

descriptive approach, 65

dialect, 10, 11, 15, 28, 29, 31, 44, 47, 63, 77, 83, 109, 131, 132, 140, 162, 175, 181, 207

Dicker, Susan, J., 23, 225

Didion, Joan, 165-169

diffusion, 12

discourse(s)...
  Anglo-American, 19, 52
  academic, 1, 17, 19, 22, 32, 47, 49, 50, 65, 73, 80, 140, 149, 171, 173, 193, 194, 195
  alternative, 1, 2
  conventions, 13, 47, 83, 116, 140, 162, 175, 182
  native, 22, 52, 77, 98, 131, 177
  political, 74, 79, 175, 177
  public, 10, 15, 16, 17, 18, 21, 30, 53, 58, 68, 74, 77, 78, 79, 86, 200

disparities,
  socioeconomic, 27, 175
  standard / nonstandard, 25

Donato, Richard, 112, 225

double negatives, 65-69, 202

Doughty, Peter, S., 81, 226

### E

Ebonics, 17, 221, 226, 229

Educational Testing Service (ETS), 53

Eisner, Elliot, W., 126, 127, 226

elaboration of function, 12

Elbow, Peter, 2, 6, 21, 39-42, 113, 141, 159, 180, 226

ellipsis, 21, 166

English as a Second Language (ESL) 3, 137, 147, 207

English 2600, 59, 60, 222

epistemology, 3, 62, 151

Evergreen, 58, 59, 155, 226

expressivist, 39, 41, 88, 138, 140

### F

Fairclough, Norman, 86, 226

Farr Whiteman, Marcia, 29, 226

Fawcett, Susan, 58, 59, 71, 226

Feldman, Edmund, B., 122, 226

Fillmore, Charles, J., 10, 226

First Language, 98, 112

Fish, Stanley, 75, 76, 227

Fitzgerald, Kathryn, 55, 56, 165, 227

Fowler, H. W., 65, 66, 227

Fulkerson, Richard, 39, 42, 57, 227

### G

Gaskins, Suzanne, 117, 227

generation, 2, 106, 130, 202, 205

generative, 41-47, 50, 62, 63, 87, 99, 200

genre, 41, 43, 47, 48, 50, 62, 63, 160, 203

Giles, Howard, 6, 10, 13, 14, 25, 36, 54, 86, 87, 179, 227

Göncü, Artin (see Gaskins)

Goodman, Yetta, M., (see Owocki)

grammar...
 drills, 42-44, 61, 143
 generative, 45
 standard, 137, 139, 160, 192

growth...
 etymological, 10
 intellectual, 117, 120,
 in language skills, 5, 72
 population, 23, 32
 skills, 4, 102-105, 110, 112, 117, 149, 206,
 socioeconomic, 36
 stimulate, 4, 101
 tracking, 226

writing, 111

Gustavson, L., (see Wartchow)

## H

habitus, 24, 25, 27

Hairston, Maxine, 1, 38, 45, 73, 227

Halliday, M.A.K, 76, 81, 155, 156, 227

Hasan, Ruqaiya, 155, 156, 227

Haussamen, Brock, 49, 50, 51, 227

Hirst, P. H., 94, 95, 228

Hispanic, 34, 147, 179, 198

Holt, John, 34, 77, 228

Horner, Bruce, 57, 61, 228

Honey, John, 16, 17

Hornick, Karen, 49-51, 228

Hudson, Richard, 160, 228

Huizinga, Johan, 114, 115, 116, 228

Hurn, Christopher, 29, 30, 228

hypothesis, 5, 141

## I

identity...
 national, 9
 personal / group, 26
 political, 13
 social, 32, 33, 44, 61

illegal aliens, 19, 20, 32

illogical, 66-69

immigration, 19, 22, 23, 33, 35, 36

incorrect(ness), 22, 51, 54, 78, 87, 131, 184

infinitive, split, 65, 102, 161, 181, 202

Intelligence Quotient (IQ), 30

irrational...
 activity, 116
 attitudes, 3, 36
 behavior, 18
 bias, 90, 205
 fears, 32
 feelings, 170
 responses, 167

isocolon, 166

Isserlis, Janet, 53, 228

## J

Jackendoff, Ray, 122, 226

Jacobson, Leonore, 30, 233

Jakobson, Roman, 136, 229

Johnson, Mark, (See Lakoff)

Johnson, Todd, R., 87, 95, 194, 206, 229

John-Steiner, Vera, 108, 109, 229

Jones, Rachel, 176, 180, 229

## K

Kamler, Barbara, R., 77, 229

Kirshenblatt-Gimblett, Barbara (see Sanches)

knowing...
  a/the language, 93, 100
  embedded, 51, 199
  how, 93, 94, 96, 101, 102, 143
  meta-, 98
  that, 93, 94, 96, 97, 100, 101, 143
  vs. doing / using, 62

knowledge...
  explicit, 16, 69, 71, 91, 95, 96, 99, 100, 102, 138, 143, 162, 164, 203, 205, 206, 207
  implicit, 62, 93, 189
  tacit, 62, 63, 70, 87, 91, 95, 96, 97, 98, 107, 133, 142, 184, 189, 205

Koch, Carl, 5, 229

Kolln, Martha, 102, 156, 229

Kreuz, Roger, (See Roberts)

## L

labeling, 32, 40, 62, 75, 143, 162, 167, 170, 172

Labov, William, 25, 28, 82-84, 131, 229

Lakoff, George, 20, 86, 95, 122, 127, 128, 129, 206, 229

Langer, Susanne, K., 85, 94, 101, 103, 123, 124, 131, 136, 205, 230

language...
  arts, English, 49, 138
  competence, 4, 13, 16, 25, 32, 41, 47, 78, 81, 92, 112, 190, 204, 209
  conscious /non-conscious, 132
  corruption, 3, 4, 8, 10, 25, 31, 72, 78, 177
  deficit, (see linguistic)
  difference, (see linguistic)
  maintenance, 9, 12, 53, 202
  maven, 79, 80, 173
  meta-, 61, 69, 70, 71, 143
  norms, 3, 9, 14, 15, 19, 22, 35, 77, 87, 196
  performance, 4, 13, 32, 78, 140, 189
  policy, 44, 57, 80
  skills, 4, 24, 63, 79, 91, 101, 127

Lantolf, James, P., 105, 225, 230

Leahy, Richard, 164-168, 170, 208, 209, 230

Leo, John, 33, 34, 47, 247

lexical, 21, 58, 156, 168, 190

Lin, Angel, 24-28

linguistic...
  capital, 27-29, 48, 75, 197
  deficit, 4, 28, 30, 31
  difference, 4, 28, 29, 32, 77, 86
  imperialism, 6
  meta-, 43, 45, 61, 71, 99, 100, 121, 143, 153, 163, 184
  remedy, 42, 140, 160

Lippi-Green, Rosina, 4, 18, 27, 34, 35, 76, 179, 230

Little, Brown Handbook, The, 66, 69, 70, 155

Liu-Gale, Xin, 50, 51, 230

Lu, Mei-Yu, 200

Lusser Rico, Gabriele, 125, 207, 233

## M

mainstream, 6, 18, 24, 34, 77, 78, 82, 141, 171, 178, 201

marginalized, 6, 25, 83, 137, 146, 197

Matched-guise Technique (MGT), 14

Matlin, Margaret, 98, 101, 121-123, 126, 230

McKenzie, Jim, 95, 230

McWhorter, John, 20, 21, 230

meaning…
  discursive, 52, 94, 103, 122, 123, 136, 194, 204, 205
  presentational, 94, 136, 204

Meehan, T. M. (see John-Steiner)

meritocracy, 27

Mexico, 32

Michigan, Ann Arbor, 29

Miller, M., (see Daly)

Miller, Susan, 55, 231

Milroy, Jim, 3, 8, 10-12, 22, 27, 31, 49, 53, 55, 59, 69, 74, 75, 76, 78, 202, 224

minority, 3, 33, 46, 47, 81, 147

modifier(s), 71, 139, 169, 175

Moffett, James, 44, 190, 231

multiculturalism, 19

Murray, Donald, 5, 6, 39, 231

mythrules, 65, 66

## N

National Council of Teachers of English (NCTE), 137

Native-American, 34

Neisser, Ulrich, 159, 231

neurotic, 18

non-mainstream, 34

non-rational, 114

non-standard, 10-12, 25, 31, 140, 168, 169, 177

normative, 36, 41, 62, 63, 132, 176

North American paradigm, 28, 37, 39, 40, 43, 54, 56, 57, 61, 130, 138, 170

## O

Obama, Barack, 64

O'Conner, Patricia, T., 8, 65, 167, 182, 231

Orwell, George, 44, 67, 68, 72-75, 231

Owocki, Gretchen, M., 61, 232

Oxford English Dictionary (OED), 9

## P

Paglia, Camille, 19, 20, 21, 232

parallelism, 21, 54, 185, 187

Passeron, Jean-Claude, 22, 24, 26, 27, 28, 50, 73, 166, 175, 222

periphery student(s), 3, 4, 26, 36, 37, 46, 50, 52, 60, 63, 75, 132, 138, 202

Peyton, Joy, K., 137, 144, 232

phrase...
  infinitive, 142, 143, 153
  noun, 61, 129, 142, 153, 188
  play, 133, 150, 192, 205, 206, 207, 208
  prepositional, 139, 142, 143, 153
  type, 186, 190
  verb, 129, 142, 143, 153, 184, 185, 188, 200

Piaget, Jean, 117-119, 121, 123, 227, 247

Pinker, Steven, 64, 64, 77 101, 102, 122, 173, 177, 232

play...
  language, 121, 133, 137, 140
  rhetorical, 3, 125, 205, 207

poetics, 136, 137, 144, 191, 229

poetry, 2, 21, 136, 137, 144, 165, 187, 191, 203, 204, 208, 232

Polanyi, Michael, 62, 63, 92, 95-97, 99, 107-109, 112, 113, 115, 125, 204, 232

polysyndeton, 21

power...
  economic, 10, 19, 20, 24, 25, 35, 48, 72, 83, 174, 183, 200
  political, 6, 9, 25

preposition, ending sentence with, 65, 161

prescription(s), 12, 15, 17, 34, 44, 47, 52, 55, 56, 58, 59, 63, 65, 66, 69, 70, 72, 75, 126, 130, 140, 181, 182, 183, 199, 202

prescriptive approach(es), 4, 5, 32, 34, 69, 133, 182, 199, 201, 207

process...
  approach, 6, 33
  composing, 5, 6, 50
  creative, 199
  developmental, 200
  drafting, 183
  education, 29, 183
  generating, 42, 87, 131
  play, of, 159
  practitioners, 47
  psychological, 115
  school, 5, 13, 33, 39, 40, 41, 42, 46, 47, 50, 58, 63, 125, 129, 141
  theory, 33
  writing, 58, 111, 137, 169, 186, 202

progressive...
  approaches, 56

education policy, 16
movement, 20

psychology...
  behaviorist, 43, 62
  cognitive, 40, 112
  developmental, 105, 110, 117, 121-128, 200
  humanistic, 45

purity, 13, 18, 22, 79, 202

Pyles, Thomas, 8, 233

## Q

Quinn, Michael, 150, 233

## R

paradigm shift, 22

Prosch, Harry, (see Polanyi)

Received Pronunciation (RP), 13

rhetoric...
  cognitive psychology, of, 40
  composition, and, 38, 39, 72, 110, 165
  courses, 55
  Greco-Roman, 43, 136, 165, 166
  ideology, 39
  procedural, 39
  textbooks, 71

rhetorical...
  analysis, 41, 208
  devices, 63, 69, 164
  effects, 112, 130, 133, 188, 191, 198
  exercise, 4, 141
  figures, 199
  form, 2
  play, 2, 125, 204, 206
  problems, 200
  question, 17
  solution, 62
  structures, 42, 127, 128, 129, 141, 146, 204
  style(s), 164, 165
  theory, 56, 137
  tropes and schemes, 21, 26, 164-168, 184, 187, 190, 203, 208

Rigg, Pat, (see Peyton)

Roberts, Richard, 156, 233

Rolf, Bertil, 92, 233

Roney, C. J., 122, 126, 233

Rose, Mike, 146, 197, 198, 233

Rosenthal, Robert, 30, 233

Ryle, Gilbert, 92, 93, 95, 98, 143, 233

## S

Sanches, Mary, 103, 200, 234

scaffolding, 111-114, 118, 193, 198, 199

Schaff, Adam, 25, 234

schizophrenic, 18

Schuster, Edgar, 15, 49, 50, 65, 69, 138, 234

Searle, John, R., 76, 234

Second Language, 52, 81, 112

selection, 12, 55

semantic(s), 95, 96, 97, 103, 106, 142, 154, 155, 156, 157, 162, 165, 166, 184, 189, 192, 205

Shafer, Robert, E., 56, 57, 234

Skinner, B.F., 41

social stratification, 27

socioeconomic, 10, 24-27, 32, 34, 55, 83, 84, 148, 198, 201, 202

Spanish, 35, 147, 179

speech community, 44, 131

standardization, process of, 3, 5, 11, 12, 22, 55, 74

standards ...
  academic, 16, 19, 31, 32, 33, 42, 73, 75, 78
  correctness, 15, 139, 176
  language, 3, 8, 9, 10, 18, 27, 31, 69, 75, 166
  linguistic, 9, 33, 73, 136, 149

Stanley, Jason., 75, 93, 234

status...
  desirable, 5, 6
  marginal, 37
  periphery, 6,
  socioeconomic, 10, 146, 148
  superior, 6

stereotype(s), 13, 26, 81, 148, 179

structuralism, 43, 60

syllepsis, 166, 189

synæsthesia, 187

syntactic, 11, 54, 78, 118, 128, 131, 142, 143, 154, 182, 185, 190, 193, 199

sub-standard, 10

suppression, 12, 31, 55

Summers, Lawrence, 75, 76

Sveiby, Karl, E., 91-95, 234

T

text production, sentence-level, 5, 43, 46, 47, 52, 93, 137, 139, 190, 204, 207

Tomasello, Michael, 103, 234

Toonkel, Rob, 24, 235

tradition(s), 1, 5, 8, 21, 37, 43, 45, 47, 62, 65, 92, ......

transition(al) (expression), 54, 71, 106, 129, 155, 157, 158, 184, 186, 187, 190

Trick, L. M. (see Roney)

Trimbur, John, 61, 193, 228

tropes, 185-188, 191, 203

Trudgill, Peter, 16, 17, 67, 221, 231

U

United Kingdom (UK), 13

University of Maryland University College (UMUC), 58, 80, 111, 164

United States (US), 33, 34

U.S. English Inc., 23, 24

### V

van Essen, Arthur, 57, 81, 235

verbal hygiene, 36, 74-76, 205

von Humbolt, Wilhelm, 158, 244

Vygotsky, Lev, S., 4, 5, 38, 41, 45, 62, 98, 103-119, 121, 131-133, 141, 190, 198-200, 205, 222, 225, 233, 235

### W

Wartchow, K., 158, 233

Weaver, Constance, 102, 235

Wells, Gordon, 73, 108, 109, 111, 199, 235

Wertheimer, Max, 124, 236

White, E.B., 65, 66, 72, 73, 102, 234

Williams, F., 29, 236

Williams, Raymond, 9, 236

Williamson, Timothy, (see Stanley)

workshop, 144-149, 153, 155, 158, 164, 171, 187, 191-200

xenophobic, 18

Zone of Proximal Development (ZPD), 110, 111, 112

### Z

Ziegahn, Linda, 109, 236

www.ingramcontent.com/pod-product-compliance
Lightning Source LLC
Chambersburg PA
CBHW082037230426

43670CB00016B/2685